For Gago, the strike always exceeds the act, the event, marking a vector of temporalities that both analyze the past and inaugurate a new futural horizon. Born from 'gestures of revulsion,' the felt urgency of leaving those domestic enclosures that threaten to define and debase women's bodies, the feminist strike is linked with the general assembly, understood as 'a situated apparatus of collective intelliegence.' Furthering the legacy of Rosa Luxemburg, Verónica Gago links the praxis of revolution to the critique of finance under neoliberalism, colonial dispossession, and patriarchal forms of state terrorism directed against women, trans, and transvestis, precarious workers and the indigenous. Working in collaboration with radical thought across continents, Gago offers in this book the most comprehensive transversal anaysis and the most compelling case for feminist praxis as the framework for an anti-fascist left. Embodied thought takes shape as affect, action, and a new understanding of collective potential. The activism for which Gago calls is already underway, and this book belongs to that revolutionary process."

—**Judith Butler**, author of
The Force of Non-Violence

Feminist International

How to Change Everything

Verónica Gago

Translated by
Liz Mason-Deese

VERSO

London • New York

For Raquel, Nati, and Luci

First published by Verso 2020
Originally published in Spanish as *La potencia feminista:*
O el deseo de cambiarlo todo by Tinta Limón 2019
© Verónica Gago 2020
Translation © Liz Mason-Deese 2020

1 3 5 7 9 10 8 6 4 2

Verso
UK: 6 Meard Street, London W1F 0EG
US: 20 Jay Street, Suite 1010, Brooklyn, NY 11201
versobooks.com

Verso is the imprint of New Left Books

ISBN-13: 978-1-78873-968-9
ISBN-13: 978-1-78873-970-2 (UK EBK)
ISBN-13: 978-1-78873-969-6 (US EBK)

British Library Cataloguing in Publication Data
A catalogue record for this book is available from the British Library

Library of Congress Cataloging-in-Publication Data
A catalog record for this book is available from the Library of Congress

Typeset in Sabon by MJ & N Gavan, Truro, Cornwall
Printed and bound by CPI Group (UK) Ltd, Croydon CR0 4YY

Contents

Habent sua fata libelli—Books have destinies of their own.

As quoted by Rosa Luxemburg

Translator's Foreword

If there is one thing we have seen in the process of constructing a feminist internationalism, it is that internationalism (and transnationalism and plurinationalism) are only possible through practices of translation. Translation from one language to other, but also from one context, and its associated histories and geographies, to another, translations across asynchronous temporalities and uneven spatialities.

In translating this book, we aim to bring some of the key innovations of the feminist movement in Argentina to a new, transnational audience. These innovations are as practical as they are theoretical, in that they demonstrate the impossibility of separating theory from practice and bodies. They include, for example, a feminist strike that creates a new notion of what it means to strike based on expanding what we recognize as work and a feminist internationalism that creates a new notion of how we define the relationship between bodies and territories and the relations between one territory and another. Fundamentally, these point to a feminist methodology that starts from mapping specific experiences of violence and exploitation and connecting them through practices of situated assemblies and coordinating networks. It is this methodology that we hope to share.

But first, a few notes on the translation are needed.

We have chosen to maintain the direct translation of certain terminology that has emerged through struggles within the feminist movement in Argentina. Namely the use of the term *travestis* and the longer formulation of the movement of "women, lesbians, trans people, and travestis." While the word "transvestites" clearly has a derogatory connotation in English, in Argentina, *travesti* continues to be used as a form of self-identification and collective mobilization. The travesti movement in Argentina has publicly organized for decades through organizations such as the Asociación de Lucha por la Identidad Travesti-Transsexual, founded in 1997, and has achieved key victories, such as the "Gender Identity Law" passed in 2012 and generally considered to be one of the most progressive in the world due to its lack of barriers for officially changing one's gender identity.

However, travestis primarily refers to a political identity. As Argentine travesti activist and thinker Lohana Berkins argued, in Latin America, the travesti community has organized itself in a context both materially and discursively distant from the North American academia and medical procedures. She defines the origins of the travesti identity: "In Latin America, the term travesti comes from medicine and has been appropriated, reelaborated, and embodied by travestis to name themselves. That is the term that we recognize ourselves as that we choose to construct ourselves as subjects of rights."[1] Much of the travesti movement has focused on fighting against labor discrimination, which forces nearly 90 percent of travestis into the informal or precarious sector, often in sex work, and for rights in that sector, as well as against discrimination in housing. Here "identity" is not separated from "class" position, and indeed it demonstrates their inseparable nature.

On the other hand, the formulation of "women, lesbians, trans people, and travestis" (and more recently gender nonconforming people) might sound redundant or unnecessary in English. However, it is the result of years of debate within the feminist movement and the construction of shared collective subjectivities. Each of those collectivities has its own history of struggle and organization and has fought to expand the meaning of the feminist movement, its concerns, demands, and practices. Those fights often involved uncomfortable assemblies and conversations, forcing all involved to challenge their previously held assumptions. They continue requesting to be named within the Argentine feminist movement, in mobilizations and gatherings, so we honor that request here. What these movements have shown is that the meaning of "woman" or "feminist" cannot be taken for granted, that the feminist movement is far from unitary, but taking that into account makes the collective struggle that must stronger.

Another word we have left in its Spanish original is *potencia*. In Spanish, there are two words for "power": *poder* and *potencia*, which derive from the Latin *potestas* and *potentia* respectively. The Spinozist understanding of power that underlies this book, identifies *poder* as static, constituted power, while "potencia" has a dynamic, constituent dimension. Potencia defines our power to do, to be affected and to affect others, while *poder* refers to power over, a form of power with the mechanism of representation that separates the bodies being represented from their own *potencia*. One of the central wagers of the feminist movement, highlighted throughout this book, is on a different type of power, not the power of the state or centralized parties, but rather a power based on our collective capacity to do. That is the type of power that surges from the feminist strike and that takes hold everywhere through the feminist internationlism proposed here.

Beyond the philosophical debates, here a feminist potencia, the work's original title, refers to that collective capacity for creation. Thus it remits to the question of desire, "the desire to change everything." This desire is productive, constituting subjects and relations, and a fundamental element of the feminist tide discussed in this book. It is an understanding that has permeated the movement that, while protesting the many forms of violence that women suffer, is primarily motivated by a powerful desire, a desire to find new ways to be together, to transform all the spaces we inhabit on a daily basis, to create new forms of life. And it does not wait for anything but is already being practiced in the multiple space-times that make up our transnational and plurinational feminist tide.

Finally, the process of translating this book also deserves to be remarked upon. If, as the old adage goes, *traductore traidore,* translation is also an act of friendship and love, as well as a creative process. The manuscript was translated as it was written, chapter by chapter, over the course of nearly a year, accompanied by a constant dialogue between the author and translator as we both participated in feminist mobilizations, assemblies, seminars, exchanges, and debates. The first Spanish and English versions were edited simultaneously, sentence by sentence, often with the author and translator sitting side by side, writing and editing mixing with translating. It was translated in the moments between feminist mobilizations, assemblies, long lunches and ongoing dialogues, at the rhythms of everyday life and of feminist uprising.

Going back and forth between the feminist movements in my new home in Buenos Aires and my old home in the United States, participating in organizing feminist strikes here and there, made this translation seem ever more urgent. While the feminist strike stuttered in the United States, facing liberal backlash and critique and failing to connect and collectivize campaigns against gender-based violence, such as #MeToo, in Argentina the feminist strike was becoming a mass phenomenon, mobilizing millions of women and transforming other movements and spaces from the inside out. Workplaces, schools, homes, bars, the street, unions and other organizations: in recent years, it seems like all conversations and interactions are somehow marked by the questions and demands raised by the feminist movement. Feminism is everywhere and unstoppable. Can a translation help spread that collective effervescence? It is our desire that this translation serve to strengthen the resonances of an already existing feminist internationalism, that the concepts, practices, stories narrated here serve to spark feminist assemblies, strikes, organizing, and conversations in other places and times. And that it allows us to continue to weave those experiences together, to coordinate, to learn from one another, and to multiply, until we change everything.

Introduction

Feminist Potencia; or, The Desire to Change Everything

In recent years, the feminist movement has made the earth shake around the world. In Argentina, the Ni Una Menos movement emerged in response to the multiple and specific forms of violence faced by women and feminized bodies, and its participants rapidly invented a new form of organizing and action: the feminist strike. Half a million women, lesbians, trans people, and travestis came out to the marches following the 2017 International Women's Strike; 800,000 women took the streets for International Women's Day in 2018 and in 2019. At the same time, massive and sustained mobilizations for the legalization of abortion took place throughout 2018, 2019, and 2020.

This text was written in the heat of those events, at a time when the feminist movement was developing a new type of protagonism. And it was written from a particular position: from *within* that organizational dynamic. This is a living record of discussions that took place while we prepared for the strikes, marched, debated in assemblies, held dozens of meetings and hundreds of conversations, and coordinated and exchanged with *compañeras* around the world. It is a record of a political process that remains *open*. My writing is situated there. And it is carried out in the register of militant research.

The book's division into eight chapters began as an arbitrary affirmation of the number we used to organize the collective demands for the first International Women's Strike on March 8, 2017.[2]

However, as sometimes magically happens, the number clicked. And indeed, it coincides with a series of problems that make up the fabric of this text. Each chapter has a title-problem, and at the same time, it can be said that the questions repeat, reappear, persist, and jump from one chapter to the next. Despite naming them as different problems, there is a way of approaching them that draws out their dense interconnections. It could be said that while the same questions are always being raised, there is nevertheless a tone, a form of light, and a velocity that differentiates each of them.

The concept of *feminist potencia* reflects this sort of *movement* by gesturing toward an alternative theory of power.[3] To embrace feminist potencia is to vindicate the indeterminacy of what one can do, of what we can do—to acknowledge that we do not know what we're capable of until we experience the displacement of the limits that we've been made to believe and obey. It is not a naive theory of power, because it does not ignore the forms of exploitation and domination that structure power; in fact, its proposals go to the heart of the subjectivities that confront existing powers. In this sense, it is an understanding of potencia as the deployment of a counter-power. Ultimately, it is the affirmation of another type of power: that of common invention against expropriation, collective enjoyment against privatization, and the expansion of what we desire as possible in the here and now.

What I am attempting to construct here is an analysis that is *situated* in a sequence of struggles, street parties, experiential tremors, and resonances of the shout "Ni una menos!" ("Not one woman less!"). There is an underlying premise to this method of working and writing: that desire has a cognitive potential. I use the slogan, coined by the feminist movement, "Desire moves us" to recognize this *movement* as the collective intellect and multitudinous expression of an ongoing investigation, with its moments of shake-up and moments of retreat, with its variable velocities and intensities.

Potencia, a notion developed in the writings of Spinoza, Marx, and beyond, can never be detached from its roots, from the body that contains it. Therefore, feminist potencia is the potencia of the body that is always individual and collective and that also always exists in variation, that is, as singular. However, feminist potencia also expands the body due to the way it is reinvented by women's struggles, feminist struggles, and the struggles of sexual dissidences that time and time again *update* that notion of potencia.

Potencia does not exist in the abstract (it is not identical to the Aristotelian concept of "potential"). Rather, feminist potencia is desiring capacity. This implies that desire is not the opposite of the possible, but rather the force that drives what is perceived as possible, collectively and in each body. This book seeks to be a manifesto of that indeterminate potencia, expressed as the desire to change everything.

What I write here is knotted together with political and theoretical concerns and exchanges in which I have been engaged for a long time, through a very wide network of friendships and complicities—not to mention quarrels and controversies. This machine comprises conversations with compañeras, experiences, and texts from many places and many eras. Like all writing, multiple voices act and can be heard within it.

At the start, I want to highlight some methodological questions concerning my theoretical vantage, particularly with regard to *situated thinking*.

Situated thinking is inevitably feminist thinking: if the history of these struggles, for all their victories and defeats, has taught us anything, it is that the potencia of thought always has a body. That body is a constant and collective (even when individual) composition, one that assembles experiences, expectations, resources, trajectories, and memories.

Situated thinking is inevitably partial. "Partial" does not mean a small part, a fragment or a splinter. Rather, it describes a piece in an art of bricolage, a specific assemblage. As such it functions as an entry point, a perspective, that shows the singularity of an experience.

Situated thinking is a process. In this case, it is the heat of the feminist strike as political process that has created a landscape capable of sustaining new existential territories.

Situated thinking is inevitably internationalist thinking. Thus, feminist internationalism is not abstract, nor does it adopt a panoramic view. Each situation is an image of the world, a totality open to the infinite empirical experience of a concept's detail and texture. By starting from those situations, it weaves a transnationalism, a cartographic practice that creates global resonance from the South. Its strength comes from its rootedness in Latin America, in multiple layers of insurgency and rebellion. And it fuels a situated thinking that defies the scales, reaches, and inventions of an ever-expanding movement, without losing the force that comes from being embedded and the requirement to be concrete.

I write from Argentina, where the movement has its own distinctive characteristics. One of the primary hypotheses of this book is that the feminist movement here has a remarkable capacity to bring together two features often considered anathema to one another: *massiveness* and *radicality.*

The coalescence of these dimensions was anything but spontaneous. It has been patiently woven and worked on, threading together enormous street events with everyday activism that is equally monumental in scope. It has histories and genealogies that do not fit neatly into the recent calendar of mobilizations, precisely because they are what has enabled this opening up of time, in the here and now, in a subterranean way.

The feminist strike will serve as a catalyst, my entry point into a process that is simultaneously political, subjective, economic, cultural, artistic, libidinal, and epistemological. By "process" I am not referring to a descriptive neutrality that "substantiates" the strike, but rather the strike itself as a process of invention, rupture, and, at the same time, of the accumulation of forces.

4

In this sense, I propose the strike as a *lens*, as a specific point of view to read and frame some of the current problematics being raised by the feminist movement. As I discuss in the first chapter, I am inspired by Rosa Luxemburg's idea that each strike has its own form of political thought and that our historical task is to theorize the strike that we have led. In this sense, the international feminist strike functions as a threshold, an "experience," something that is crossed, after which one cannot go back to having the same relationship with things and with others. Many of us were transformed in and by this process.

I will use the idea of strike as a lens in a double sense:

1) *In an analytical sense.* The strike allows us to detect how certain forms of work and value production are rendered invisible in a diverse range of territories. It constructs a diagnosis of precarity based on our strategies for resisting and politicizing sadness and suffering. In this sense, that diagnostic becomes an anti-fascist and anti-neoliberal tool today.

2) *In a practical sense.* In our refusal to accept the invisibility of all our forms of work, the strike allows us to challenge and surpass the limits of what we are, of what we do, and what we desire, constructing a historical shift with respect to the position of victims and the excluded. In this register, the practice of the strike is a redefinition of a powerful form of struggle in a new historical moment. Against the narrow model of who can strike—white, male, waged, unionized workers—we have expanded its political capacity, languages, and geographies. Thus, questions arise that completely remake it: What types of bodies, territories, and conflicts fit into the strike when it becomes feminist? What type of generality is it committed to?

And many more questions arise from there. Can the feminist strike redefine the very notion of class on the basis of movements and struggles that do not use that vocabulary?

To reformulate the notion of class via subalternity, coloniality, and difference—as important theorizations and struggles from diverse geographies of the global South have done—also means to call into question, once again, a long Marxist history that takes homogeneity as the central characteristic of the class, and that takes for granted that "unity" is the objective result of the development of capitalism. Feminisms, through the strike, contest the boundaries of what is defined as labor and, therefore, the working class, opening the category back up to new experiences and demonstrating its historically exclusionary meaning. Even more: the strike broadens feminist experiences, taking them to spaces, generations, and bodies not included in earlier feminist practice. Moreover, it points to something beyond the "patriarchy of the wage" and its heteronormative rule.

The strike, as an undulating, long-winded process, draws a map of conflicts that dilute the rigid borders between life and work, body and territory, law and violence. The strike becomes a practical tool of political investigation and a process capable of constructing *transversality* between radically different bodies, conflicts, and territories.

In Chapter 2, I analyze the diagnosis produced by connecting different types of violence to the current needs of capital accumulation. In this way, I attempt to describe how the question of violence has escaped from its enclosure under the concept of "domestic violence" and the modes of its domestication through the responses attempted by institutions, NGOs, and philanthropic and paternalistic forms of management. Thus, the method that those institutions have criticized, that of "mixing everything up," is what makes it possible to trace the relationship between sexual violence and financial violence, between labor violence and racist violence, between police violence and obstetrical violence. Above all, it is this diagnosis that produces a strategic displacement: an escape from the figure of the victim, from permanent mourning, or from necropolitical accounting of femicides that is imposed on us.

Following this line, in Chapter 3, I reflect on the notion of *body-territory*, a concept elaborated by different compañeras from Central America to name the anti-extractivist struggles that begin with women's resistance—especially those of Indigenous, Black, and Afro-descendant women, along with different feminist collectives. I also use the concept to analyze how the struggle for the legalization of abortion in Argentina has overflowed that particular demand and its global repercussions through the Latin American pro-choice movement (the so-called green tide), as well as to understand what was at stake when the former daughters of genocidal military leaders decided to de-filiate from their families, while the daughters and nieces of political militants have continued to re-filiate in a register of rebellion.

Chapter 4 leaps to a different genealogy—the struggles of the unemployed in Argentina—to ask: What was invented by those collectives that took their pots and pans out onto the streets, not to bang them but to collectively produce and distribute meals to the hungry, that took reproductive tasks outside of household walls in the midst of the 2001 crisis? From there, the chapter outlines a critique of political economy from a feminist perspective in order to discuss a key point: the historical affinity between popular economies (all those economic activities that overflow the so-called formal economy) and feminist economics, and the ways the strike facilitates their mutual affection. A debate over aspects of value theory from the perspective of feminist economics is a fundamental element of this move, allowing for the definition that the movement has been constructing as anti-capitalist, anti-patriarchal, and anti-colonial. Additionally, it allows for connections between the critique of extractivism targeting common resources in our region, on one hand, and on the other, a critique of financial extractivism that is expanded as popular indebtedness.

Chapter 5 explores the kitchen where the strike was cooked up: the assembly as a space where political diversity elaborates its differences, where listening generates proximity, where the rhythm of thinking also gives a beat to breathing and the gestures of being together.

Chapter 6 unpacks the thesis of the Feminist International: What type of transnationalism from below is the movement building? What are the multilingual, migrant, moving territories that weave internationalism into a concrete force based on each struggle? The rootedness of feminisms, the communitarian reinvention for which feminisms create space, and the geographic imagination that they feed are part of a cartography that is continuously expanding.

However, the neo-fascist counteroffensive that characterizes the most recent alliance between neoliberalism and conservativism arises in response to this specific force. Chapter 7 explores how the ecclesiastic campaign against so-called "gender ideology" targets this force, as does the moral and economic crusade that leads to massive impoverishment, while proposing that anti-neoliberalism consists of a return to the family and to work for a boss.

Each of these chapters includes, in turn, an excursus: a more theoretical excursion into debates, ideas, or polemics that are related in some way to the problem in question, but that can also be read on their own.

Finally, Chapter 8 consists of eight theses, a sort of synthetic manifesto.

Multiple and overlapping temporalities have been involved in the writing of this book: many parts were written as the events were taking place, meaning that there is not a unifying, retrospective gaze. Yet, the rhythm that has driven it is that which opens up when we nurture a collective desire to change everything.

Chapter 1

#WeStrike: Toward a Political Theory of the Feminist Strike

Since 2016, the strike has successively taken on several names: "national women's strike"; "international strike of women, lesbians, travestis, and trans people";[1] "international and plurinational feminist strike"; and even "feminist general strike."

It has been woven together into a saga, somehow crazy and relentless in its force and continuity. The strike is not an isolated event; it is structured as a process. In that sense, it is still underway and open ended. In the space of less than three years (from October 2016 to March 2019), the strike became a tool driving the movement of women and dissident bodies in a new direction at the international level that continues to this day.

In Argentina, that movement was fueled by a slogan—"Ni una menos"—that convened the first, massive, mobilization in June 2015 against femicide, which would grow into the strike one year later, shouting "We want to be alive and free!" However, the strike also brought a historical accumulation of previous struggles to the stage. In genealogical terms, there are four lines that should be taken into account. The first is the women's movement, whose main reference is the Encuentro Nacional de Mujeres (National women's gathering) that has been held annually in Argentina since 1986, as well as initiatives such as the National Campaign for the Right to Legal, Safe, and Free Abortion, founded in 2005. The second is the human rights movement, led by the Mothers and Grandmothers of the Plaza de Mayo and their campaign for truth and justice for those "disappeared" under the military dictatorship of the 1970s and '80s. Third is the long history of movements of sexual dissidences, going from the legacy of the Frente de Liberación Homosexual (Homosexual liberation front) to the lesbian militancy in the 1970s for autonomous access to abortion to trans, travesti, intersexual, and non-binary activism. Fourth is the line of social movements, especially the unemployed movement, in which women's participation has been fundamental over the past two decades. Throughout this book, I will examine, in feminist terms, each of these lines and their modes of connection, contamination, and radicalization. Building on these struggles, the strike produced a qualitative leap: it transformed mobilization against femicide, focused on the sole demand "Stop killing us," into a radical, massive movement, capable of linking and politicizing the rejection of violence in a new way.

When the idea to call a "strike" emerged in the heat of a multitudinous assembly, it showed the potencia of an action that allowed us to go from mourning to taking our rage to the streets. In the word "strike," we perceived the strength of being able to summon and speak with all of our voices: housewives, workers in the formal and informal economies, teachers, members of cooperatives, the unemployed, the part-time self-employed, full-time mothers, militants, domestic employees, students, journalists, unionists, retail workers, women organizing neighborhood soup kitchens, and retired women. We came together based on our *doing*, and in our multiplicity we became accessible as a common ground.

Through the strike, we started to draw practical connections between the forms of violence that are tied together in sexist violence: the economic violence of the wage gap and the countless hours of unrecognized, unpaid domestic work, as well as the disciplining that results from a lack of economic autonomy; the violence of exploitation and its transfer into the household as masculine impotence, which implodes in situations of "domestic" violence; the violence of the defunding and looting of public services, resulting in the burden of extra community work. In this way, we showed how sexist violence has to do with much more than gender.

By using the word "strike," we began to weave connections between women's leading role in popular economies (where they are as criminalized as they are hyper-exploited) and in conflicts over the use of urban space, and the extractivist megaprojects that are encroaching on indigenous and community territories, attended by violence against the women leading those movements in defense of their territories. Connecting the strike to these issues also frees time for ourselves: both to think and to act, to grieve and to fight; to say enough is enough, and to find one another.

In this chapter, I consider the strike as a *new form of practical cartography* of the feminist politics that is today taking to the streets en masse. The strike's capacity to serve as both a practical horizon and as an analytical perspective emerging from struggle is what has allowed it to propel a popular and anti-neoliberal feminism from below—one that connects webs of economic violence to the violence targeting women's bodies and feminized bodies.

How was the strike reinvented and transformed by a movement led by subjects and experiences that do not fit into the traditional idea of labor? Why does the strike, as it is reappropriated from the labor movement, manage to translate new grammars of exploitation into new grammars of conflict in the here and now? How is the strike, in its expanded meanings, capable of connecting domestic labor with financial exploitation? Why did the strike enable a new type of international coordination?

The strike as a process weaves together the intensification of insubordination in multiple forms: different modes of protest and assembly; varying uses of the strike; occupations of diverse work and neighborhood spaces. Based on this multiplicity, the very idea of the *general strike* takes on another meaning, leading to other questions: From a feminist viewpoint, how does the multiplicity of actions included in the notion of the strike reveal and sabotage forms of exploitation and value extraction that today are no longer concentrated only in areas recognized as "labor"? How does the strike express a mode of political subjectification, a way of crossing borders and exceeding the limits of the possible?

Starting from these questions, it follows that adopting the lens of the feminist strike also serves as a means to understand the reconfiguration of contemporary capitalism—its specific modes of exploitation and value extraction, as well as the dynamics that resist, sabotage, and challenge it. The strike is a way of blocking the continuity of the production of capital, understood as a social relation. The strike is also an act of disobedience to the constant expropriation of our vital energies, plundered by exhausting routines. Therefore, more questions emerge: What happens to the very practice of the strike if it is understood and practiced based on sensibilities that are not recognized a priori as belonging to a *class* and that, nevertheless, challenge the very idea of class? How does this "displacement" of the strike, its out-of-place use, remap the spatialities and temporalities of production and antagonism?

A Feminist View on the Heterogeneity of Labor

The strike becomes a specific apparatus for politicizing violence against women and feminized bodies because it connects it to the violence of contemporary capitalist accumulation. In this sense, the strike produces a global map: it makes visible transborder circuits and organic relations between accumulation and violence. To convene the strike, we launched the slogan #NosotrasParamos (#WeStrike); in so doing, we forced that traditional tool of the organized labor movement to mutate, to be reconfigured, reconceptualized, and reused to reflect lives and work that escape the confines of the union (and its economy of visibility, legitimacy, and recognition).

The strike, as it has been reinvented by contemporary feminism, shows how precarity is a common condition, but also one differentiated through class discrimination, sexism, and racism. It becomes a tool for understanding violence as a juxtaposition of contemporary capitalism's forms of exploitation, and it turns feminism today into a form of organization, a practice of alliances, and a transversal and expansive narrative.

What does it mean to politicize violence through the strike? First, it means taking the strike as an action that situates us as political subjects against a systematic attempt to reduce our pain to the position of a victim to be repaired (in general, by the state). To be a victim, therefore, requires faith in the state and demands redeemers. The strike puts us in a situation of struggle. It does not forget the importance of mourning, but it removes us from the "state" of mourning.

Second, the strike is an exercise of mass suspension and sabotage of the political and economic order (in Argentina, half a million women were mobilized in each of the marches that followed the strikes in October 2016 and March 2017; 800,000 participated in March 2018, and a similar number in March 2019, on the heels of even more massive mobilizations for the legalization of abortion). Who went on strike and mobilized? It was not the workers traditionally recognized as such, but rather that heterogeneity of historically invisibilized labor. Mapping the strike thus becomes a tool for visibilizing hierarchies of work in a feminist register, giving visibility and value to forms of precarious, informal, domestic, and migrant work. This means no longer considering these forms of labor as *supplementary* or *subsidiary* to wage labor, but showing how they are fundamental to current forms of exploitation and value extraction, and also constitutive of the precarious and restricted condition of collective sustenance.

Third, the strike shaped an organizational horizon that

enabled it to play host to multiple realities, which together resignified, challenged, and updated the very dynamic of what we call a strike.

Argentina has one of the highest unionization rates in the world: two-thirds of waged workers in the country. In this context, the historic meaning of the strike was transformed by its feminist reinvention. First, it revolutionized who could call the strike: it ceased to be an order emanating from above (from the union hierarchy) to which workers simply adhered or complied. Instead, today the strike has become a concrete and situated question-investigation: What does it mean to strike from each different position? A first phase of this narrative consists of explaining why one cannot go on strike at home, or as street vendor, or as a prisoner, or as a freelancer (i.e., to identify ourselves as those who cannot strike). After all, there is no clear or identifiable boss, no one with whom to enter into immediate negotiations, and no clearly defined working hours during which to strike. Yet that *impossibility* immediately becomes its strength: it forces those experiences to resignify and broaden what is suspended when the strike must accommodate those realities, widening the social field in which the strike is inscribed and where it produces effects.

In a collective research-action intervention in 2005, the Madrid-based collective Precarias a la Deriva (Precarious women adrift) asked: What is your strike?[2] We return to this question, but on a mass scale, radicalizing it in opposition to the offensive of sexist violence that puts us in a state of assembly and emergency action. A concrete question—"How do we strike?"—multiplies the strike: in Paraguay, the call was used as a protest against the poisoning of communities with agro-toxins. In Honduras and Guatemala, the organization of the measure was strongly affirmed by the call against "territorial femicides" targeting community leaders. A communiqué from women in Colombia's FARC guerilla movement appropriated the call, which they signed "#NosMueveElDeseo"

(#DesireMovesUs), indicating that they would also be striking in the jungle. In Brazil, strikers' demands highlighted the church's advances against struggles for bodily autonomy. This organizational horizon, submerged in that dynamic of open conflict, recenters the class, anti-colonial, and mass dimension of feminism, because the situations that revolutionize the tool of the strike from within are those that the strike would disregard if it were to apply solely to free, paid, unionized, masculine labor with defined limits to its tasks.

Taken in its capacity as an anomaly, in its displacement of place, the strike has allowed for mapping, from the perspective of insubordination, the forms of labor exploitation—territories and vital webs that are made visible and given value by deploying a feminist lens. This point of view has been elaborated based on a common and transnational kind of action, leading to the production of an analysis in the form of a diagnostic—one that is elaborated in the assembly, and is not merely analytic. The practical exercise, the question of situated investigation, has been to map the unrecognized and unpaid ways in which we produce value and to elaborate a diverse collective image of what we call *work*, *territory*, and *conflict*.

A strike of women, lesbians, travestis, and trans people carries a force that overflows the space of labor because what is paralyzed and defied in the sabotage amounts to much more than a job. For a few hours at least, a mode of life in which that job is one piece among others is not recognized, the roles of the sexual division of labor are paralyzed, and the political arbitrariness that organizes the borders between work and nonwork are illuminated, as well as the historical struggles between confinement and autonomy, between recognition and rupture.

The strike exceeds and integrates the labor question. It does not leave it out, but at the same time it redefines it and brings it up to date; it problematizes and critiques it in relation to obedience. The strike multiplies this question's reach without diluting its historical intensity. It overflows it because it includes the realities of non-waged, unrecognized, unpaid jobs that have to do with forms of domestic, reproductive, mandatory, and free work, but also work linked to popular economies and the self-managed forms of life's reproduction. Viewing work in a feminist register thus allows us to think about a politics of this reproduction that takes up and traverses the domestic, social, neighborhood, campesino, and suburban territories, and their hierarchized articulation with the territory recognized as "labor."

The strike also exceeds and integrates the labor question because we are striking against the structures and the mandates that make capital's valorization possible. Those mandates (from the heteropatriarchal family to forced maternity, from clandestine abortion to sexual education) are not merely cultural or ideological questions. The mandates respond to the very imbrication of patriarchy, colonialism, and capitalism. Elements considered to be "noneconomic" are key to feminist economics as an expanded and radical critique of the patriarchal notion of the "economy."

In this sense the strike is turned into a vector of transversality: it goes beyond being a specific tool, whose legitimacy and use is prescribed for waged and unionized sectors associated with the "police-like materialism" of some unions (as Rosa Luxemburg put it), to become a formula of insubordination for realities and experiences that are supposedly "excluded" from the labor world. Such transversality thus challenges the supposed impossibility of the strike and demonstrates its possible uses, by shifting it to other territories, where it vindicates a legitimate anomaly and a new, practical potencia.

We could say that the feminist strike expresses three dimensions that have been strengthened sequentially from one strike to the next. First, the strike is constituted as a process, not as an event. This entails a concrete production of the time of the strike as a time of organization, of conversation, of building a common web, of coordination in assembly; the strike also produces subjectivations that elaborate a new type of radicality through the encounter with one another, and the effort to remain organized. The strike is not a detached and isolated date on the calendar, nor is it the creation of an event that is an end in itself.

Second, the strike produces intersections between struggles and creates transnational connections. It does so by involving a class dimension, linking violence against women and feminized bodies to forms of labor exploitation, police and state violence, and corporate offensives against common resources. This means it broadens the dimensions of conflictiveness, including questions of identity, while going beyond their neoliberal multicultural capture. The strike remaps social conflict *in practice*. By de-liberalizing the politics of recognition, quotas, and identitarian traps, the popular, Indigenous, communitarian, peripheral, slum, and Black feminisms from Latin America thus politicize the precarity of existence as a sequence that is inseparable from dispossession and exploitation.

Third, because of all of this, when we narrate the geography of fear and risk (because many of us carry a map of warnings that alerts us to multiple forms of abuse and violence), it is in terms of a fear that is translated not into victimization, but into *strategic capacity*. The map of sensibilities of the different forms of exploitation that are experienced every day in relation with others fuels radical ways of thinking about territory and, in particular, about the body as territory (body-territory).

Our '17

The strike of our revolutionary 2017 traces a serpentine line going back a century, echoing and connecting with the strike of March 8, 1917, which was driven by the textile workers of Petrograd against the hardships of the war and in repudiation of tsarism. The overflowing and radicalization of that strike led to the beginning of the Russian Revolution. Another origin may be closer to home. Perhaps the strike of our revolutionary '17 started brewing in the *maquilas*, those enormous assembly plants dotting the border between Mexico and the United States. That is where many of us have turned, in an attempt to understand what was also killed in us each time one of those women workers was killed. It was those murdered women who made Ciudad Juárez famous as the concentration of a true "femicide machine."[3] What mode of freedom were these young women inaugurating by migrating to those factories that became part of a gruesome sequence, as well as key to global capital? This question was tattooed on each of us. We are its contemporaries, and in some way, the maquila is the beginning of the feminist strike in which we as strikers also played a leading role, and that it now falls to us to think about it.

There could have been no international strike of women, lesbians, trans people, and travestis in 2017 without the expanded geography of Ciudad Juárez, without our fears and our desires, which become mixed up there, to the rhythm of flexibilized production and the border, our practices of escape and conditions of exploitation that we never would have imagined that we would be able to handle but that we decided to confront. Who is killed in Ciudad Juárez? Julia Monárrez explains that "they are predominately young women, they are brown, they are students, they are workers, they are girls, but all of them are economically marginal."[4]

March 8 commemorates other young migrant women, too: sweatshop workers who went on strike in the Uprising of the 20,000 and later died in the March 1911 Triangle Shirtwaist Factory fire in New York. Thus, in a discontinuous manner, it brings together memories of these women workers' contempt and organization with the women workers of Juárez and the force that the International Women's Strike in 2017 propelled, as a common measure, in fifty-five countries. That form of action was repeated, weaving together even more layers of organization on March 8, 2018, and March 8, 2019 and again in March, 2020.

When we speak of the international feminist strike, then, we are referring to a transnational, but not abstract, measure. The feminist strike, following the genealogy that starts with the maquila, expresses the need to mourn those bodies that only come into sight as a series of cadavers surrounded by horror, always in anonymity, that recur in every femicide in Latin America, the rates of which have multiplied over the last decade.

Over the past five years, feminist struggles have also developed a capacity for analysis and have come to understand these murders not as sexual crimes, but as political ones.[5] When we read with trepidation the number of deaths that are repeated between the factory, the nightclub, piecework, and the border, we understand something that connects us to those women, even in a desert that we have never seen but that feels close to us. Because something of that geography is replicated in a peripheral urban neighborhood; in a slum that is also dotted with informal textile workshops; in a nightclub outside the city; in homes imploding with domestic violence; in the risks taken by migrants; and in the communities being evicted by transnational capital's mega-enterprises. It is the composition of a common body that produces a kind of resonance: a politics that makes the body of one woman the body of all. That is what draws us to that old slogan, chanted in all the marches: "If they touch one of us, they touch us all!" Then we understand that there is something in the lives of the women of Juárez that exists in all our lives: the impulse of a desire for independence, a decision to forge a destiny that one wagers on, trusting in one's own vitality, the movement and the risk fueled in equal parts by fantasy and desperation. In Ni Una Menos Argentina, we identify the decision to strike as also a decision regarding our mobility and desire for autonomy. #NosMueveElDeseo:

desire moves us, thus politicizing it. By naming the impulse of movement, we explicate the subjective place where we locate political force. The phrase was replicated here and there, in the jungle and in neighborhoods, in schools and during marches, in homes and in assemblies. It named a common truth. And it allowed us to coordinate multiple spaces, trajectories, and experiences to constitute a specific link between moving and stopping, blocking and transforming, striking and removing our bodies and our energies from the reproduction of capital, fueled by everyday violence. The slogans that accompanied the strike initiative summarize a sentiment shared here and there: "If our work isn't valued, produce without us!" "If we stop, we stop the world!"

The feminist strike responds—with both a political language and form of action—to a mode of violence against women and feminized bodies that seeks our political neutralization and negation. That mode of violence seeks to confine us to the position of victims (while also almost always casting us, indirectly, as guilty of causing the violence that we suffer). By halting our activities and our roles, by suspending gestures of ours that confirm patriarchal stereotypes, we use the tool of the strike to build counter-powers against the femicidal offensive that synthesizes a specific intersection of different forms of violence.

It follows that femicidal violence is not only confined to domestic violence. New forms of indebtedness to maintain daily existence are part of the violence of precarity that triggers intra-family violence. Sexist violence expresses an impotence that responds to the display of a desire for autonomy (in fragile and critical contexts) by feminized bodies. This desire for autonomy is immediately translated into practices of contempt toward masculine authority, to which it responds with new dynamics of violence that can no longer be characterized as only "intimate."

Ciudad Juárez expands beyond Mexico because it functions as a sort of laboratory, anticipating how a certain labor and migrant energy of women expresses a political dynamism (a set of historical struggles) to escape from domestic confinement, of which transnational capital takes advantage. It is a desire for escape that the capitalist machine exploits, using the yearning for popular prosperity as fuel in order to translate it into dispossessive forms of labor, consumption, and debt—at its peak, becoming the femicidal machine.

It is through these temporal and geographic displacements that I want to account for an important reinvention of the strike, that creates a new origin story that turns on its *production of proximity* between struggles that seem chronologically and spatially distant. There is a twofold movement here: the creation of connections between struggles, which are neither spontaneous nor natural, and are produced not in a purely analytical register but through insubordination.

This dynamic, the forging of connections, is also seen in an abundance of times and spaces of creation. For example, a 2015 fanzine written by imprisoned women in Mexico entitled *Women on Strike, the World Falls* fictionalizes the beginnings of the feminist strike from within the prison.[6] These displacements of the strike also open up the very meanings of its placement, of its politics of place and of its appropriation of time. This is what militant intellectual Raquel Gutiérrez Aguilar narrates as she passes through the Bolivian prison of Obrajes, in the city of La Paz, where the strike expresses the possibility of a different sort of political community.[7] Thus the strike is transformed into a tool of refusal and contempt that *transversalizes* situations at the same time that it composes them, starting from subjectivities that have been historically excluded or subordinated in the labor and political spheres.

#NosotrasParamos (#WeStrike) was the slogan launched by Ni Una Menos that was later interwoven with others. To say "we strike" suspended at the same time it enabled. Striking is a negative gesture, of blocking, yet it enables an indeterminacy that places us in a state of investigation: What do we do by striking? What is stopped when we strike? What other things does this form of striking allow us to do?

The feminist movement has words, but it is not only made up of words, as if they floated around collecting meanings here and there. It is important to avoid thinking about the notion of the strike as a "floating signifier," as those who use the Argentine theorist Ernesto Laclau's theory refer to it: the sort of term that, because it is undefined, anything can fit into or be projected onto, a linguistic declination of logical and discursive connections.[8] The strike is able to be transversal, is able to give collective voice to so many kinds of people, precisely because it is rooted in the shared materiality of our precarity. It is these shared conditions that give the strike its meaning, rather than the inverse (as if realities would require that signifier in order for their common composition to be legible).

The first national women's strike in Argentina took place in the pouring rain on October 19, 2016, a few weeks after the women's strike for abortion in Poland. It was experienced as a vibrating sound that formed what psychoanalyst Suely Rolnik has called a massive "resonant body."[9] What was heard trembling was that shout that is made by moving one's hand over one's mouth. A pack's howl. A warlike disposition. A conjuring of pain. A very old and yet very new shout, connected to a way of breathing.

That day, we were mourning the murder, by colonial methods, of sixteen-year-old Lucía Pérez in the city of Mar del Plata.[10] She was raped and impaled to death at the same time that 70,000 women, lesbians, trans people, and travestis were meeting at the Encuentro Nacional de Mujeres in Rosario, the largest ever recorded in the gathering's thirty-three-year history. The previous year, when the encounter was held in Mar del Plata, there had been brutal repression on the final day and, on returning, we heard news of the travesticide of Diana Sacayán.[11] We had found out about the crime against Lucía on the eve of October 12, the date that "commemorates" the conquest of America. Therefore, the colonial imagery seemed inscribed between the lines: both the method and the date of the murder contained layers that resonated in the collective colonial unconscious.

Following the wave of rage that inundated social media came a message from Ni Una Menos: "Let's meet in an assembly." The need for a face-to-face encounter against the terror and paralysis that we felt when we saw the crime, a crime that they tried to make exemplary and instructive, allowed us to go beyond virtual lament. In that assembly, the idea-force of the strike emerged. Apparently excessive according to conventional "measures" of force to be organized in a week (irrational, that is, from the point of view of many people who were not present!), in the assembly itself, the strike was perceived as completely possible and realistic. The assembly, held in a warehouse belonging to the Confederation of Workers of the Popular Economy (CTEP)[12] of the Buenos Aires neighborhood of Constitución, produced another type of rationality and devised its own form of decision making, as well as something else: ways of putting that decision into practice. I want to propose the formula of a *realism of the assembly*: it is in that space where there is a collective evaluation of strength, and the ability to elaborate possibilities that did not preexist the assembly as a space of encounter. But the assembly is also constituted as an apparatus that is capable of anticipating and eventually casting out the risks and threats that will attempt to capture that common force. It is also in that sense that I refer to a realism: the assembly is not only an enthusiastic celebration of encounter and, therefore, an "illusion" of force, but a machine of perception-evaluation that takes responsibility for limits without accepting them a priori as restrictions.

What Is (Not) to Be Done?

There is a temporality of the strike that effectively puts into practice a refusal: a way of saying "enough!" to the violence and the way in which our time slips through our fingers; a refusal of the physical and psychic exhaustion that sustains extenuating precarity. It is saying "no!" to the fact that the multiplicity of tasks we carry out is not translated into economic autonomy, but rather is reinforced as compulsory and free labor. It is a refusal of the invisibility of our efforts and labors, and it builds on an understanding that this invisibility structures a political regime based on systematic disregard for those tasks.

The strike, then, disrupts its own temporality as a "date." It began to be imagined—in the imagination that navigates such tight confines—in the maquila; it continued in homes; it transpired in assemblies; it was discussed in unions and community soup kitchens; it became a collective breath in the streets; but it had been brewing since times of sabotage enfolded in ancient memories. What, then, is the experience of time produced by the feminist strike? In what sense are we able to analyze violence against women and feminized bodies as an offensive of capital? How do we respond to state regulation that limits our gestures and language? How do we continue strengthening our feminist struggles within the popular and autonomous horizon that the strike fueled?

The feminist strike, unlike the traditional labor strike (that is, of the masculine, waged, and unionized labor movement) is not only linked to "professions." It simultaneously refers to certain *specific* tasks linked to production and reproduction, and therefore to a *generic* question: it explains why certain tasks correspond to a certain sexual division of labor. In this register it is both a *labor strike* and an *existential strike*.

That generic and generalized activity for which the strike is carried out means that it is not an "identitarian" strike, as claimed by certain union leaderships that saw their monopoly of the strike being questioned. Thus they argue that the feminist strike is only "symbolic" since it would not "really" alter the productive sphere and would, rather, be a demand for recognition—that is, an action that merely seeks the recognition of identity.

The key to the feminist strike is *disobedience* in a broad sense, one that both exceeds the legal framework of the "union" strike, while "using" its protection for certain specific situations. What is radical about the feminist strike is that it opens up questions about who we are disobeying (if it is not only the figure of the boss), what and who we are striking against (if it is not only bosses condensed in leaderships), and how interrupting the relation of obedience that capital imposes on us creates a space for thinking about different lives.

Striking, in this feminist meaning, involves a two-part movement, which is much more explicit than the factory strike —above all, because the strike unfolds and spills over into the street, the community, and the home. Thus, this practice opens up the spatialities of the strike; it multiplies them while showing how spheres that have been arbitrarily segmented and partitioned are, in fact, connected.

As scholar-activist Silvia Federici said of the March 8, 2018, strike, it was about "stopping the activities that contribute to our oppression and, at the same time, producing those that expand the horizon of what we want as a different society." There is, then, a double dynamic to the strike: to stop certain activities, *to free up time and energy* in order to give time and space to others (both existing ones and those to come). Striking in workplaces, in households, in schools, as proposed by the feminist strike, liberated time to dedicate it to the assemblies and mobilizations throughout the day. This form of strike is not merely staying home from work (one variant of the traditional strike) or going on strike from one particular job, but rather opening up the question of the strike everywhere, occupying the streets and the whole day of the strike. If our occupations and roles oppress us, to strike is to defy them, to create the conditions of possibility for other ways of existing.

The frantic organizing activity during the days following the decision-making assembly in October 2016 included meetings with all types of organizations, while word traveled on its own to different countries across the continent, and the calls and languages in which it was expressed multiplied. In our method of overflowing borders and limits in our practice (the excessiveness of the strike, of the time of the measure and the measure of time, of the "rationality" enacted by the call), we realized that in various places in the world, thousands of women and sexual dissidents had the same practical need to mobilize. They shared a desire to escape the confinement forced by private mourning, resulting from death and forms of violence that put existence itself in danger, that threaten any gesture of autonomy, solely for being women, lesbians, trans people, and travestis.

Organizational frenzy. Transnational resonance. Discussion over how much strike time we could "guarantee." Everything feeds a question that has already been launched: what is the time of the strike? That day we stopped the country, in a coordinated action, for one hour, but we also did so in thousands of different and interlinked ways throughout the whole day. There were strikes in hospitals and schools, in factories and retail businesses, in the subway system and universities; there were assemblies in small towns and in large cities, mobilizations everywhere, and flags hanging from the windows and balconies of all the houses that declared themselves on strike. Throughout the day we resisted doing anything other than organizing ourselves to be together. We made time itself shake, opening it up, exploding it.

What does it mean to strike if the *measure* of the strike does not respect, does not adjust to, and even goes beyond the "workday"? It means that the temporality in play does not coincide with working hours. But what are working hours for someone who combines domestic work with odd jobs, with state benefits and/or intermittent unemployment? When do you stop, if after work you keep working at home and in the neighborhood, in all those community spaces that, in fact, expand and overflow the domestic sphere, and reformulate work itself? When will we cease to be subjugated by the endless work imposed on us by gender roles?

There are two forms of *time* in the strike. One is the *unmeasurable quality of work time from the feminist perspective*. It is what accounts for excessive work, without a measurable amount of time, without clear limits. Feminist theories have popularized the notion of the *triple working day*: work outside the home, work within the home, and the affective work of producing relations and networks of care. To strike in that multiplicity of times is a *subtraction* that seems almost impossible because it takes place in that excess, where life and work are assembled and where reproduction is made visible as production. In the temporality of the strike, the multilayered consistency of working time is made visible from a feminist point of view: How is the very time that is counted as work time "produced"? How are workers produced by their vital and everyday reproduction? That is why to strike in this register is to rethink everything.

On the other hand, there is the time that is counted as the coordinated time of absence, sabotage, and blockage carried out anywhere at the same time: a strike of eight hours, twenty-four hours, one shift? Something of that very distinction is being undone and, at the same time, is being raised as a political strategy.

As Italian and North American feminists debated when they launched the Wages for Housework campaign in the 1970s, a fundamental question is highlighted in reproductive labor, the labor of producing and reproducing life every day: Can reproductive labor be measured with a wage? How do you calculate how many hours should be paid by a wage that remunerates domestic tasks? Furthermore, how can the intensity of work that involves care and affect, and that involves unlimited subjectivity and not simply a series of repetitive, mechanized tasks, be measured?[13]

That domestic labor must be compulsory and free to serve its function is pointed out and systematized by Silvia Federici in her book *Caliban and the Witch*. This text has circulated widely in Latin America following its translation into Spanish in 2011 and has nurtured debates in diverse spaces, as part of practices of popular feminist pedagogy.[14]

What we learn from Federici, whose theorization returns to the political experience of Wages for Housework, is that the specific mode of exploitation that capitalism organizes for women first requires them to be socially discredited. Only in this way is their enclosure and privatization justified. In capitalism, the domestic is produced as a space of "enclosure": women are *confined* to the home, they are limited to this sphere baptized as the "private." Later, they are forced to work for free and their tasks are rendered politically invisible.

But Federici warns of another danger: the specific relationship between reproductive labor and the wage under the formula of the "patriarchy of the wage."[15] The stipulation that domestic, affective, and care work be free and compulsory, she argues, is the key to the productivity of the wage, its hidden part, its secret crease. Why is it hidden and secret? Because capitalism itself exploits that work through the sexual division of labor, creating a hierarchical relationship between the sexes (and more generally toward feminized bodies) and subordinating, while politically devaluing, free labor.

In the 1970s, Angela Davis also debated the universality of the figure of the "housewife," arguing that those women enclosed in their homes only accounted for the status of some women, while universalizing a particular model of femininity. Black women's experience in the labor market that Davis historicizes, however, was also a reflection on the servile character taken by domestic work after women were stripped of their position as "expert workers" during the colonial era, which saw the advent of an economy that was based on the household but not limited to it. This point is fundamental. The distinction that Davis makes between an economy based in the household, but able to project economic protagonism outside the home, on one hand, and on the other a secluded domestic sphere where work is not recognized as such, reveals the political production of the household as a space of confinement. This shows that the problem is not the existence of the home or of domestic economies, but that of the division between a capitalist economy of profit that only recognizes activity in the public sphere (i.e., nothing more or less than the "labor market"), and the private and inferior domestic economic (the reign of free and unrecognized work). Davis also emphasizes that Black women were not only housewives; indeed, upon being dispossessed of their economic protagonism in domestic economies based in the household, they were the first to be forced to enter the labor market, and even so they never stopped being treated as "strange visitors" in factories. The articulation between patriarchy, capitalism, and colonialism is evident here.[16]

The debate that Davis raises with the Italian feminists is very important: it focuses on questioning the "emancipatory" capacity of the wage. She argues that the oppressive and frustrating nature she attributes to domestic work would not be extinguished by receiving a wage as monetary repayment for those tasks that continue to be the same. To the contrary, the wage would legitimate "domestic slavery." Davis takes as an example the women who work as domestic employees and maids who, despite being paid, fail to increase the social status of that work.

Davis's critique, however, overlooks the criticism the Italians themselves made of the "domestic wage," proposed as a paradoxical demand: that is, as a specific demand and at the same time as an "impossible" measure, since it demonstrates capitalism's reliance on unpaid work as part of its structural logic. They also pointed to the "ordering" role of the wage: it operates by maintaining the division between the public and the private, hierarchically dividing spatialities and sexes.

Both theories raise common points via different entryways. First, they note that the wage under capitalism is a narrow framework for thinking about liberation from the oppressive character of domestic labor. That is why both Davis and the Italian Marxist feminists explicitly denounce the political role of the wage. Second, both argue that domestic labor is oppressive to the extent that it is part of a certain mode of confinement, one that is unpaid and obligatory. Both questions then are ways of demonstrating the original articulation between gender, class, and race.

What happens when the home is not synonymous with enclosure? Here the debate opens up over whether or not capitalism can produce value by getting rid of domestic life. But what sort of domestic life are we talking about? Davis refers to the South African case, showing how an attempt was made to dismantle households on the grounds that they were considered spaces that fomented resistance to apartheid. Yet, at the same time, she wonders how the completion of reproductive tasks could be ensured with an infrastructure of support that would not obligate women to bear the brunt. In the case of Italian women, and the debate that Silvia Federici continues today, capitalism's inability to automate reproductive tasks (a utopian imaginary of technological development) ensures that reproductive labor is not only oppressive and obsolete (as Davis affirmed in the 1970s), but also a space that deploys another type of productivity if it is freed from its compulsory and family-based character. It is along these lines that we can return to the key point Davis makes about a domestic economy that projects political power.

The Domestic Wage and the Social Wage

This earlier historical debate, which spanned continents and involved many participants writing from varying conjunctures, can now be brought back to a discrete and concrete situation in Argentina: the debate over state subsidies to remunerate reproductive tasks. Comprised of these tasks that make up a good part of feminized work beyond the formal waged economy, the economy of self-management or the "popular economy" is distinguished politically from concepts of the "informal," "marginal," and "excluded economies." The discussion about how to compensate these tasks, which have become social and communitarian *because of the crisis*, has to do with a politicization of the subsidies coming from the state by social movements, whose history goes back to the 2001 Argentinian economic crisis.

Since then, a political question has taken shape: What forms does living labor take, today, outside of the factory? In an Argentinian context, this question has grown in importance ever since the eruption of movements of *piqueteros* (unemployed workers) at the beginning of this century. Such collective movements dislocated the workers' "picket line"— that classic deployment of force in the factory—by taking it to the streets and highways. Since then, a myriad of forms of work "without a boss," exemplified by the hundreds of factories and companies that have been recuperated by their workers, have emerged as a response to systematic layoffs, bankruptcies, and capital flight. Such projects have given rise to forms of self-management that have combined welfare benefits packages

31

won from the state with a strong desire for autonomy, territorial enterprises managed by popular assemblies, and the valorization of community work, all framed by the urgent need to survive in an increasingly desperate situation.

The political genealogy of the valorization of reproductive labor, particularly in popular economies whose leadership is clearly feminized (i.e., starting within social movements and then achieving institutional recognition), is a key point raised today by feminist economics. What sort of dialogue is possible between the 1972 Wages for Housework Committee and the benefits packages that today are being expanded in Argentina?[17] How have these benefits packages, largely targeted at women, recognized—in an ambivalent way—care work and feminized community labor?

That valorization has to do with how those tasks spill beyond the confines of the home: into self-managed soup kitchens, day cares, health care initiatives, and so on. This spillover is due to the crisis that destroyed the masculine "heads" of households through massive unemployment. But, more than anything, it is the effect of the politicization of the crisis through community and popular organizational dynamics.

There is a key point here that I will attempt to develop at various points throughout this book and that forms an essential component of my broader hypothesis about the affinity between the popular economy and feminist economics: the dispute over the social "revalorization" of reproductive tasks in a context in which their political function has become a new source of dignity and prestige in neighborhoods, as their protagonists become socially and politically recognized. This situation opens up challenges to "authority" in the face of new thresholds of cruelty in the webs of violence, whose favored target is women and feminized bodies. In this sense, there is a fundamental tension in popular economies: they move between the *family-based* orientation imprinted on subsidies by the state (through the request for considerations where the family "obligation" is used as reassurance: requirements include vaccinating children, making them attend school, and so on) and their operation as part of an overflowing of the domestic confinement of reproductive tasks that has already occurred, largely driven by the crisis.

As I indicated previously, in the 1970s, the framework was the discussion about the sexual division of labor, which highlighted the consolidation of hierarchies that organized unpaid domestic labor and the invincible border that marked the public outside. That division was put in practice by a concrete tool: the wage, that remunerated labor done "outside" the home, consecrating money's power of command within the household. That function, thanks to feminist theorizations, became known as the "patriarchy of the wage" and was later popularized by the phrase of Federici herself: "They call it love, we call it unpaid labor."

The wage, as a patriarchal apparatus, maintains domestic confinement as a place where an "invisible infrastructure" is produced that fuels, sustains, and enables the "independence" of the "free waged worker." Its condition of invisibility is historically and politically produced. Domestic tasks are those that have to do with social reproduction in general and, therefore, with the very conditions of possibility of exploitation in capitalism. That they have been devalued time and time again— precisely so that they do not count, so that they are not remunerated, so that they are not recognized as immediately productive, and so that they are not politically vindicated in their centrality —is the effect of capitalist-patriarchal-colonial exploitation.

Does the "patriarchy of the wage" continue operating in the same way today? What does the patriarchy of the wage mean when the wage itself is increasingly a privilege of "stability" only available to a few? I will develop this point more extensively in Chapter 4, but for now it suffices to affirm: the feminist strike takes on the crisis of the patriarchy of the wage and opens up debate about how forms of patriarchy are being reinvented today beyond the wage.

33

The Becoming-Internationalist of the Strike

In Argentina, the call to strike one year after the rise of the far-right government of Mauricio Macri was a gesture that no "organized" political force had made until that moment. We called for the strike beyond the trade union parameters and, at the same time, denounced their negotiations with the neoliberal government. "Yes we can, women were the first to strike against Macri," was heard later in the Plaza de Mayo. "While the General Confederation of Labor drinks tea with the government, women take the streets!" was another slogan that pointed out the displacement effected by the strike, and the debate around work in relation to the neoliberal measures underway, as well and the union's passivity. The mass resonance of the call to the streets, given what we knew was simultaneously happening in other countries, made it an unforgettable day of collective effervescence, where we shared scenes of everyday contempt, gossip about revolt—anonymous whispers on a day that, as we sang in the rain, we stopped the world and found ourselves.

But this was only the first, the one that would inaugurate a saga. The force of that strike led us to decide to call an international strike on March 8, 2017. Thus it began to be amassed, communicated, debated, and above all, built in multiple spaces, by diverse classes, in conjugations that enabled the strike to accommodate and expand with heterogeneous realities, with geographies that, although distant from one another, are connected by overlapping zones, struggles, and realities that are not reduced to the borders of nation-states.

On that day in March 2017, we felt the earth shake beneath our feet. But during the preceding months, we had moved with the certainty that what we were doing, or stopped doing, was decisive. We had organized assemblies, attended small meetings here and there, talked, wrote, listened, fought, conspired, and fantasized. We even dreamed at night about what was left to do in the coming days. Compañeras around the world would simultaneously do similar things: coordinated by slogans and intuitions, by practices and networks we had been weaving for some time, as well as by gestures that we did not even know lived inside of us. We were magnetized by a strange shared feeling of rage and complicity, of potencia and urgency. But, more than anything, we were amazed by the surprise of that multiplicitous and effective coordination. As we operated, we were connected by images that accumulated as a password: from the streets to the internet, and from there to our retinas, sealing themselves as part of a transnational, multilingual imagination. We wove, with the horizon of those days, a new internationalism. And the strike unfolded as *rupture* and as a *process*.

The strike, then, has another double dimension: *visibilization* and *flight*. It not only seeks the recognition of invisible labor. It is also a wager on its refusal. In the combination of the two, the very radicalization of what we are going to name as work is at stake. Flight at the same moment as recognition. Simultaneous desertion and visibilization. Contempt at the same time as it is counted. It is in that two-sidedness that relations, times, and spaces are perceived based on their *becoming*.

That disjunction between visibilization and flight is understood not as a contradiction, but rather as the opening to various modalities of the strike. The strike took up another mode of demands: condensed in a practice that does not make demands, but rather expresses precisely that desire to change everything. Therefore, the strike also integrates and overflows specific demands. That was the experience of the preparatory assemblies—open calls to gather and organize the strike that took place in the preceding month. It integrates them because it does not underestimate concrete demands about budgets, laws, necessary modifications to institutions, or specific complaints. And it overflows them because placing bodies in common on the street enables a stoppage in order to give ourselves time to imagine how we want to live and to affirm that our desire is for radical change. But these two planes are not experienced in opposition. To put it in classic terms: it is not reform *or* revolution. There is a simultaneity of temporalities that do not function in contradiction. Having concrete demands does not imply the idea that recourse to the state is the most effective response to violence: this diagnosis does not impede fighting for and winning resources that, by not being thought about as ends in themselves, are assembled with other dynamics of transformation.

In that way, the state is not invested with a capacity for "totalization." This means that, in opposition to state-centric perspectives, ours does not continue to prioritize the state as a privileged site of transformation. And, at the same time, it does not ignore the state in its limited political capacity, which is, therefore, capable of partially modifying certain realities—for example, in relation to the allocation of resources. This position renews political theory in feminist terms and replenishes other coordinates for thinking about radical change.

Every Strike Contains a Form of Political Thought

For the militant revolutionary and theorist Rosa Luxemburg, fascinated with the mass strike during the 1905 Russian Revolution and its implications for the international labor struggle, each strike has its corresponding form of political thought. That phrase seems to me like a talisman, and one worth emphasizing. On the one hand, she studies a combination of elements to characterize the strike as a process and not as an isolated event: "so very many important economic, political and social, general and local, material and psychical, factors react upon one another in such a way that no single act can be arranged and resolved as if it were a mathematical problem." It is that rhythm and multiplication of elements that make Luxemburg think that the strike is a living body:

It is the living pulse-beat of the revolution and at the same time its most powerful driving wheel ... If the sophisticated theory proposes to make a clever logical dissection of the mass strike for the purpose of getting at the "purely political mass strike," it will by this dissection, as with any other, not perceive the phenomenon in its living essence, but will kill it altogether.[18]

On the other hand, in understanding the strike as a process, Luxemburg is dedicated to investigating the different strikes that preceded the great strike of 1905 in Russia. Therefore, when she describes its expansion, an aquatic landscape appears. "It flows now like a broad billow over the whole kingdom, and now divides into a gigantic network of narrow streams; now it bubbles forth from under the ground like a fresh spring and now is completely lost under the earth." Undoubtedly, she is accounting for a multiplicity of actions to conclude that "all these run through one another, run side by side, cross one another, flow in and over one another—it is a ceaselessly moving, changing sea of phenomena." Adopting the strike as a lens allows us to deploy the strike's political thought as we experienced it, and to understand its processuality and multiple geographies.

I bring up Rosa Luxemburg here not only because of that clue that she provides us with, but also because today her thought can inspire us along three lines of investigation-intervention:

1) Feminist movements, in the multiplicity of the here and now, can return to her critique of war precisely to understand the so-called war against women. Of course, while these are very different kinds of violent conflict, Luxemburg's reflections nevertheless continue to provide vital signposts for thinking about what this warfare attempts to dismantle. (In the following chapter, I will go into more detail on the discussion around the very idea of a "war" as a way of thinking about forms of violence against women and feminized bodies.)

2) In the same way, Luxemburg's theory of imperialism can

be reappropriated and updated in relation to capital's constant need to expand its borders and, in the case of the labor of feminized bodies, to think about how the violence of the process of accumulation particularly impacts those economies in which women are the leading players.

3) Finally, her theory of the strike as a process continues to be key for thinking about the temporality and the movement itself of a historical accumulation of forces that, by starting from the practical criticism of violence against women and the reappropriation of the tool of the strike, proposes the challenge of weaving a new internationalism and political work at multiple scales.

Unprecedented Alliances

The time of interruption that the strike produced was seized thanks to a fabric of unpredictable conversations and unprecedented encounters. We speak of unexpected alliances, as Mujeres Creando from Bolivia name them,[19] to account for the potencia that is unleashed from the way in which we interconnect, mix, and work together based on our differences, weaving the urgency to say "Enough is enough!" For the world is organized so that we do not find one another, so that we look at each other with mistrust, so that the words of other women and feminized bodies do not affect us.

What was it that created this possibility of encounter between women of the popular economy and housewives; between students and sex workers; between employees in public hospitals and hospital workers; between the unemployed and the self-employed?

To answer this, we have to look more closely at the time that preceded the strike itself, and must stop by the kitchen where the strike was cooked up: the assemblies. And not only those that were called for by the organization, but also ones that were replicated at different scales and in various places in the face of conflicts as they transpired.

This dynamic of assemblies and the production of alliances enabled us to leave the confines of gender discourse, which seeks to limit us to speaking about femicides and positioning ourselves merely as victims. That is, it allowed us to break through the fence that makes it so that feminized voices are only listened to if they narrate an episode of pure horror and violence, without that narrative's inclusion in political enunciation that unravels the causes of violence and asks what forces are necessary to confront it. But it also allowed us to go beyond solely self-declared feminist organizations in order to bring in compañeras from unions, social movements, community spaces, organizations of Indigenous peoples or Afro-descendants, student groups, migrant collectives, art groups, and others. The assemblies are a space where those unusual alliances flourish; they also imply frictions, debates, and disagreements, as well as partial syntheses of what we are proposing.

In fact, the deepening of the strike was first demonstrated in the assemblies ahead of its announcement in 2018, where the qualitative leap, in organizational terms, was powerful. The number of attendees tripled: in the city of Buenos Aires alone turnout often exceeded 1,000. There were debates within each union about how to approach the strike. As one union activist described the scene: "I have never seen such a truly federal process of discussion." The 2018 strike increased in density by weaving together, once again, a social conflictiveness that was occurring in workplaces and, at the same time, it overflowed them because with the strike we practically redefined what we call work "places," incorporating the street and the household, creating new ways of looking at "jobs" as such. In that movement, which overturns spatiality and leads the strike to unexpected places, we also modify the concrete possibility of "striking," of "blocking," and ultimately of organizing ourselves by broadening and reinventing the strike itself.

I want to pause and focus on one of the preparatory assemblies initiated by the Ni Una Menos collective, along with many other territorial organizations, for the March 8, 2018, strike in Villa 21–24, a slum in the city of Buenos Aires. The majority of the participants were workers from the popular economy who carry out tasks of social reproduction in the neighborhood. Many worked in community soup kitchens, which became increasingly important in the face of the inflationary crisis that had been unleashed over the preceding year. They insisted on something that brilliantly points out the singularity of the feminist strike: they said both that they could not strike, and that they wanted to strike. That phrase opens up a situation of problematization; that is, a moment of thought. The *supposed impossibility* summarizes the practical dilemma of the feminist strike. In the case of women workers in the popular economy, the desire to strike was demonstrated by those who are assumed to be excluded from the prerogative (a quasi "privilege," from a certain perspective) of that labor tool traditionally associated with the organized, waged, and masculine movement.

They could not strike, they argued, because they have a responsibility to feed neighborhood residents, especially the children. But they wanted to strike because they wanted to be part of that collective action, and to be in the street with thousands of other women. This affirmation, which at first glance seems contradictory, broadened the strike. It complicated it, forcing it to live up to the multiplicity of tasks that redefine the very idea of work from a feminist point of view. Thus an idea emerged: "Why don't we hand out raw food? We'll leave the food at the door of the soup kitchens, but raw food, removing all the work of cooking, serving, washing," Gilda, one of the workers, summarized. The political occurrence unblocked the situation, adding another layer to the very practice of the strike. The idea was turned into graffiti that was spread across the neighborhood: "Today, March 8, we distribute raw food—Ni Una Menos." The assembly thus became a way of evaluating the logic of the sensory qualities of things—the raw and the cooked—from the point of view of women's labor.

Another one of them, Nati, clarified during the same assembly: "I want the strike to make people notice my absence." This supposes that the absence is not perceived, that it is corrected, replaced, precisely because there is a presence that permanently remains invisibilized and naturalized. A discussion ensued about the lack of recognition and the invisibility of reproductive tasks, the naturalization of "services" of cooking, cleaning, attending, calculating quantities. As if they were the real "invisible hand" of the economy that Adam Smith talked about. At the same time, they discussed how this work was building the neighborhood's concrete popular infrastructure, producing common services that have a clear political value. The question becomes urgent when faced with the scenario of crisis. Austerity has a differential impact on women in these neighborhoods: they are the ones juggling everything so that there is enough food, and, to start, they reduce their own intake so as to not decrease collective distribution. These women literally put their bodies on the line so that austerity is felt as little as possible in the daily lives of others.

In these situations of collective problematization, the specific exploitation of women's labor becomes a point of view that allows for the reconceptualization of the very notion of the bodies implicated in that work. That work is named, it becomes visible and recognized in its concrete manifestations as based on everything that is put to work in contemporary economies, as overflowing the map of formal waged labor. But by doing this based on the strategic thinking required by the question of how to strike, those forms of exploitation are revealed by the very possibility of disregarding them and not only in terms of an analysis of submission.

In this sense, the feminist strike functions as a *chemical catalyst*:[20] it demonstrates relations of power; it shows where and how they are inscribed and function; it discovers the bodies, times, and spaces over which they are applied and also the mechanisms for their disobedience. The strike becomes the key to an *insubordinate* practice when it begins operating as an element of disobedience and not simply as part of a repertoire of actions of negotiation.

The Debate *in* and *with* the Unions

In the case of Argentina, one of the particular features of the process was the tense and conflictive, yet constant, dialogue with unions of varying ideologies. This dialogue was decisive at the moment of seeking alliances. Initially, the union leadership strongly resisted giving up their monopoly over the tool of the strike. What was interesting was that the debate took place within unions themselves, empowering the young women within them, who were fighting to force the structures to open up spaces of democratization.

This was inseparable from the protagonism of women of the popular economy, including street vendors, women doing piecework out of their homes, trash collectors, community caregivers and cooks, and others, joined together in the CTEP as a particular union-esque formation. Those popular economy workers both demanded to be recognized as workers by other unions and demonstrated the limits of the "union" strike. Like the women in the villa's soup kitchens, they force us to think about the strike of those who "cannot" strike, because they would risk losing their daily income.

However, two points need to be emphasized about the participation of popular economy workers. On the one hand, at that conjuncture in Argentina, in which president Mauricio Macri—representative of the power of transnational financial groups and agribusiness associations—governed with measures that went directly against the wage, women vindicated the tool from a position supposedly "outside" of work that, nevertheless, is able to debate and reshape work itself. In this, it can be said that contemporary feminist struggles have a *piquetero genealogy*, referring to the struggles of the unemployed in Argentina. Those unemployed, who were supposedly condemned to the outside (so-called "exclusion"), were able to debate and reformulate what they called dignified work through the mass struggles that they developed at the beginning of this century.[21] At that time, the majority of the countries' unions refused to recognize the unemployed as workers, marking another line of analogy with today's feminist movement. On the other hand, the feminist strike *processes and takes responsibility* for the crisis of wage labor that *has already occurred*, occupying, socializing, valorizing, and reorganizing the labor of social reproduction. Here another continuity with the movement of the unemployed can be traced: it raises the issue about the current limits of inclusion through precarious waged labor and the permanent management of unemployment as a threat of exclusion from the perspective of the supposed "victims." That movement reveals the break with the figure of victimhood.

The broadening of the strike action (like the displacement of the picket from the factory to the highway beginning in the late 1990s) functions as a practical denunciation of the ways power structures (including some union leaderships) negotiate austerity. The expansion of the strike measure does not leave out wage disputes, but, at the same it, it redefines them and forces them to face the reality of non-waged labor. It multiplies the meanings of the strike without diluting its historical force. It relaunches the strike as the key for understanding how the transversality of social conflict is at play in the intersection of exploitation and sexist violence.

In the manifesto calling for the international strike on March 8, 2017 (which was quickly translated into several languages), we denounced the ways capital exploits our informal, precarious, and intermittent economies; how nation-states and the market exploit us when they put us in debt. And we declared that those forms of exploitation go hand in hand with the criminalization of our migratory movements. We made it clear that this feminist movement, by taking itself as a political subject, has the strength to denounce violence against women and feminized bodies as a new form of counterinsurgency, one that is necessitated by the expansion of the current modalities of exploitation and multiple forms of dispossession. The strike is shown, therefore, as a gesture of revulsion, not of negotiation. It is a rebellion against its decorative uses (as a folkloric occasion or preestablished date on the calendar) or its reduction to a "symbolic" effect that is only communicable on social media. The communication initiated by the strike phenomenon is sustained by the potencia of bodies in the street, by the eruption of words that create a new way of naming, by the rage unleashed by the violence, by the necessity of thinking about forms of self-defense and of explicating the new modes of exploitation and extraction of value.

Here, another point is worth highlighting: feminism becomes more inclusive because it is taken up as a practical anti-capitalist critique. Therefore, we can evoke Luxemburg again: the strike is not a "purely technical" weapon that can be "decreed" or "prohibited" at will. To the contrary, by including, highlighting, and valorizing the distinct terrains of exploitation and extraction of value by capital in its current phase of accumulation, the strike as *blockade*, *challenge*, and an act of *contempt* allows us to account for the conditions in which struggles and resistances today are reinventing a rebellious politics. Therefore, the use of the strike proposed by the movement of women, trans people, lesbians, and travestis expresses and disseminates a change in the composition of laboring classes, overflowing its classifications and hierarchies—namely, those that are so well synthesized by the patriarchy of the wage. And it does so from the register of a practical feminism, rooted in concrete struggles.

In February 2017, the Ni Una Menos collective met with the general secretary of Equality of Opportunities and Gender of the General Confederation of Labor (CGT), in their mythical building on Azopardo Street. The reception reminded us that the women's movement can be a nongovernmental organization, but it cannot call a strike. Our interlocutor insisted on this, expressing her concern with the "foreignization" displayed by the movement's internationalism. She also warned us that radicalization in our country "has always ended badly," referring to the armed struggle during the 1970s. There was something comical and anachronistic about her words: the secretary was worried that solidarity was our "weapon," interpreting the slogan "solidarity is our weapon," which originated with the feminist movement in Poland, as the promotion of an armed movement.

A year later, at a February 21 workers' march, the leaders of the union federations announced, from a shared stage, that March 8 was the next date for workers' mobilization, because it was the international feminist strike. The meeting we had with one of the male members of the CGT's triumvirate at its headquarters had ended with the leader's promise that he would be fulfilling tasks in a soup kitchen on the city's periphery on the day of the strike. On the eighth he sent us a photo of himself serving food to children. For the first time in its history, the CGT used the word "feminist" in an official communiqué, informing their members about the strike. Both scenes are vignettes of displacement, driven by a force from below: over the course of the entire year, the feminist movement was shown to be truly active, building the strike as a process.

The multiplication of the assemblies was connected with social conflict, from layoffs in factories to evictions of the Mapuche community, giving the movement a capacity for transversality that no other political actor could achieve. This implied having the skill to include conflicts that until recently were not considered part of feminism's concerns, reinventing feminism itself, but above all, transversalizing a mode of action and feminist problematization in all political spaces. The affirmation of the strike as a process accumulates concrete reference points in specific places because it delineates a feminism that is constructed as popular and anti-neoliberal.

However, it did not take long for arguments against feminism to emerge from union leaders opposed to the feminist strike. Such argument included the following:

— "Feminism functions as a form of sectarianism": it leaves out men and weakens the unity of demands. The women's movement is here presented as a sort of "external agent" to unionism, erasing the intersectionality of alliances and experiences, along with the potencia of questioning masculine authority and its logic of patriarchal construction *within* unions.

— "Women are not prepared to take the spaces of power that they demand": an intransigence is attributed to them that makes them supposedly unable to negotiate. It is not recognized that the feminist movement is putting into play a different logic of movement building, which, furthermore, uncovers the limits and inefficiencies of a conciliatory and extremely patient negotiation.

— "For the feminist movement to call a strike delegitimizes and weakens the power of the union leadership, in a moment of attacks and campaigns to discredit unions": they blame feminism for taking the initiative in the face of the unions' sectoral inaction.

— "The action of the feminist strike takes away force from other union actions": in this way, they ignore and disregard the inclusive form produced by a feminist understanding of conflicts.

These arguments structured the unions' reaction, in the face of a confluence of struggles linking diverse territories of work (domestic, community, waged, precarious, care, migrant) from the feminist view, which allowed for the radicalization and deepening of demands *within* the unions as well.

Despite these objections, the international strike on March 8, 2018, was accompanied by a historic achievement: in the heat of the preparatory assemblies, a "feminist intersindical" (interunion) was formed. In an unprecedented milestone, women leaders from all of the federations (five from Argentina), which have historically had political differences, held a joint press conference on March 7, 2018, to announce the transversal call to action. Today that confluence continues functioning and organizing common assemblies in places of labor conflicts and confronts the government's initiatives to translate demands about gender into neoliberal proposals (e.g., Argentina's November 2017 gender parity and pay gap law).

Difference and Revolution

The feminist revolution reshapes and reconceptualizes the meanings of both work and the strike. This is what allows the strike to function as both a *cartographic method* and an *organizational apparatus*. Here I draw on lines of analysis that historically have placed emphasis on the "making" and the "composition" of the working class, to demystify and oppose a certain crystallized idea of a class "identity" or "consciousness."[22] There are also decisive feminist theorizations about the conjunction between class and feminism as a method against the "male handling of the class struggle"[23] and about class as an element of racist discipline.[24] The strike, as it is taken up by feminism, forces us to reinvestigate what working-class lives are today. In this sense, starting from the *impossibility of the strike* opens it up to its *possibility in terms of the multiplicity of labor forms*, showing that the feminist movement is not simply a set of sectoral or corporate demands. To the contrary, it launches a question that affects the entire working class in its redefinition of class itself. As such, it opens a situated field of investigation.

47

The strike does so, first, because it shows how all of the exclusions that historically constituted the "class" have been dismantled and disputed through concrete struggles. Today the class is a multiplicity that has expanded the borders of what we understand as the "working class," thanks to those struggles that redefine who are considered to be productive subjects based on specific conflicts. At the same time, the class never ceases to be a partiality: a division in society between those, following Marx, who depend on their labor power in order to relate to themselves and to the world, and those who do not.

The *expansion of the class through the multiplication of labor* demonstrated by the current feminist movement is due to the fact that it does not accept the premise that workers are only those who receive a wage. In this sense, by expanding the tool of the strike, we provoke a crisis in the patriarchal concept of labor because we question the idea that dignified work is only that which receives a wage; therefore, we also challenge the fact that recognized work is predominately masculine. Like in a game of dominoes, this implies questioning the idea that productive work is only that which is done outside the home.

Thus, feminism takes up the problem of redefining labor— and, therefore, the very notion of class—because it demonstrates the heterogeneity of unrecognized tasks that produce value and disobey the hierarchization and division that the wage creates between workers and the unemployed. It is a political movement: by decoupling recognition of work from the wage, it rejects the idea that those who do not receive a wage are condemned to the political margins.

The feminist movement, especially the movement of popular feminisms (which brings together a multiplicity of Latin American experiences under diverse names), shows that we cannot delegate to capital—through the tool of the wage—recognition of who are workers. That is why we say #TrabajadorasSomos Todas (#AllWomenAreWorkers). Now, that statement does not operate as a blanket that covers and homogenizes an abstract class identity; rather, it functions because it reveals the multiplicity of what labor means from the feminist point of view, with all of its hierarchies and all of its struggles.

When it is connected to difference, the class dimension does not turn class into a privileged element for understanding conflict (which, by flexibilizing the notion of class, risks ultimately putting it in the center again). It is something that is more radical, precisely *because* it emerges from the feminisms of the peripheries: the question of class can no longer be abstracted from the colonial, racist, and patriarchal dimension without being revealed as a category that covers up hierarchies. In this way, we also put another idea of *productivity* into play: productivity is not confirmed by whether or not we are exploited under the wage form. Rather, the reasoning is different: the form of exploitation organized by the wage invisibilizes, disciplines, and hierarchizes other forms of exploitation.

This opens up another fundamental line of investigation: How do financial apparatuses update the colonial pact today with forms of domination and exploitation that, as Raquel Gutiérrez Aguilar indicates,[25] are revealed as a fundamental point for understanding the war against women in its role as counterinsurgency? Here it is essential to create connections between the *most precarious territories of labor* and the *most abstract apparatus of finance* in order to think about new forms of exploitation and value extraction and, especially, the role of women's bodies and feminized bodies in them.

The collective and multitudinous body of the feminist movement is now disputing the body in terms of its potencia: that is, it is defending the indeterminacy of what the body can do. In other words, the very idea of labor power. That is where its multiplicity, its expansion, comes form. With this understanding, the body ceases to be individual confinement and the object of liberal rights, and instead becomes interwoven with insurgent territories, putting social wealth into dispute.

Excursus: The Collective Invention of an Origin

The collective invention of a fable is a way of dismantling, critiquing, and tearing apart the origins that consecrate our secondary place—which is described as natural, pre-political, and generally muted. It also consists of telling alternative stories.

The attempt to narrate and conceptualize the feminist strike aims to vindicate our power of collective fabulation and, therefore, that of the invention of a logic that defies what is considered "political" rationality. For that reason, it invents its own origin, to the point of imagining a movement that does not have origins but is composed of displacements.

The theory of the social contract (which abstractly guarantees the order in which we live, and compels us to obey those who govern us) projects an idealized previous state that gives rise to it: the state of nature. In philosophical debates, it is said that this state is a sort of imaginary site (or, as Hobbes described it in the seventeenth century, as existing in the Indigenous populations of America).[26]

But we can make a different hypothesis: that women are the concrete reference for the materiality of the state of nature, due to the embodied form of their political existence, which in turn *naturalizes* and *invisibilizes* them. Thus, arguing that the state of nature is fictitious is a double negation: it strips existence and dignity from nature (denigrated as nonrational), and it denies the effective persistence of that state of nature in the feminized mode of existence. And, let's add something else: it mystifies women as an exploitable natural resource.

Religious, political, mythological stories narrate the origin of things. Indeed, British political theorist Carole Pateman has shown that by repeating the story of the social contract as the origin of the political pact, women accepted a subordinated role under the covert form of a sexual contract that we "signed" in advance.[27] An always-hidden hem, the sexual contract is that marriage contract that, in turn, operates in relation to the employment contract. Both are inseparable from the social contract, that is, from the way the political order functions; from the way in which social obedience is structured, where women are uniquely obligated both in relation to the unpaid work that we do as well as to the fidelity that we must promise.

In Pateman's unparalleled account, the "civil contract origin story" of societies is a fiction made to the measure of men. On the one hand, it synthesizes a specific dispute over the power to "give birth." The contract grants men a "specifically masculine creative power": the capacity to generate new forms of political life. In this sense, men also make a body to their measure. This fable is part of the *gestation* of modern patriarchy, which distinguishes the power that men exercise over women and feminized bodies, via a form of political right. It is here that the male body is revealed as a rational and abstract body with the capacity to create order and discourse.

On the other hand, these "origin" stories are mounted over material expropriations: conquests and appropriations of communal and Indigenous lands, conquests and appropriations of female and feminized bodies (of both slaves and migrants). The figure of the individual is shaped through that dispossession. There is no "natural" possibility of such a subordination of women, without having *previously* stripped them of any possibility of economic autonomy. There is no confinement and impoverishment of women, no way of making them dependent and submissive, without a previous dispossession of their capacities for self-management and their own economies.

Political creativity—in the alliance between patriarchy and capitalism—thus becomes a strictly male power, based on an earlier expropriation. And the contract that acts as a body (as a body of text and a civil body) for that creativity organizes a whole system of subordination and delegation, one that later takes the name of rights and obligations. Pact and contract.

But who signs? Pateman says that it is white men (who no longer represent the old power of the father, but a power distributed fraternally, among equal men), and that this contract is, in turn, three in one: a social contract, a sexual contract, and a racial or slave contract that legitimizes the government of whites over Blacks. Thus, what it organizes is not a paternalism, but a specific form of masculinity.

Yet, it is not men that are spoken of, but rather something more abstract: individuals. It is a party that women are apparently invited to, if they dress the part: that is, if they recognize the political fiction of liberal equality and speak its language, even as they are excluded from it. However, there is a trap. As women—as aspiring individuals—they are only allowed a single contract at the beginning: that of marriage. The sexual contract thus establishes the political right of men over women as the first clause, which is transcendental to all other contracts. It is a contract with a "specific content": that of "loyal service," which in turn structures access to the female body as a male prerogative, as well as the sexual division of labor, organizing the patriarchal meaning of what we understand as femininity. Because along with fidelity, we "sign a pact" to do free domestic labor.

Pateman makes the point, again with extreme clarity: despite the individual and metaphysical language of contracting wills, an examination of the contracts of which women are a part (marriage, prostitution, surrogacy) shows that what is at stake are *women's bodies*. The philosopher's thesis is acute: the sexual contract is the *repressed* part of the social contract that is always *displaced* under the form of the marriage contract.

Marriage and prostitution contracts reveal the core—and recall the origins as a founding fiction—of modern contractual patriarchy because it both "denies and presupposes women's freedom," and it cannot operate without that assumption. Freedom and contract are linked at the same time as women's power is confined: the freedom to make decisions about gestation in one's body and to not remain enclosed in the domestic sphere. In women, however, the body is something that is *not* property (a quality that is necessary in order to be an individual). Sexual difference thus turns into political difference.

Women, then, are presupposed as individuals (because they can sign the marriage contract), yet they are not, because they are not owners of themselves (since they signed the contract that consecrates their "natural" subordination to men). A similar structure functions in the parable of the Aventine, which French philosopher Jacques Rancière recalls as the "unequal fiction": the owner who gives orders to the slave presupposes that he has a faculty of comprehension and language, a humanity that Rancière calls the "equality of intelligences," without which it would not be possible to comply with the order.[28] But that humanity is immediately denied by the affirmation of the hierarchy: the distinction between the one who commands and the one who is forced to obey is later translated into a "natural" distinction, in which slaves are no longer rational beings.

In a way, the double standard of women as *individuals who are not individuals* functions similarly. However, it can be used to their favor, as Pateman proposes: the figure of the woman opens up a critical path that can lead the feminist perspective beyond the liberal horizon. It is not about a race to finally become full individuals, in the way propagandized by the women who "lean in" to the top levels of corporate management or political power. Quite the opposite: it demonstrates that the figure of the individual as owner is inexorably masculine, an idea that is foundational to patriarchy: that way of converting the power men exercise over women into political power, and the reassurance of the sexual division of labor.

Their paradoxical relation to *exclusion* is fundamental to this way of understanding women's situation: they are both excluded from the contract as well as (in a certain way) included in it. Women are simultaneously an object of property and a person. This reasoning can be interwoven with forms of argumentation that critique the very figure of exclusion. As the French theorist Michel Foucault indicates, the notion of exclusion "does not take into account—is consequently unable to take into account—or analyze the [struggles], relations, and specific operations of power on the basis of which, precisely, exclusion takes place."[29] The notion reinforces an almost metaphysical distinction between inclusion and exclusion, in which exclusion is a complete outside, a desert.

Women, then, are trapped if we want to be included in the world of equal opportunities that is promised to individuals. Because women and migrants (and feminized bodies) will never reach the status of full citizen or individual, their condition raises a critique of "exclusion itself": it denounces its symbiotic and synthetic relation with the very structure of inclusion.

This schema can be used precisely to think about sexual difference as a political hierarchy: it is not so much that one sex is excluded at the expense of the inclusion of the other, but rather that exclusion (for example, of domestic labor in respect to the wage) explains the very way in which inclusion is internally structured by specific forms of exclusion (for example, in the way in which the wage "includes" domestic labor as a family allowance). This brings us back to the relation that organizes the "patriarchy of the wage." And it is the same dynamic that projects sexual difference in terms of difference between public and private space. Here, public space (civil, masculine, and white) demands attributes and capacities that imply the repression (or the inclusion through exclusion) of the private sphere (natural, of sexed bodies).

However, if we manage to dismantle the figure of the woman (and feminized bodies) as *excluded*, we get closer to the possibility that her mode of existence can *decompose* the individual, contest its limits, move against and beyond it. On the one hand, if this exclusion is intrinsic to the functioning of the formula of inclusion, to escape it allows for dismantling of the binary. On the other hand, precisely by being a corporeal figure, it proposes a relation with the body that is not that of property. We could add that it is instead a relation with the body as composition. The body never depends solely on itself.

Chapter 2

Violence: Is There a War on and against Women's Bodies?

Can we speak of *war* to name the escalation in deaths of women, lesbians, travestis, and trans people (80 percent of which occur at the hands of current or former lovers, boyfriends, or husbands)? Clearly it is not a war in the sense of a confrontation between two symmetrical sides or under clear rules of engagement. But it does seem necessary to qualify the type of conflict that today, in Argentina alone, involves the death of one woman, lesbian, travesti, or trans person every eighteen hours. That number continued to rise even after the first International Women's Strike in 2017, reaching its terrifying zenith in the month immediately following the strike. As the modalities of crimes diversify, the tendency is for them to become more and more gruesome. It is an escalation with no end.

Why do they kill us? The reconceptualization of sexist violence has been a key element of the feminist movement in recent years. This has emerged in two ways. First, we have pluralized its definition: we stopped talking "only" about violence against women and feminized bodies, and have instead connected it to a set of other forms of violence, without which its historic intensification could not be understood. Speaking of violence starting from femicides and travesticides positions them as its culminating point, but it also poses a challenge: to not limit ourselves to its necropolitical accounting, the tallying of femicides and victims.

In this sense, a recognition of the pluralization of violence is strategic: it is a concrete form of *connection* that creates *intelligibility* and, therefore, enables a displacement of the *totalizing figure of the victim.* Pluralization of the meaning of sexist violence is not only about quantifying and cataloging different forms of violence. It is much more complex; it is a way of mapping its *simultaneity* and its *interrelation.* It connects imploded homes with lands razed by agribusinesses, with the wage gap and invisibilized domestic work; it links the violence of austerity and the crisis with the ways in which those are confronted by women's protagonism in popular economies, and it relates all of this with financial exploitation through public and private debt. It ties together ways of disciplining disobedience through outright state repression and the persecution of migrant movements, with the imprisonment of poor women for having abortions and the criminalization of subsistence economies. Moreover, it highlights the racist imprint on each one of these forms of violence. Nothing in this web of violence is obvious: to trace the modes of connection is to produce meaning, because it renders visible the machinery of exploitation and extraction of value that involves increasing thresholds of violence, which have a differential (and therefore strategic) impact on feminized bodies.

This work of weaving—and the strike is a fundamental tool for its deployment—functions precisely like a spiderweb: only by producing a political cartography, connecting the threads that make different forms of violence function as interrelated dynamics, can we denounce the ways their segmentation seeks to enclose us in isolated cells. Such a cartography implies overflowing the confines of "gender-based violence" to link it with the multiple forms of violence that make it possible. In this way, we escape the "corset" of pure victims with which they seek to pigeonhole us, to inaugurate a new political language that not only denounces violence against women's bodies, but also includes other feminized bodies in the discussion and, moreover, moves from a single definition of violence (as domestic or intimate, and therefore secluded) to understand it in relation to a web of economic, institutional, labor, colonial, and other violence.

In this political fabric we can also collectively evaluate the ways violence differentially impacts each one of us. Understood in this way, "violence" is not an enormous capital-letter word, producing that other equally enormous, equally abstract, capital-letter word: "Victim." This is the second new element of the reconceptualization of violence: the forms taken by violence against women's bodies and feminized bodies are analyzed starting from particular situations, based on specific bodies. It is from there that a comprehension of violence as a complete phenomenon is produced. Each person's body, as a trajectory and experience, thus becomes the entry point, a concrete mode of localization, from which a specific point of view is produced: How is violence expressed? How does it take particular form in each body? How do we recognize it? How do we fight it?

This embedded understanding of violence enables a questioning that runs transversally across each space: from the family to the union, from the school to community center, from the border to the plaza. But it does so by giving this questioning a material, familiar, corporeal anchor. While violence displays differentials of oppression and exploitation that are expressed in different concrete bodies, it also nurtures, starting from that difference, a historically novel "interclass sorority," as the Argentine feminist sociologist Dora Barrancos has indicated.

However, an important clarification is needed: the common element is not violence; rather, the common is produced by the *situated and transversal questioning of violence.* Drawing connections between forms of violence gives us a shared perspective that is both specific and expansive, critical but not paralyzing, that links experiences. Mapping forms of violence based on their organic connection, without losing sight of the singularity of the production of the nexus between them, allows us to do something else: produce a language that goes beyond categorizing ourselves as victims.

Finally, the issue of violence proposes two other fundamental questions: What does it mean to produce feminist forms of self-defense when confronted with increased violence? And, going further: What would it mean for the feminist movement to be able to produce its own machines of justice?

Where Is the War Today?

The war against women, lesbians, travestis, and trans people finds expression in four specific scenes, which are at the foundation of femicide today. They are the substrate prior to the production of violence, or, paraphrasing Marx, its hidden abode, where there is a logic of connection between them. This logic of connection is supplied by finance, whose specificity I will highlight throughout this book. These scenes frame a reading of the violence of neoliberalism that accounts for structural adjustment measures, as well as the way that exploitation takes root in the production of subjectivities that are compelled to precarity and nevertheless fight to prosper in structural conditions of dispossession.

The four scenes of violence to which I refer are:

1) The implosion of violence in homes as an effect of the crisis of the figure of the male breadwinner, and his subsequent loss of authority and privileged role in relation to his position in the labor market;

2) the organization of new forms of violence as a principle of authority in popular-sector neighborhoods, rooted in the expansion of illegal economies that replace other modes of provisioning resources;

3) the dispossession and looting of common lands and resources by transnational corporations, and thus the deprivation of the material autonomy of other economies; and

4) the articulation of forms of exploitation and value extraction for which the financialization of social life—particularly through the apparatus of debt—is a common code.

I would like to propose that there is an organic relationship between these four dimensions. Next I will return to the characterization of "war," and then go back to the beginning: What sort of force responds to this offensive? In what sorts of economies is the autonomy of women, lesbians, travestis, and trans people inscribed? Here it will be necessary to return to some elements of the feminist strike. Finally, I would like to suggest that a displacement occurs here: it is because there is war *on* the body of women and feminized bodies that there is war *against* women.

The implosion of the home

It is male "dignity," sustained by what Silvia Federici calls the "patriarchy of the wage," that is in crisis.[1] For men, the wage has served as an "objective" measure of their dominant position in the labor market, even as more women participate in the waged labor force. In this sense, it has functioned historically as a political tool: it ensures both the control of "obligatory" and "unpaid" work in the home for which women were responsible, establishes a representative of the boss within the household, and affirms hierarchy within the labor market. It is not that the patriarchy of the wage no longer operates by seeking to exercise that power and monopoly over the management of money. But its crisis runs deeper: today, for the majority, the wage is not guaranteed as a means of reproduction. Due to the collapse of the wage as an objective measure of male authority, sexist violence becomes "excessive" or "beyond measure" in the home: masculinities are no longer contained by the value that the wage provides them, and so they find compensatory affirmation of their authority in other ways. The crisis of unemployment, precarization, and increasingly harsh conditions of exploitation make it so that domestic violence structures the patriarchal domination previously mediated and measured by the wage (even if domestic violence was always a legitimate, albeit latent, element for "internal" discipline).

At the same time, a greater desire for autonomy is expressed by women who do not feel contained or constricted by domestic ideology, since they have already accumulated experiences of extra-domestic work (badly paid and undervalued, but functional as a way to desert the domestic mandate), and generations of youth that have cultivated forms of contempt for the patriarchy of the wage or have directly experienced its decline. The accumulation of disobedience, intensification of autonomies, and depreciation of the figure of the waged male provider destabilize the structured modes of obedience in the monogamous, heteronormative family. In light of this situation, devalued masculinities find themselves in a desperate and violent search to relegitimize themselves. Illegal economies, especially those linked to drug trafficking and recruitment into (illegal and legal) security forces, provide that promise of masculinity.

New violence in the territories

Where does the "civil war" between labor and capital take place today? Marx identified it in the working day, but now we see it broadened in both spatial terms (beyond the factory) and temporal measure (beyond the recognized working day). What violent forms does this civil war take under today's neoliberal conditions if we look at it from the perspective of social cooperation, in which the illegal and a-legal, migrant and popular economies, as well as domestic and community work, are the key elements of new proletarian zones?

Over the past decade, unprecedented forms of violence markedly reorganized social conflict, driven by new forms of territorial authority linked to illegal economies in collusion with police, political, and judicial structures. These new forms of territorial authority confronted the popular, highly feminized economies, which were structured on the basis of social movements. It was finance, with its high level of abstraction, that took charge of this articulation, from below and from above, of subjectivities that had to procure prosperity without taking for granted the privilege of the wage as their main income. In Latin America, this was produced in connection with a neo-extractivist type of insertion in the global market (I will return to this in the following chapter). The new forms of violence are translated into an intense segmentation of hierarchized spaces based on differential access to security, which promotes a "civil war" for the defense of property between peripheral neighborhoods and the wealthy areas, but also within the more popular zones. The use of public and private security forces seeks to constrain all of those who, under the effects of the stimulus to social inclusion by means of consumption through debt, do not have equal conditions of access to property or its defense.

Today, illegal economies "organize" the vacuum left in many spaces by the retreat of wage labor. They provide employment, resources, and belonging, as well as a mode of affirmation of male authority, all of which are confirmed through territorial control on a daily basis. This supposes an accelerated passage of the thresholds of violence that structure the everyday. It is not a coincidence that the other path of recomposition of that male authority is through recruitment in state security forces—the only widely available work in Argentina. In this way, legal and illegal forces of confrontation substitute for the majoritarian model of waged authority, decisively contributing to the increase in violence and the implosion of homes discussed above, as the violence of those security forces spills over into the home. There is one more "economy" that must be accounted for, one that is booming and growing: the churches that offer access to employment, and promises of prosperity, as they manage to weave together a network of resources in increasingly critical everyday situations. Illegal economies, on one hand, and the theology of prosperity or charity, on the other, forge different modalities of an economy of obedience in a context of everyday impoverishment.

The dispossession and looting of community land and life

Understanding the offensive of agribusiness and extractivist industries on the continent requires an analysis of the ways Latin American countries have been inserted into the global market. Here, Rosa Luxemburg's analysis stands out for its contemporary relevance: the formulation of colonial capitalist expansion against what thinkers of her era called the "formations of the natural economy"—what we might describe as the advancing march of capital's frontiers. This means the advance of the frontiers of capital through the dispossession of lands to put an end to the self-sufficiency of peasant and Indigenous economies. She emphasized the mortgage debts of US farmers, as well as Dutch and British imperialist policy in South Africa against Black and Indigenous populations, as concrete forms of political violence, tax pressure, and introduction of cheap goods.[2] Diverse struggles have started to use the concept of body-territory to situate the resistances against neo-extractivist attacks primarily led by women. Such is the case of Berta Cáceres, whose murder the movement has named as a "territorial femicide."[3] This point not only connects to a notion of the body as more-than-human, but that also refers to the question of nature from a non-liberal point of view. That is, it is not about an abstract conservationism, but about confronting the modes of dispossession of the material possibilities of life—ones that today structure a direct antagonism between multinational companies and states, and the

63

populations that are looted, displaced, and redirected in new dynamics of exploitation.

Finance as common code

This analysis of the extractivist paradigm in rural settings must also be expanded to urban and suburban spaces. There, too, we find finance in multiple aspects of the "extractive operations," from real estate speculation to mass indebtedness. In this register, it is necessary to conceptualize extractivism in broader terms, as a way that the capture of value by capital is operationalized today.[4] Just as capital accumulates by dispossessing peasant and Indigenous landholders, and extracting common resources from the earth, many of its leading forms in more urbanized spaces engage in a similar sort of plunder, in a retrospective capture or appropriation of socially cooperative activities that are, to some degree, autonomous from capital.

Finance thus "lands" in popular economies, long after they've been organized—that is, in those economies that emerged in moments of crisis, fueled by the modalities of self-management and work without a boss—and it exploits the ways in which the subaltern fabrics reproduce life in a way that cannot simply be reduced to "survival." A multiplicity of efforts, savings, and economies are "put to work" for finance. This means that finance becomes a code that manages to homogenize that plurality of activities, income sources, expectations, and temporalities. Finance has been the most skillful and quick to detect that popular vitality and root within it a system for value extraction, one that operates directly upon the labor force as living labor. This mode of financial exploitation of social cooperation that does not have the wage as a mediating part—so crucial to understanding contemporary capitalism—therefore is best grasped as "extractive."

Against the Pathologization of Violence

There are advantages to accounting for the specific economy of violence against women, lesbians, travestis, and trans people as a sort of *war*, rather than via the personal pathologies of bad men. Doing so outlines a systemic phenomenon that evades attribution to the psychological motivations of some men, which end up being understood in terms of crimes of passion. Such an interpretation ends up exonerating violent forms of masculinity, treating its crimes as exceptional, as isolated pathologies, and making a casuistry of "deviance." This explanation based on an individualist psychology, and the very idea of "health" that patriarchy proposes for males, is questioned in the streets, is condensed into graffiti, is conceptualized in songs. It is painted on the walls: "He is not sick, he is a healthy son of the patriarchy."

The notion of war emphasizes a dynamic of forces in conflict, and it clears away the neutralizing language of "epidemic" or "outbreak," which would obscure that conflict. But there is another dimension to the exculpatory diagnosis of pathologization: it blames the feminist movement's collective emergence in the streets. In their analysis of the increase in femicides, these kinds of arguments denounce the "preventive inefficiency" of massive marches,[5] suggesting that mobilizations do not have the capability or efficacy to prevent or diminish femicides, and therefore, that their usefulness is doubtful. They compare the increase in feminist mobilization and the increase in crimes, arguing, on the one hand, that there is a direct causal relation —that the disobedient presence of feminized bodies in the streets is itself the cause of violence. On the other, such arguments seek to confirm the "ineffectiveness" of mobilization to counteract femicidal violence.

Meanwhile, other discourses speak of a mimetic "illusion" of strength held by women, lesbians, travestis, and trans people, one that pushes them to take on "empowering" attitudes that lead to their deaths.[6] This argument speaks of an "effect of contagion" of the collective, claiming that rather than protecting the victims, it exposes them even more.

Those discourses attempted to read the massive #EleNão (#NotHim) mobilization in Brazil in a similar way: by trying to blame it for the subsequent electoral victory of the ultrafascist Jair Bolsonaro. A psychologizing, guilt-producing language was also used: the march of women and LGBTQI people "awoke the monster," they said.

The multitudinous effervescence of the movement is discredited as false, deceitful, and, above all, risky (compared to the "contagion" of a virus): it leads to trust in an experience of collective strength that is, supposedly, only dangerous and illusory—or further, counterproductive. Thus, it is a twofold strategy; these discourses attempt to make us feel guilty *and* impotent. The notion of war, on the other hand, situates us in a different economy of forces.

The "Internal" War

Today the household has gone from being an allegedly pacified place to a battlefield marked by open, if asymmetrical, conflict. Domestic violence itself does nothing other than show scenes of a domesticity that is exploding, and the home as the site of gruesome everyday experiences. The home is no longer the warrior's place of rest, as was proposed when the sexual division of labor assigned women the task of romanticizing the house (under the command of the "patriarchy of the wage"). Today the house is where the "warrior" (one of the classical figures of patriarchal control) seeks to wage "internal" war as a symptom of his impotence and humiliation suffered in the workplace, among other existential territories. Rather than an explosion, the image of an implosion is more apt. Violence is deployed inward. It pierces through bodies. It unravels relationships.

However, a characterization of sexist violence as something that is only connected to the domestic sphere reinforces women's isolation in the home, confirming its borders as marking a "private" space. It is the "great enclosure" of women within the domestic sphere—something Federici speaks of, remarking that Foucault forgot to account for it among his genealogies of prisons, schools, and hospitals—that also allows for violence to be confined, as something that is suffered "inside," in other words, privately, intimately. "I only feel unsafe when I am in my house," explained a woman in the assembly at Villa 21–24 of Barracas, a slum in the south of Buenos Aires, in the midst of preparations for the international strike on March 8, 2018. Her statement inverts the traditional idea of the home as a space of shelter and refuge: "Luckily, when I have a problem, I tell my compañeras, who arrive before the police and are more effective than the panic button and restraining order."

Confronting violence this way, so that it is no longer a private issue, allows us deepen our analysis of how the webs of violence expressed "domestically" are directly linked to political, economic, labor, institutional, media, and social violence. By no longer placing our faith in solutions from the state, we alter the plane of "solutions" or responses. When we are confined to the home and the solitude that we sometimes feel when we are enclosed there, we become prisoners to the rhetoric of "saviors." This comes not only from organizations that think solely in terms of rescue and refuge, but also from judicial and police institutions that are ineffective insofar as they are complicit in the same violence they wish to denounce. To escape confinement is to get away from the logic of rescue and refuge as the only options, and instead build denser fabrics of defense and protection. Self-defense, thus, displaces the question to be resolved onto the organization of collective care under conditions of structural dispossession.

The discourse of redeemers and saviors is intrinsic to the victimization of women, lesbians, trans people, and travestis.

Without the figure of the victim, the framework of rescue does not work. This perspective allows us to critique how much of the focus on the trafficking of women relies on this discourse and also to understand why that approach receives support from nongovernmental organizations and international financial networks, under the spiritual guidance of the church.

Similar to what happens with migrant workers, the notion of trafficking and its connection with slavery forms a part of this whole. Based on an exceptional case that is taken as emblematic, and using images that are capable of swaying public imagination (a textile worker handcuffed to the sewing machine or a young woman tied to a bed), those discourses seek to explain what they consider to be an intrinsic, *natural* submission as a general framework for understanding trafficking. This framework leaves no room for the freedom and autonomous rationality that persists despite difficult and desperate conditions.

Understood this way, the discourse of trafficking and slave labor as a totalizing perspective leads to a paternalism that is nothing other than a way of exerting control, as opposed to a more complex idea of the autonomy of women, lesbians, trans people, and travestis in difficult, violent, and adverse contexts—situations they respond to with more than mere resignation. In this sense, the trafficking discourse impedes any understanding of such forms of violence that would allow for a more profound explanation of the issue. The problem is that their argument about violence completely leaves out (1) an explanation of the exploitation of women and feminized bodies that is not moralizing; (2) the role of international funders in creating such a focus on the issue; and (3) the complex game of desire, calculus of progress, and risk that women and feminized bodies put in motion under diverse modes of migration, as well as when young women "flee" from their home. This analysis is a necessary condition for understanding how contemporary capitalism functions at its core.

68

By negating the strategic rationality that many of these trajectories put in play (through planning, frustration, recalculation, learning, sacrifice, appropriation), these types of analyses underestimate any knowledge in the name of an infantilization that renews, again and again, the colonial savior logic and, above all, that shows the impossibility of giving space to the rationality and voices of those involved in such processes. This problematization does not ignore extreme cases. The question is why exceptional cases are turned into the truth of the whole phenomenon, and proposed in the media as the indisputable totalization of a much more varied and complex reality.

The perspective of trafficking constructs the figure of the woman—and especially the migrant woman, or daughter of migrants—as the perfect victim. It moralizes and judges her actions, while it legitimizes the actions of organizations, funders, and the savior rhetoric, which makes those women completely passive. To counteract that focus, it is necessary to account for the infrastructure and logistics that organize mobilities beyond the figures of "traffickers" and "slaves," since trafficking tends to be characterized from the perspective of this all-encompassing narrative. Trafficking is not only a normative frame, but also progressively gains strength in media discourse and political disputes, flattening a reality that is much more entangled than what the category seeks to simplify into a specific conservative orientation.

This is made even more complex in the case of young women and girls who "disappear" from their homes for a time, who reappear and leave again. This reality is increasingly common, especially in slums and peripheral neighborhoods, and it challenges the perspective of the usual—juridical and political—approach to these issues. The notion of trafficking fails to effectively understand, investigate, or politicize these situations. It is a discourse that obstructs the very possibility of recognizing how those complex economies of movement, of fleeing, of linking young women with parallel or illegal circuits, conjugate a desire of autonomy that is processed in conditions of extreme violence and precarity. Forms of domestic violence are at the root of these forms of flight. These women and girls flee from a very violent home to other forms of violence. Sometimes, they come back to the neighborhood and home, and it is not clear that they want to "return." Search campaigns led by the family and neighborhood are often the most effective way of finding these young women and girls, for they are the only pressure that makes police and juridical denunciation effective. But when I say that it is not clear that they want to return, I want to emphasize that the place to which they return is generally one that is not desired, one from which they attempt to flee. This does not mean that the possibilities in the place to which they flee are better, but rather that they create a path, in a pragmatic way, for that desire of flight.

This "coming and going" problematizes the more traditional understanding that typifies these dynamics of flight purely as "kidnapping," or as the irrational obtundation of the youth with promises of drugs or alcohol. As in the case of migration, it is more about flight from a "depraved trinity," as sociologist and migrant rights activist Amarela Varela characterizes it in regard to the migrant caravans of Central American women that have crossed borders toward the United States in recent years: femicidal violence, state violence, and market violence.[7]

Blame and juridicalization of young women is insufficient: investigations of the cases do not advance, dismissed because they cannot "fulfill" the definition of trafficking. This also socially "discredits" the young women: when they "reappear" in the neighborhood, they are signaled as guilty, and their very appearance is considered to "disprove" the violence in which they are then re-ensnared. So the most urgent problem becomes ignored and illegible: how their drift beyond the domestic space is appropriated, how their "escape" from violence takes place in extremely fragile conditions and at the cost of other forms of violence, and how, nevertheless, a will to autonomy persists in their flight.

Therefore, it is necessary to bring together different elements to criticize the one-dimensionality of the trafficking discourse as a rationality that simultaneously victimizes and passivizes women's trajectories, especially those of youth and migrants (or daughters of migrants), under a biased global policy that we must stop seeing as "neutral." As I indicated, we must register this dynamic within the circuits of the popular, informal, a-legal, and illegal economy (an intersection that is not at all clear and is increasingly intertwined in a dispute over forms of "authority" over territories). Here violence, exploitation, and also *a desire* to flee domestic spaces imploded by violence are articulated with logistics and infrastructure (of varying legalities) that make "mobility" possible for young women in conditions of extreme precarization.

I want to problematize the element of having "no will." The forced recruitment that defines the figure of trafficking, both legally and subjectively, impedes understanding of the complexity of the majority of the actually existing situations, where the removal of will is never complete (there is an ambiguous voluntary component to flight) yet is still produced in a web of violence inscribed in the very situation of the conditions of "flight."

The terminology of "trafficking" and "slavery"—which emphasizes the extreme side of that involuntary condition—and the merely legal acceptance of the calculation that the trafficking framework supposes,[8] discredit other rationalities that have to do precisely with a way of fleeing domestic violence, abuse, and poverty in the home. Above all, it isolates a problematic in which what is at stake is a very concrete dispute over the normalization of hyper-exploitation that characterizes contemporary capitalism. In the case of the young women and girls, this is seen in the patriarchal appropriation of their desire to flee. The critique of violence cannot be made by denying the action of these youth who, in desperation, exercise their desire, taking an extreme risk, but by calculating that it is important not to submit to an initial violence—that of the household—and where autonomy is confronted with more complicated forms of its appropriation and exploitation.

War as an Interpretative Key

Michel Foucault proposed war as a principle of analysis of the relations of power and, more precisely, the model of war and struggles as a mode of intelligibility of political power. He also argued that there is a sort of permanent war, a constant fixture behind all order, such that war is the "point of maximum tension of the relations of forces," but also something that is itself comprised of a web "of bodies, of cases, and of passions": a true entanglement over which a "rationality" is assembled that seeks to appease the war.⁹

Silvia Federici often speaks of "a state of permanent war against women," in which the common denominator is the devaluation of their lives and work by the current phase of globalization. Federici's theoretical coordinates are set by the intersection of a Foucauldian perspective with feminism and Marxism. Federici argues that capitalism, since its transatlantic beginnings, has persecuted and fought "heretical" women with ferocity and terror. That is why, in her book *Caliban and the Witch*, she ties together three concepts: *women*, *the body*, and *primitive accumulation*. There she asks fundamental questions about that emblematic figure of rebellion: Why does capitalism, since its foundation, need to make war against women who hold knowledge and power? Why is the witch hunt one of the most brutal and least remembered massacres in history? Why must friendship between women be made suspicious? What did they seek to eliminate when they burned those women at the stake? How can a parallel be traced between witches and the Black slaves on plantations in the Americas?

The war against women, as Federici characterizes it, is an "original" moment that is *repeated* in each new phase of "primitive accumulation" of capital: in other words, that which is deployed over the social field, prior to a time of extreme instability of the relations of command-obedience and exploitation. The idea that there are historical moments when violence becomes a productive force for the accumulation of capital, as sociologist Maria Mies argues in her book *Patriarchy and Accumulation on a World Scale*, is fundamental for understanding the current phase of dispossession at various scales.[10] Carrying out war against women and their forms of knowledge-power is the condition of possibility for the beginning of capitalism, Federici argues, but we are left with the question of what this means in the present. We must test the hypothesis of an updated witch hunt, mapping the new bodies, territories, and conflicts of its contemporary iteration.

Historically, reactionary violence against women responded to their growing power and authority in social movements, especially the "heretical" movements and guilds. Federici identifies a "misogynist reaction" to that massiveness, to the reproductive control that women practiced among themselves, their techniques of accompaniment and complicity. "Clean sex between clean sheets": that was the objective of the capitalist rationalization of sexuality, which sought to turn women's sexual activity into labor at the service of men and procreation. Additionally, it was a way of making women sedentary. Federici argues that it was much more difficult for them to become vagabonds or migrant workers, because nomadic life would expose them to male violence, precisely in the moment of the capitalist reorganization of the world when misogyny was on the rise. However, as she insists, such violence was not only a hidden story of its beginnings. That is why her image still feels

73

so relevant, at a time when all female nomadism, from taking a taxi at night to abandoning a partner or leaving the home, is increasingly the occasion of sexist violence.

Women's bodies, Federici continues, came to replace spaces held in common (especially lands) following their enclosure in continental Europe. All at once, women were submitted to a new form of exploitation that would give rise to a growing submission of their work and of their bodies, which were increasingly understood as personal services and natural resources. The women *privatized* in this way were those who took refuge in bourgeois marriages, while those who remained out in the open were turned into a servile class (from housewives to domestic workers or prostitutes).

But to regard such women as "rebels" does not refer to any "specifically subversive" activity. "Rather, it describes the *female personality* that had developed, especially among the peasantry, in the course of the struggle over feudal power, when women had been in the forefront of heretical movements, often organizing in female associations, posing a growing challenge to male authority and the Church."[11] The images that portrayed them—in stories and caricatures—described women mounted on the backs of their husbands, whip in hand, and many others dressed as men, ready for action. In this sequence, friendships between women also became an object of suspicion, seen as counterproductive to marriages and as an obstacle to the mutual denunciation promoted, once again, by male authority and the church.

Many of these scenes continue to resonate in the present; I identify at least three dynamics that call attention to how this framework persists in our conjuncture: (1) the relationship between feminized and dissident bodies and common lands/territories, both of which are understood as surfaces of colonization, conquest, and domination; (2) the criminalization of collective actions led by women, as the energizers of rebellious social movements; and (3) male and church authority as a key

74

that is constantly present for the call to order of capitalist accumulation.

The Colonial Dimension

"New forms of war" are what Argentinian anthropologist Rita Segato calls the current modes of violence that take women's bodies as their target. They are "new" because they update a geometry of power that goes beyond the nation-state, since it is often other actors who exercise violence, overwhelmingly linked to illegal capital. At the same time, a connection to the past persists amid the novelty, especially in its colonial dimension. That dimension is expressed in the properly colonial methods of murdering women (such as impalement, acid, and dismemberment), but above all in the exercise of the affirmation of authority based on the ownership of bodies. This classical form of capitalist conquest (authority = property) today requires something extra: an intensification of scales and methodologies. In other words, it is what Segato defines as "a world of lordship," what we might think of as a regime of appropriation that radicalizes the colonial form.[12]

Suely Rolnik emphasizes the colonial dimension of aggression against feminized bodies, proposing the category of the "colonial-capitalist unconscious."[13] This term refers to the traumatic effects of the "fear and humiliation" of colonial processes —in their various phases and repetitions—which organize "operations" of subjectivation that are "more subtle than the macropolitical movements that resulted in independence from the colonial statute." I want to extract and specify three premises from Rolnik's argument.[14] First, the colonial unconscious operates by producing a "dissociation between the political, the aesthetic, and the clinical." In other words, it disciplines and creates hierarchies between knowledges that are taken as "separate." Then, this dissociation condemns us to despising

75

the body's knowledges and structures as "colonial repression": "the object of that 'repression' is the body itself in its ability to listen to the diagram of forces of the present and the paradoxical dynamic of its frictions with the dominant forms of reality, an aptitude from which it extracts its power of evaluation and its potencia of action." Lastly, "the abolition of the 'repression' of the body's knowledge and the actions in which it is updated" become a fundamental practical dimension on the horizon of transformation.

Power of evaluation and potencia of action are two essential practices of subaltern knowledges and feminist epistemology. They confront that division, which is so patriarchal and always in fashion, between those who *think* and those who *do*, those who *conceptualize* and those who *struggle*—in short, between stereotypical notions of comfort and risk. The colonial element of this division is what stands out, in which *knowledge* is an overvalued power of the elite and *doing* a modest resource of the subaltern.

On the other hand, considering practices based on both their power of evaluation and their potencia of action mobilizes a key element against the colonial-capitalist unconscious. The knowledges of the body of which Rolnik speaks today become the new object of suspicion and repression when they produce forms of socialization between women, lesbians, trans people, and travestis, becoming true political technologies of friendship, trust, rumor, and authority.

The misogynist and violent reaction also rises in response to these knowledges of the body. Therefore these knowledge-powers express the rupture of "minoritized" subjectivities (historically relegated and unappreciated) that flee from submission through recognition, from pure identity politics. In the case of women, lesbians, travestis, and trans people, a slogan such as #EstamosParaNosotras (#WeStandForOurselves) implies, among many other things, an impulse to stop adapting to heteronormative desire whose unilateral and violent deployment is the foundation of sexist affirmation. More precisely, the decomposition of the minoritized body, Rolnik says, dismantles the "scene" in which the dominant body is constructed, and in which the violent reaction is the attempt to maintain the stability of that scene, at any cost. The war against women could thus be rethought as a war against feminine and feminized characters who turn the knowledge of the body into power. It is no coincidence that she concludes with a discussion of the figure of the "witch" as a mode of existence that provides an "ethical compass," positioning knowledges of the body as acts of subversion against the colonial-capitalist unconscious. Those knowledges operate in concrete situations (over which they are evaluated and over which they act), and they bring us face to face with the borders of a regime of power whose colonial structure contains fundamental clues both for evaluating its failures and the possibilities of flight. It is against those rebellious knowledge-powers that colonial war has been waged. They are powers and knowledges that are strategic, both in defensive withdrawal and in the persistent desire to disobey.

Beyond Victimization

Segato has developed the precise diagnosis of a "pedagogy of cruelty," a term that has since become common parlance. She has analyzed gender-based crimes as "expressive violence," leading her to interpret the murders of women in Ciudad Juárez as violence that sees the female body as a tapestry on which to write a message.[15] Commenting on Segato's work, Raquel Gutiérrez Aguilar and I argued: "There is a novelty, even in its repetition. War takes on new forms, puts on unknown clothes. The textile metaphor is not a coincidence: today its main canvas is the female body. It becomes the privileged text and territory for marking violence. A new type of

77

war."[16] We also spoke about the "opacity" of a social conflictiveness in which femicides are inscribed. This opacity is not simple confusion, lack of information, or the impossibility of interpretation, and it is not a coincidence. Such opacity should be analyzed as a strategic element of that newness: as a truly counterinsurgent dimension that seeks to dismantle the rebel capacity of certain body-territories.[17]

In Latin America, the reality of femicide demands that we return to the question of its meaning: What message is transmitted by these crimes that, now, seem no longer to be circumscribed by the home, but take place in the middle of a bar, a day care, or on the street itself? It exercises a "pedagogy of cruelty," which is inseparable from the intensification of "media violence" that operates by spreading that aggression against women, distributing a message, and confirming a code of complicity between a mode of practicing masculinity. This is what Segato is referring to when she speaks of femicide as carrier of an "expressive violence" that is no longer only an instrumental violence.

The prevalence of such violence against women, lesbians, trans people, and travestis (which takes multiple forms, from dispossession to harassment, abuse to discrimination) is key to understanding a line of interconnected violence, one that has to do with the ways exploitation and value extraction are reconfigured today. Moving beyond the perspective of violence as victimization does not take us away from the problem of violence, nor does it free us from understanding its specificity. To the contrary, it relocates it. I already spoke of a strategic displacement: it is the intersection between gendered violence and economic and social violence that allows us to go beyond enclosing violence in a limited gender-based perspective. Its specificity emerges from that connection, not from a process of isolation. This specificity stems from a situated perspective that facilitates an understanding of the different forms of violence as a totality in movement, and each of them as a partial synthesis.

This connection allows us to build and move ourselves on a plane of intelligibility that gives meaning to violence to the extent that it links the domestic sphere with the world of work and the exploitation of our precarity, as well as with new forms of financial exploitation that are assembled beyond the wage. It is this connection that explains how the impossibility of economic autonomy leads to immobility in homes that become hell, and how migration becomes a line of flight that is worthwhile, even as its risks grow ever greater.

The material possibility of making a critique of contemporary violence, then, has three intersecting elements: (1) a map of the world of work in a feminist register that allows us to reevaluate non-waged economies; (2) the emergence of a political ecology from below that deploys a non-liberal comprehension of the earth and resources, in a broad sense, because it emerges from struggles in favor of communitarian life; and (3) struggles for justice, understood as an extension of the work of collective care.

Therefore, we avoid, as I indicated above, the thematization of domestic violence as a "ghetto" that determines corresponding "responses" and "solutions," which are also isolating: a new secretariat (of the state), or a new section (of a union), or a new program (of health care).

Once this displacement and linkage of different forms of violence produces a feminist diagnosis that starts to become common sense, we see how the neoliberal and conservative reaction attempts to recodify the violence. That reaction interprets violence as insecurity and, therefore, as the need for greater control. In general, governmental institutions attempt to respond to femicides through punitive, racist, and sexist reprisals: that is how the political system recodifies these forms of violence, in order to include them in a general discourse of *insecurity*. This reinforces classist and racist stereotypes (e.g., that men are dangerous in accordance with their class and their nationality), while it proposes the request for a "heavy hand" as the only way out. The solutions of punitive demagogy thus appear as magical proposals.

Excursus: The War *on* Women's Bodies

The war *on* women's bodies, which I want to talk about here, can be understood in relation to those heterogeneous ways in which autonomy and contempt expand the limits of what a body can do.

Thinking about what type of war is being developed against women, lesbians, travestis, and trans people allows us to understand capital's current offensive to relaunch its control. But, before that, in terms of method and political perspective, we must account for the type of autonomy that is being deployed if we are to understand the magnitude of the misogynist reaction against it.

A widely circulated photo from Chile's 2018 feminist mobilizations for democratic and feminist education showed a masked youth with a patch sewn on her ski mask that read: "I am at war." When the balaclavas go from the jungle to the streets of the metropole, what sort of war are we talking about?

Being at war is a way of taking on an array of forces. It means finding another way of living in our bodies. It makes visible a backdrop of violence that differentiates "terminal" bodies from others in that weft. To be at war is to liberate forces that are experienced as contained. It is to stop covering up the violence.

In that sense, to be at war means assuming that we are being attacked, and there is a decision—which is a common force—to no longer pacify ourselves in the face of everyday violence. It has to do with a way of traversing the fear, not simply believing that it ceases to exist.

If the writer Simone de Beauvoir said that one is not born a woman, but becomes one, it was in order to reveal the historical construction of the female nature that *limited* us to certain tasks, functions, and obligations. Becoming, in *The Second Sex*, expresses a negative process of which we have to become conscious: it is the way in which becoming women emerges as synonymous with turning into *non-free* subjects. Becoming is a process of subjection, especially to maternity.

The French thinkers Gilles Deleuze and Félix Guattari gave it the opposite meaning (but one that would be impossible to understand without de Beauvoir's precedent): becoming-woman is to leave one's assigned place, to get down from the family tree, to escape the patriarchal mandate. In this sense, becoming has nothing to do with progressing or adapting, nor with enacting a model or reaching a goal (there is no evolution, as the philosophers say). Becoming, to the contrary, "is the process of desire."[18]

However, the becoming-woman alerts us to a theft. They rob us of a body in order to produce a two-part, binary organism, thus making us into a body that is not our own. First they rob the young girl of her body: "Don't use that posture"; "You're not a girl anymore"; "Don't be a tomboy." Thus, becoming-woman is a type of youthful movement: not because of age, but due to the capacity to circulate at different velocities and in different places, to go through passages, until turning into the process itself. Becoming-woman is the key of other becomings: a start, a rhythm, a vertigo that is opposed to the majority, which is understood as a state of power and domination.

"Becoming what you are": if we had to identify an origin (or better, invent one provisionally) for the issue of becoming, we could go to this sentence from Friedrich Nietzsche. Lou Andreas-Salomé—the philosopher's interlocutor and lover—wrote about the *impulse of transformation and change of opinion* as two key elements of his thought: thus, her reading highlights a process of transforming one's self—that is, becoming—as an indispensable condition of all creative force.[19] The aphorism "We should all become traitors, exercise disloyalty, constantly discard our ideas" functions as a call to a materialism whose fidelity is no longer to convictions or ideals, but to the process of transformation itself. In any case, what would a fidelity to becomings *be*?

Salomé—who would later become a friend of Freud and one of the women precursors to psychoanalysis—makes an interpretation of the philosopher that gives special emphasis to the emotional tone of his thought, to highlight "the subtle and secret sentimental relations that a thought or a word can awaken," and also how intuition and truth are intertwined in his work to the point of producing a towing effect, an increase in energy. The relation between intuition and necessity, elaborated in this way, nourishes a new objectivity.

These knowledges—Salomé indicates—are linked to artists and women because they are the ones who "produce the impression of the fullness of force, of the living, of the full spirit, of the invigorating." Becoming turns into war. "Eternal war that *one is*": each person as composed of opposing elements, from which a higher form of health can sprout. As Nietzsche would say, "The price of fertility is to be rich in contradictions"; you just have to have the strength to bear them. Premises that are fundamental for a certain feminist perspective emerge from here: First, the idea that "everything is *non-truth*," that is, that the violence of the totality is a suppression of concrete situations and partialities; therefore, there is no absolute truth, only *perspective*. Second, the notion that there is a certain preponderance for affective life to overtake intellectual life: the content of truth is considered secondary in respect to its content of will and feeling, such that becoming involves an economy of forces. In that passage, truth is no longer discovered; it is *invented*. But there can be no truth without a declaration of war.

These premises are common knowledge to survivors. In her *Cancer Journals*, the Black lesbian feminist Audre Lorde is a survivor who says she needs to not write as a survivor.[20] She does so, rather, as a warrior who has not abandoned fear. Who goes from the biopsy to the detection of a tumor in her right breast. Who is fighting battles and victories in the face of death. Who deals with the vertiginous fantasies of a disease that can assault the entire body. Who resists the ups and downs before and after the decision for a mastectomy. She investigates her body as a battlefield where a combat between very different powers plays out: that of the erotic and self-care, against the cosmetic and surgical machinery; that of racist and aesthetic prejudices and the fear of not being desired, or of herself losing the desire to make love, against the healing power of a network of friendships. They are powers, Lorde shows, that require self-training. And a language that is also like a new skin.

It is said that young Amazon women remove their right breast to be better archers. Lorde brings the image of these determined fifteen-year-olds to her pages several times, almost as unexpected mythological allies. Or perhaps they are not so unexpected for this woman, who writes that "growing up as a black, fat, almost blind woman in the US" also requires knowledge of the bow and arrow to survive.

Lorde says that, as opposed to the (idealist) illusion of the end of fear, it is about recognizing fear as part of one's own nature, precisely in order to stop fearing it. To familiarize oneself with it is to disarm it. To refrain from assuming it will magically disappear, so as to avoid paralysis when it arrives. To traverse it. To coexist with it to the point where one can guess its tricks. In this sense, the diary that she writes stops being intimate; in other words, it radicalizes her intimacy to the point of making it a political manifesto, the interpellation of a foreign sister or a wise teacher, of whom Lorde sometimes. From there, a direct question arises: What are the words you still have not found? What do you need to say? What are the tyrannies you swallow every day, and that you attempt to make yours until they make you sick and you die from them, still in silence?

Chapter 3

Body-Territory:
The Body as Battlefield

In what sense can women's bodies be thought of as a territory of conquest? Sociologists Maria Mies, Veronika Bennholdt-Thomsen, and Claudia von Werlhof theorize women as "colonies," as territories to be looted, and from which wealth is extracted with violent force.[1] Based on an analogy between the female body and the colony, they draw connections between what capital exploits as "free resources" from domestic labor, from peasant labor, and from the labor of the inhabitants of cities' slums, explaining that this exploitation is simultaneously colonial and heteropatriarchal. Mies, in turn, formulates the notion of the "domestication of labor" in describing the labor of seamstresses in the lace industry in India. She refers to the milieu of reproductive work in the lowest strata of "productive labor" as a favored arena of colonialism.[2] In these scenes, the categories of the productive and the reproductive are reconfigured; they do not so much refer to specific spaces, but rather to assemblages under a specific relation of *subordination*. Here a central hypothesis emerges: *domestication and colonization are inseparable*, since they constitute a specific relation both as a way of exploiting the labor force and of subordinating territories. Mies's emblematic study is focused on that relation, explaining the organic relationship between patriarchy and accumulation on the global scale. The subjugation of women, nature, and the colonies, with "civilization" as the watchword, inaugurates capitalist accumulation with the sexual and colonial division of labor as its foundation. The feminist movement, in its different historical moments of growth, traces that same connection, but in a register of *insubordination*. The feminist inversion of domestication and colonization means opening up the question of what practices are capable of *depatriarchalizing and decolonizing* in the here and now, and from an urgently needed *internationalist* perspective.

The task of updating this understanding is currently being carried out by the communities that confront extractive megaprojects (from mining to soy monoculture, from petroleum extraction to forestry), largely led by women. For years, these struggles have been battling against such projects, which have been a fundamental element of the steady relaunch of the neo-developmentalist discourse in Latin America over the past decade. In turn, their efforts allow us to draw a map that connects the global South with other regions of the planet through extractivism and the systematic expropriation of land, and the ways such structures maintain an "imperialist mode of life."[3]

These struggles have invented the idea-force of the *body-territory*. The notion ties together a perspective that explains how the exploitation of territories is structured in a neo-extractive mode today, and how that also reconfigures labor exploitation, mapping the ways the dispossession of the commons affects everyday life. That is why it is *strategic* in a very precise sense: it expands our *way of seeing*, based on bodies experienced as territories and territories experienced as bodies. That image of the body-territory reveals the battles that are occurring here and now, pointing to a field of forces that it makes visible and legible on the basis of conflicts. The body-territory is a practical concept that demonstrates how the exploitation of common, community (be it urban, suburban, peasant, or Indigenous) territories involves the violation of the body of each person, as well as the collective body, through dispossession. There are consequences to stripping a community of its water so it can be used by mining companies. The women resisting the installation of the Rositas hydroelectric dam in the Río Grande basin in Santa Cruz, Bolivia, recount how it forces them to go look for water in the city, paying for the bus there and back, plus a charge for each container that is transported, the effort involved in the trip, organizing childcare or taking children with them, carrying the containers on foot for part of the way. Of course, all of this is done in the name of "development."

The conjunction of the words "body" and "territory" speaks for itself: it says that it is impossible to cut apart and isolate the individual body from the collective body, the human body from the territory and landscape. "Body-territory," compacted as a single word, de-liberalizes the notion of the body as individual property and specifies a political, productive, and epistemological continuity, of the body *as* territory. The body is thus revealed as a composition of affects, resources, and possibilities that are not "individual," but are made unique because they pass through the body of each person to the extent that no body is ever only "one," but always with others, and also with other nonhuman forces.

The compaction of "body-territory" also forces us to recognize that no one "lacks" either a body or a territory. It is not a matter of *lack*. And this allows for the illumination of processes of *dispossession* in another way.

This move inverts the idea of private property, in which one must always acquire what one does not have. A movement that begins from the standpoint of lack hides the *initial expropriation* that produces it, covers it up, and proposes it as an origin. That is why the images transmitted by these contemporary struggles are so strong: they show how so-called primitive accumulation acts in the *present*. That process that Marx described as the inaugural moment of capitalism has been intensely debated precisely in order to think about its *contemporaneity*.

Struggles against neo-extractivist megaprojects demonstrate that *dispossession* is a continuous logic that also includes a second moment: one that has to with *possession*. Now, we are faced with a "possession" that cannot be reduced to and does not replicate individual and private property and, therefore, does not reproduce the political scientist C.B. Macpherson's ideas on the limits of "possessive individualism."[4] This supposes decentering the individual as the privileged space of dispossession and, in that sense, not taking the individual ego as the starting point. This discussion refers to the psychoanalytic terms that outline the definition of subjectivity, as can be seen in the debate between Judith Butler and Athena Althanasiou on the very concept of dispossession.[5] The potencia of feminisms that speak of the body-territory is that they propose another notion of possession, in terms of use and not of property. In this way, they demonstrate the logic of the common as the plane of that which is dispossessed and exploited; and, finally, because this is what allows for the deployment of a political cartography of conflict.

An affirmation that there is no original *lack* of body or of territory is a key point for these forms of feminism, which emphasize the importance of situating themselves: each body is a territory of battle, an always-changing assemblage, open to becoming; it is a fabric that is attacked and needs to defend itself; and at the same time, it is remade in those confrontations, persisting as it practices alliances. Therefore, to join them in a single concept complicates the very notion of body and territory.

What does it mean to have a body? What does it mean to have a territory? First, one "has" a body-territory in the sense that one *is part of* a body-territory, not in the sense of property or possession. "Being part of" then implies a recognition of the "interdependence" that shapes us, that makes life possible. It is no minor detail that the women defending territories are also called defenders of life. The reference to life is not abstract, but rooted in the spaces, times, bodies, and concrete combinations in which that life unfolds, is made possible, is made dignified, is made livable. Therefore, it is not a naturalist, purely physiological, concept of life (which would be mere survival). "Life" refers to a vital register: it involves not only the defense and protection of the common, but also the production and expansion of shared wealth.

There is a hypothesis in operation at the heart of the concept of body-territory. That hypothesis is that the women and dissident corporealities who nourish and are nourished by those struggles produce and situate the body as an extensive territory. That is, not as the confinement of individuality, limited to the boundaries of one's own body understood as "property" backed by individual rights, but rather as expanded material, an extensive surface of affects, trajectories, resources, and memories.

Precisely because the body understood as body-territory is a concept-image that emerged from struggles, it manages to highlight knowledges of the body (about care, self-defense, ecology, and wealth) and, at the same time, to deploy the indeterminacy of its capacity: in other words, it foregrounds the necessity of *alliance as a specific and unavoidable potencia*. Alliance is not an individual's rational choice, nor is it a narrow calculation. It is a calculation, yes, but in the sense of calculation as a moment of a *conatus*, a form of perseverance in existence that is always collective and individuated. That *defensive* deployment that is embodied in the names of the coordinators and initiatives of struggle (in defense of land, of water, of life, and so on) is also *inventive*: it gives rise to new modes of organization, of sociability, new tactics of exchange, to the creation of existential territories, points of view. These are practices that defend and invent, that conserve and create, that protect and update, and, in that movement, produce value in a broad sense.

Therefore, the expansion and spillover of the body as a body-territory is the concrete place from which *expanded* extractivism is confronted today: that is, all the forms of dispossession, looting, and exploitation (from the literal extraction of raw materials to digital and financial extractivism) that the machine of capitalist valorization articulates. That the body-territory would be the situation that enables contempt, confrontation, and the invention of other modes of life implies that these struggles put knowledges of the body into play precisely in their becoming-territory. Yet they also make it indeterminate, because we do not know what a body, as a body-territory, can do. The body-territory is, for that reason, an idea-force that emerges from particular struggles but that has the potencia to migrate, resonate with, and compose other territories and other struggles.

Extractivism as a Political Regime

Berta Cáceres was assassinated on March 3, 2016, in Honduras for leading the struggle of her Indigenous people, the Lenca, through the Council of Popular and Indigenous Organizations of Honduras (COPINH) against large-scale infrastructure projects associated with Plan Puebla-Panama: the railways and hydroelectric dams necessary for mining exploitation.[6] She had explained it clearly: "If women do not speak about their bodies among themselves, if they do not recognize their rights to pleasure and to not experience violence, they will not be able to understand that militarization is a practice of territorial invasion that is linked to violence against women, by using sexual violence as a weapon of war."[7] In the majority of these conflicts, women's leadership opens up tensions within the community itself. Many women indicate that they "put their bodies on the line," even in cases of direct conflict, but that later they are displaced when it comes to making political decisions, when the politicians and business leaders ask to dialogue with the men of the community or the leaders of campesino unions. This question is key because it also updates the "subversion of the community" historically practiced by women.[8] Researchers Claudia López and Marxa Chávez, analyzing the Tariquía conflict in Bolivia, speak of an "oppressive enclosure" to name the power structure that combines violence against women with the neo-extractive advance:

> Women have challenged multiple mechanisms of patriarchal mediation throughout their defense, which have been enacted by larger regional and national organizations and state-instructed unionism. These structures attempt to impose and reproduce logics that asphyxiate and permanently block women's actions and strategies. In this war, there is an expansive dynamic we call oppressive enclosure, a power structure founded on violence against women's bodies.[9]

Indigenous and community feminisms, by proposing this register of the body-territory, place a demand on all forms of feminism: decolonization as a practical dimension that is inseparable from de-patriarchalization. María Galindo, from the Mujeres Creando collective, puts it clearly: "The colonial structures in our society are patriarchal and the patriarchal structures in our society are colonial; one thing cannot go without the other."[10] A whole series of investigations deploying feminist perspective are nourishing these debates on the critique of extractivism. Here I will only name a few: Mina Navarro speaks of "multiple dispossessions" in Mexico and the struggles for the commons that confront them.[11] More recently in Bolivia, Silvia Rivera Cusicanqui has detailed the conflict over the construction of the TIPNIS Highway in a register of women's territorial defense against the colonial-extractivist turn of the Movement for Socialism–led government.[12] In Chile, several analyses present women's resistance to being treated, in terms of body-territory, as "sacrifice zones," for example in the regions of Puchuncaví and Quintero.[13] In Peru, extractivism as a "biopolitical project" is presented in terms of the conjunction of "patriarchies, sexism, and discrimination based on gender" in mining activity.[14] In Ecuador, perspectives such as that of Cristina Vega and Cristina Cielo have analyzed how the devalorization and intensification of reproductive tasks are the "silent complement of Ecuador's productive matrix based on exportation of raw materials."[15] In Colombia, mapping the relationship between illegal networks and criminal groups associated with mining extractivism demonstrates that "processes of violence that specifically affect Indigenous, Afro-descendant, and campesina women have increased."[16] Lorena Cabnal, based on the conceptualization of communitarian feminism in Guatemala, has long raised the issue of the relationship between mining and sexual violence.[17] And, above all, there has been an enormous collective production of manifestos and declarations, of encounters and meetings, systematizing and updating approaches to various situations and conflicts in the region. The question of extractivism in Latin America, then, goes back to the process of capitalist colonization, but it nevertheless continues through successive reorganizations on the part of the creole elites, due to their rentier impetus and, therefore, the inherently colonial character that is translated onto the republican states. Different historical analyses show how this rentier character has been associated with a modernization project that, time and again, hides the predatory and archaic character of the elites associated with the metropoles of global capital.[18] Today, the feminist critique of extractivist looting recomposes and deepens this critical archive, investigating the ways it is organically linked to violence against women. This has also led Silvia Federici to update her hypothesis on the new witch hunt and the renewed enclosure of common goods and spaces.[19]

The sequence of the extraction of raw materials in Latin America spans five centuries, connecting forms of accumulation, specific dynamics of the exploitation of labor power, simultaneous forms of violence, and increasingly large scales of extractive operations. In that sense, we could say that it has always involved a political regime. However, today it is its new elements that must be theorized. Feminist struggles and analyses offer a crucial perspective for highlighting this newness (which is, in turn, part of a historical repetition) by producing a *displacement* from which another vocabulary of *sovereignty* emerges. It is not the juridical principle of the state (the notion of sovereignty deployed to legitimize these extractive projects), but rather sovereignty over one's own body (understood as body-territory). This idea of sovereignty is conceived in terms of pleasure and resistance against the neocolonial advance, using a grammar that puts another political economy and another, non-state-centric geography (which does not mean it refuses to think about the state) into play. That way of experiencing the extensive body is also what allows us to understand why a war is waged there today. Saying that extractivism is not only an economic mode, but also a political regime, makes visible the articulation between sexual violence and political violence in a machinery of looting, dispossession, and conquest. But it also allows us to think about other dynamics of looting, dispossession, and conquest connected to other territories. Particularly, it enables us to form a link with the territory of debt and consumption, where financial apparatuses expand their frontiers of valorization that (as I will explain in the following pages) are a fundamental part of the *expanded* conceptualization of the extractive operation. By linking both dynamics—literal extractivism exerted over raw materials and the extractivism of finance, carried out especially against populations that are considered to be "excluded"—we can bridge the forms of *exploitation* that are renewed through a mapping of the heterogeneity of labor in a feminist register.

Open Veins

The best-known image of extractive expropriation was popularized by the title of Uruguayan writer Eduardo Galeano's

1971 book *Open Veins of Latin America*. A powerful image of drainage and a medical allegory, the text synthesized for a mass audience both that historically unchanging factor and the framework of dependency theory that proliferated in Latin America in the 1960s and '70s. When former Venezuelan president Hugo Chávez gave a copy to Barack Obama as a gift at the Summit of the Americas in 2009, the book's sales skyrocketed again, highlighting the lasting validity of the diagnosis. However, this analysis obscures the elements that make the current extractivist moment different and, in turn, it has been adopted as part of an "independentist" discourse that progressive governments in the region have used to try to represent themselves as anti-imperialist in the midst of the neo-extractivist boom.[20] An element of novelty in the present period is seen in the primary destination for exports. China's emergence as a "central country" in terms of demand has led to an intense political debate as it displaces, at least in the imaginary of some interpretations, the imperialist map with which extractivism was associated in earlier historical moments of intensive raw material accumulation. This is not a minor point, since it is closely linked to the political legitimacy that the progressive governments in the region gained by arguing that taking advantage of the historical high in commodity prices (or the so-called commodity boom), from which they benefited, is a geopolitical contribution to the displacement of US hegemony.[21] A second key argument, in terms of the construction of legitimacy and newness, is that this extraordinary rent that was maintained as an income for over a decade is what has enabled a specific role of state "intervention." This had fundamental consequences. First, it was the "material" base that maintained the funding of social programs and welfare-benefits packages that were the main part of the interventionist policy, relaunching a whole discourse of recovered national sovereignty, even if these modes of intervention clearly left out public infrastructure.[22] Second, this mode of state "intervention" (even funded and focused in that way) was the basis for the rhetoric that claimed to oppose the financial hegemony that had characterized the region in the period running from the military dictatorships through the processes of democratic transition, and that ultimately led to the various crises at the turn of the twenty-first century. The overlap between the effective denationalization of some segments of the state[23] and methods of redesigning national intervention, in others areas, is a synchrony that cannot be understood in terms of the truth or falsity of the state's capacity for intervention, less so its "independence" from finance (as implied by the slogan "The return of the state" that spread as propaganda in the region). Instead, these overlaps produce new physiognomies of what we could properly call the state. For that same reason, the key point is the connection between three dimensions that produce the state today and allow for its characterization as "progressive," "post-neoliberal," or "twenty-first-century socialist" in different countries in the region, and that are crucial for thinking about their crises today. I am referring to (1) the combination between a dependent and subordinate mode of insertion in the global market, along with forms of intervention in the terrain of social reproduction that express both, (2) a capacity for taking root in de-waged urban and suburban territories through social policies won by social movements, and (3) a relaunch of the forms of valorization through finance that includes the so-called "excluded" sectors. In this register, the region's "progressive" governments opened up a discussion about possible models of "nationalization" and social organizations that tested, with different outcomes, their capacities to control and manage resources. The social repercussions of terms such as *buen vivir* or *vivir bien* (good living, or living well)—which were quickly associated with the constitutionalization of the forms of the social, solidarity, and popular economies embodied in the constitutions of Ecuador, Bolivia, and Venezuela—must also be understood in that complex intersection. In this discussion, neo-extractivist conflicts must be framed precisely: they are concrete disputes over the management of resources, over the meaning of living well, and over forms of sovereignty. A theorization of neo-extractivism from the perspective of struggles for body-territory, as simultaneously a *logic of valorization* and a *political* (and not only economic) *regime*, allows us to understand the extractivist logic as a new colonial form of dispossession and exploitation. However, doing so requires an expansion of the notion of extractivism, as going beyond raw materials and beyond peasant and Indigenous territories, into urban and suburban ones. This expanded notion of extractivism illuminates a hypothesis: that the extractive logic has become a privileged mode of producing value in the current phase of accumulation, in which finance plays a key role. It is this logic that allows for an update of the very notion of exploitation, and an explanation for why women's and feminized bodies are a preferred territory of aggression.

The notion of body-territory emerging from struggles led by women territorial leaders is in this sense strategic, because it is a point of analysis and of practical action that explains both the extensive and intensive character of contemporary extraction, as well as the organic relation between capital accumulation and heteropatriarchal and colonial violence. It does so by producing a feminist diagnosis of that conflict based on concrete struggles, which determines the political composition of a multiform antagonism at various scales. The linkage of these struggles by today's feminist movement is a reconnection of precisely that which seems to be unrelated: aggression against the bodies of women and sexual dissidents postulated as body-territory, on one hand, and on the other, a neo-extractivist political regime that is connected with financial hegemony in a nodal way.

Expanded Extractivism

Today, extractive industries have expanded their focus to go beyond natural resources, be they minerals, gases, or hydrocarbons. We must also add to this list the growing frontiers of *agribusiness*, including soy as well as other important and lesser-known monocultures, such as palm oil.[24] However, the displacement of the extractive frontier also has effects on other social, political, and economic dynamics, for which land (and its depths) is not the sole privileged space. We are referring to an extractive dynamic in contexts of urban real estate speculation (including informal speculation), virtual territories of "data mining" and the operations of algorithms, and, in a more fundamental way, the popular economies whose vitality is extracted through apparatuses of debt. We have used the notion of *expanded extractivism* to refer to this displacement of the frontiers of the "extractive zones."[25] This *expansion* accounts for a two-part movement. On the one hand, it concerns the multiplication of references to extractive language in order to define technologies and procedures that convert elements into "raw materials," which become strategic for the privileged operation of capital. On the other hand, it demonstrates the need to conceptualize extractivism beyond a specific technical procedure strictly related to raw materials, in order to make it intelligible as a logic of valorization. At the same time, by highlighting the role of finance, this conceptualization opens up a novel reading of the relationship between finance and production. It no longer speaks of the hegemony of finance as synonymous with the end of production (as finance is understood when compared to an industrial type of regime); rather, it highlights the specific productive dimension of finance.[26] This perspective does not limit the spatiality of extraction to the multiplication of "enclaves."[27] Instead, it points out the connectivity between heterogeneous spaces. In this sense, when we speak of expansion we are referring to a *dynamic* of the expansion of the frontiers of valorization, in which finance is the common operator or code. However, we must be careful not make a division between a financial extractivism as what occurs in the "First World," and an extractivism of raw materials in the "Third World" or "global South." To the contrary, the analysis of this "expanded extractivism" also seeks to undo that binary that reproduces a *naturalism* of certain regions, as compared to a sophisticated *abstraction* of others. The argument is complex because it supposes that the diversity of the articulation based on the financial dynamic is capable of linking social inclusion, consumption, and debt in social sectors that are usually considered marginal, excluded, or surplus populations[28] or, in the philosophical lexicon, as "bare life."[29]

Extraction thus becomes an operative modality of capital in which the expansion of the margins of valorization demands a colonization of new areas, sectors, and forms of production that exceed the productive forms *coordinated* by capital's command. This shows finance in its productive character as much as in its extractive one. In other words, it is not a matter of a fictitious speculation or a non-real economy, as it tends to be characterized by the industrialist discourse to account for a dynamic that does not include the labor force in waged terms. In this sense, we can say that extraction is produced directly upon forms of social cooperation, where finance lands, takes root, and inserts itself into a multiform vitality that it *exploits*. It does so in axiomatic terms: that is, by making a command code immanent.

Finance "weaves" together a "literal" type of extractivism, on one hand, referring to raw materials (even if defined by its constitutive relation with finance through the funding of megaprojects and the manipulation of commodity prices), and on the other, an extractivism in an *expanded* sense: extraction that operates upon popular vitality through mass indebtedness in urban and suburban territories, as well as other extractive

97

modes, such as the management of data through platforms. In this way, the *extractive* logic is a dynamic that produces value and that is capable of articulating the tendency toward permanent abstraction (capital's utopia: getting rid of the need for *living labor*), with the violence of multiple forms of dispossession (accumulation by dispossession and privatization in general), and the exploitation in the future of an increasingly precarious labor force (the rentier architecture over labor).

The concern about the political form of extractivism leaves open the question of *command* of that process of valorization and its territorial landing, of its link with popular and illegal economies, and of how the role of the state is reformulated. Furthermore, it raises the question of how to think about the relationship between extractivism and violence against women and feminized bodies. *It is the analysis rising from the feminist struggles that allows for the proposal of the simultaneity of those planes of social conflict today.* This analysis does so in two very precise senses: it enables an understanding of how extraction operates (1) *over* bodies and territories (as capture and exploitation) and (2) *against* social cooperation (as hierarchization and privatization) with intense levels of violence. The perspective deployed by struggles understood in a feminist register provides the foundation for thinking about such cooperation beyond the hierarchical binaries between remunerated and non-remunerated labor, production and reproduction, production and consumption, home and labor market. It creates a map of the contemporary heterogeneity of living labor, of all those who persist against dispossession and new forms of exploitation.

"We do not ask for ownership of the land; we are proposing another art of inhabiting the land," said Moira Millán, one of the Mapuche leaders at the feminist assembly in the Argentinian city of El Bolsón in September 2017. This phrase synthesizes the displacement produced by the notion of body-territory with respect to the grammar of private property. She was referring to the attempt to reduce the debate to property terms, a trick to create individual titles to later enable the (forced) sale of lands. In that type of swarm, literal dispossession is articulated with financial titling. Therefore, today this mode of Indigenous conflict resonates with diverse forms of urban conflict, tracing a complex map of real estate speculation by the large corporations in Patagonia and in the north of Argentina (whether due to agribusiness, mining projects, or hotel complexes), which qualify an increasingly acute territorialization of conflicts in terms of confrontation, and which is also reproduced, in a fractal way, in urban slums. That is, the dynamics of dispossession require ever-stronger thresholds of violence to carry out evictions and displacements, and to orient them through individual titling, or the criminalization of those who do not accept this, and resist.

Therefore, I insist that the notion of body-territory also opens up a debate about the surrounding spatiality that is normalized by individual property. Body-territory can be postulated as an image that is antagonistic to the abstract character required by the individual property owner of (neo) liberal modernity. "Abstract" means no more or less than the masculine naturalized as the universal.[30] In other words, if it is possible to abstract the body, it is because that body is marked as masculine. The body-territory is that which does not allow for abstraction from a corporeality that is marked precisely by its impossibility of being governed or defined by mere property law. From the beginning, the body-territory is marked by its capacity for combat: one of simultaneous care, defense, healing, and strengthening. It is also the site of the beautiful call of the compañeras from the Red de Sanadoras Ancestrales del Feminismo Comunitario Territorial (Network of ancestral healers of territorial communitarian feminism), of Iximulew, Guatemala, to produce *acuerpamiento* (embodiment) based on the struggles.

The Body-Territory in the Abortion Debate

By recognizing the impact of thinking based on the body-territory, we can account for the radical and profound character of the debate over the legalization of abortion in Argentina. After being presented for thirteen consecutive years by the National Campaign for Legal, Safe, and Free Abortion, since 2018 that demand has taken on a mass dimension, unprecedented in the country's history. Here I want to highlight the capacity of contagion, and connection, of certain language and images of struggle that impregnate realities that are very different from those in the places they emerged. I also want to emphasize the feminist movement's versatility in *territorializing* concepts in diverse practices and, at the same time, producing situated experiences of translation, reappropriation, and enrichment of those languages and imaginaries. Finally, I want to provide a concrete image of the transversality of practices that are not homogenized in a singular vocabulary but that allow the meanings of struggles to multiply.

Why did this notion of body-territory become operative in —that is, gain the potencia to name—the debate over abortion? There are several reasons. First, Mauricio Macri's neoliberal government tried to dissociate the dynamic of the feminist strike from the struggle for abortion. They announced that the abortion law would be discussed in the legislature on March 8, 2017 (which was proven false a few days later), thus attempting to minimize the effect of the strike and take abortion off the strike agenda. Even so, in the following months, an unprecedented scene unfolded, in which mobilizations for abortion became increasingly massive and heterogeneous.

This was possible precisely because of the way the struggle for abortion had been threaded together with other feminist struggles that had politically and cognitively linked violence against feminized bodies with a systematic attack on each of us. That systematic attack is the foundation of the heteropatriarchal regime of government. The realization that there is no form of government that does not intrinsically presuppose women's subordination is the a priori that was put in crisis with the struggle for abortion, which went beyond the limits of the individual body and the territory of law.

The overflowing of the parliamentary terrain was made clear through its appropriation by the feminist campaign. For the first time, the public sessions were transmitted live and followed by thousands of people; they included more than 800 voices, becoming a truly public platform of argumentation, confrontation, and exhibition. They forged a pedagogic space, which was taken particular advantage of by the generations of youth who dealt with those arguments in schools and everyday conversations. But they also managed to impose a discussion on the media agenda, thanks to an unprecedented polyphony of debate.

The overflow onto the social terrain was clarified by the mobilization's expansion. This took place, first, through the practice of the *pañuelazos*: mass actions in which participants waved the green handkerchiefs symbolizing abortion. The so-called green tide flooded spaces everywhere, including schools, slums, unions, plazas, and soup kitchens. Through this extension, the body that had been put up for debate also took on a *class* dimension. On the one hand, this occurred because discussion about the clandestine condition of abortion directly referred to the costs that make it differentially *risky* according to one's social and economic conditions. On the other hand, this dimension emerged because the Catholic Church hierarchy attempted to invert the class-based argument, pointing to abortion as something "foreign" and "external" to the popular classes.

Religious leaders and some political leaders focused their opposition on an argument claiming to be anti-neoliberal: that "the poor do not have abortions," that abortion is "imperialist" and a "fad" imposed by the International Monetary Fund, demonstrating the depth of patronization in play. In their pretension to show themselves as the sole anti-neoliberals, the church spokesmen directed this argument particularly toward "poor women": to those who they assume they must protect, those whose decision-making capacity they take away in the name of their social condition, those who they only recognize as resistant when they are mothers. In that way, the Vatican attempts to trace a class distinction that would justify the notion that poor women have no other option than Catholicism and conservativism, because their only option is maternity. Thus, the church attempts to reduce having an abortion (that is, making decisions about desire, maternity, and one's own life) to an eccentric gesture of the middle and upper classes (which, of course, can make use of different economic resources). Their objective is to *invert* the class-based argument: for them it functions as justification for the clandestine condition of abortion. For the church, the right to decide must be kept away from the popular neighborhoods. This crusade to infantilize "poor" women is its spearhead, because if it is disarmed, the church itself would be left without its "faithful." What is most brutal is the way, in order to maintain this position, that they must turn a deaf ear to what the women of the slums themselves and their organizations have to say. Those women have mobilized around the slogan "Stop speaking for us." They have retaken and narrated their own experiences of having clandestine abortions, rejecting the moralization of their practices, and have woven coordinated actions, including the pañuelazos. It was the transversality of feminist politicization that allowed for an expansion of the discussion into sites where it had not previously reached, even as abortions were a massive, albeit secret, reality.

In the struggle for the legalization of abortion, the body in dispute thus exceeds the conquest of individual private rights. The massive mobilization demanding legal, safe, and free abortion overflows the request for legislative recognition at the same time that it calls for it. This is due to the fact that it reveals the dispute over the sovereignty of a body-territory that allows for the connection of anti-extractive struggles with those for abortion. In those days of mobilization, in a conversation with compañeras from the Movimiento Campesino de Santiago del Estero (MOCASE), they recounted how, for the first time, they were debating in peasant communities what had been a taboo topic up until then. In conversations in assemblies, a link was drawn between abortion rights, the subjugation of the land, and the impossibility of autonomy that this implies.

The debate went beyond the sole framework of public health and abortion as a preventative question of undesired pregnancy, to open up the question of desire. With the slogan "Maternity will be desired or it won't be" and the demand for comprehensive sexual education in the educational curriculum, the campaign deepened debates about sexualities, corporealities, relationships, and affects that displaced the question in a radical way. This even allowed for variations on the slogans in support of legal abortion, not only in the hospital, but also in vindication of autonomous networks like the *socorristas* (life savers, a national network of health care and social workers who provide information and support for safe abortions in Argentina), who have been practicing abortions "anywhere"; not only of sexual education, but also the discovery of one's sexuality; not only of contraception for the purposes of preventing abortions, but also for the purposes of pleasure; and not only an abortion that would prevent death, but one that would allow you to decide.

The weft between the dynamic of the strike, on one hand, and the green tide, on the other, forged a connection between the modes of differential exploitation of feminized bodies. It wove a register of intelligibility between non-remunerated (or poorly remunerated) labor and expensive and unsafe abortions, tying together the forms of precarization of our lives, the modes of control exerted in the name of labor market democracy, and the ecclesiastic condescension of desire and autonomous decision making.

What Spatiality Does a Body-Territory Create?

We already discussed the body-territory as a concept that is antagonistic to the abstract character required by the individual property owner. I will add a second thesis: the becoming-territory of the body is a spatiality that appears in opposition to domestic enclosure. This is because the body-territory is that which flees the individual environment (and thus the contract as the privileged political bond), that of citizenship that is always retracted, of exploitation always hidden as a natural service. Therefore, the body-territory drives the invention of other "existential territories," to cite Félix Guattari's beautiful formation.[31]

To translate this into spatial terms: we have already left the domestic enclosure. Additionally, other domestic territories are constructed that do not bind us to unrecognized free labor and that do not demand a promise of fidelity to the husband–property owner. We take over the street and turn it into a feminist hearth. The occupations, assemblies, and massive vigils, carried out on the streets while Congress debated abortion, invented another type of spatiality: one where the place of politics was reorganized and reinvented under the open sky. At the same time, such a politics is not constructed in opposition to "the domestic," but rather to its restricted formulation as a synonym of "enclosure."

This spatial inversion marks a new type of political cartography. It dismantles the traditional opposition between the household as a closed space and the public as its opposite: new architectures are constructed, for these homes are open to the street, the neighborhood, communitarian networks; they are a roof and walls that shelter and host without enclosing or clois-tering. This is a practical balance that emerges from a concrete reality: many households, in the heteropatriarchal meaning, have turned into hell. They are the most unsafe spaces and the site of the majority of femicides, along with countless acts of everyday "domestic" violence.

With this new mode of constructing politics, it is almost too obvious to chant that those legislating do not represent us. A feminist version of "They all must go," which synthesized the 2001 crisis,[32] seems almost unnecessary. We have already surpassed that threshold. It was made clear that the regime of representation that is maintained with its back to the streets has nothing to do with the feminist way of doing politics and making history. But more than that, we showed that politics is already being carried out in other spaces, ones that have the force to produce a non-patriarchal domestic sphere. Thus, the question is: Why is it that the domestic must be kept private?

My hypothesis is that the so-called domestic scene deploys, and in turn contains, two situations that were made visible in the debate around abortion. The first occurs in the Argentine Senate, where senator Rodolfo Urtubey of the Justicialist Party argues that there can be "rape without violence," when, and perhaps also because, it occurs within the family. What does that mean? That the home, in its patriarchal meaning, is the place where rape is permitted. Because the home is constructed as "private" when it legitimizes men's violent and privileged access to women's bodies and feminized bodies (which includes children). The private, then, is what guarantees the secrecy and legitimacy of violence. It is also what permits the famous "double morality." Here we are in the heart of what theorist Carole Pateman has analyzed as the *patriarchal pact*: the complicity between men based on hierarchy that, in our democracies, is converted into a form of political right. This corporative male complicity, which Pateman denounces, is *foundational* to the modern political regime, which is organized based on the subordination of women and feminized bodies.[33] Therefore, any issue related to the sexes is a directly political question.

With this we see that even in Congress—supposedly a space belonging to the public sphere—they are legislating to preserve the domestic space as one of confinement, as a place of secrecy. What Congress is legislating is no more or less than the desperate attempt to maintain the home as the patriarchal reign, in the face of an emerging politics that constructs other spatialities and dismantles the division between the public and the private that is responsible for the hierarchy between the "realms." Therefore, when the Senate votes to reject the legalization of abortion, what it sanctions is male power over women's bodies, the foundational scene of which, I insist, is rape.

The second situation is the contempt shown by Congress toward the masses in the streets clamoring for the legalization of abortion. From the congressional perspective, because the street is occupied by women and sexual dissidents, it loses its public character and is thus treated as if it were a domestic space. How so? With regard to the mass mobilization, representative power repeats the same historical pattern of nonrecognition that it did with feminized tasks. Just as it has invisibilized the ways in which we produce value, by doing practically everything that allows for the world's production and reproduction, feminized and dissident ways of weaving sociability and collective care have been systematically excluded from the accounts of all democracies. The maneuver of ignoring the masses in the street seeks to render invisible a multitude that shouts, "Now that they see, the patriarchy is going to fall!" The maneuver of nonrecognition aims to enclose the open space of the street. It also shows how *mobile* the categories of the public and the private are, or rather, how the geometry of power that makes them function as a grid operating according to sexual difference is translated into political hierarchy.

This invisibilization—which is a specific regime of visibility —is created at the cost of expropriating the potencia from our bodies while, at the same time, "exploiting," benefiting from, representing us. August 8 thus presented a twofold scene: Congress discussed rape in the domestic sphere as a justification for maintaining the clandestine, illegal, and unsafe status of abortion, while trying to ignore what was taking place on the streets, as if the street were no longer a public space when taken over by the feminist masses. This scene offers historical clarity on an already-inverted power: there can be no compliance in the face of such belittlement. No submission to invisibility. No resignation to going uncounted. There can be no accommodation to once again not being part of, or being the infantilized part of, democracy, and therefore under bondage. The body-territory expresses the disobedience of a distribution that is simultaneously political, economic, and affective, as well as critical of the patriarchal public-private geometry whose counterpart, as we will see in Chapter 5, is the distinction between the social and the political.

Disarming the Domestic Enclosure

A metaphor has been circulating that considers the home as a new feminist space. More precisely, it asks us to consider: What would a non-heteropatriarchal home look like, given that the very definition of home seems to eclipse this very possibility?

There are two scenes from this discussion in Argentina that I want to highlight. The first is that of the "former" daughters of the men responsible for genocide during the country's last military dictatorship, which lasted from 1976 to 1983. The dictatorship was one of the most brutal and cruel in the region in terms of state terrorism, with the disappearance and murder of more than 30,000 people through a system of concentration camps, in which those kidnapped were tortured under clandestine conditions. The daughters of the men responsible for these crimes against humanity publicly "came out of the closet" at the Ni Una Menos march on June 3, 2017, where they told their stories, denounced their progenitors, and debated the constitutional premise that has barred them from testifying against their fathers.[34] The force of their public words was constituted around a hypothesis: state terrorism traced a line of continuity between the concentration camp and the family homes of the men committing genocide, in such a way that their children lived in an extension of that camp. This idea supposes that there is no state terrorism without its intimate ties to the patriarchal family. It therefore corrects a fairly widespread idea that many military officers were "good" or "affectionate" within their homes, "objectifying" their actions as something having to do with work (the idea that they "were just doing their jobs"), which was external and corporate. It is precisely that border between domestic life and public life that disappears.

On the other hand, what some narratives reveal today is an attempt to transfer "family" and domestic dynamics onto the concentration camp. Florencia Lance, the daughter of an army pilot accused of carrying out death flights,[35] recounts a striking scene. Starting in preschool, they would celebrate her birthday in the Campo de Mayo concentration camp: "The ritual was that a green bus, one of those big Mercedes-Benz, would come by to pick us up, and my friends would get on to go spend the entire day in that place."[36] Another story is told by Andrea Krichmar, invited by her school friend to "play" at "her dad's job." Her friend was the daughter of Rubén Chamarro—alias the Dolphin—vice-admiral of the navy, director of the Navy School of Mechanics (ESMA), and directly responsible for the Task Group 3.3.2.[37] Additionally, the families were routinely convened for mass and ceremonies in the barracks. For example, Mariana Dopazo, the former daughter of Miguel

Etchecolatz—police chief during the dictatorship and now serving a life sentence for crimes of homicide, torture, illegal detention, and infant kidnapping—recalls attending birthday parties "in some Police Circle of La Plata."[38]

The patriarchal function of the repressive system is seen both in domestic spaces that are assumed to be "preserved" from violence, and in the attempt to normalize the spaces of horror through "familiar" presence. These former daughters have worked to publicize the imbrication of state terrorism with the patriarchal family. They are the ones who have shown that home can be hell, as many survivors have named the ESMA concentration camp. The first to defiliate was Rita Vagliati, former daughter of Buenos Aires police chief Valentín Milton Pretti. She wrote: "Nor can I stop feeling the relationship between their crimes and what existed in my family. I cannot forgive him for wanting to torture and kill and for having touched me and my siblings. That he held us or caressed us."[39]

There would be no way for the dictatorship to have combined civic, ecclesiastic, business, and military action without operating under the banner of "saving" the West and Christianity. They presented the threat of "subversion," in reference to the guerrilla, as a civilizational threat. It would have been impossible for the spatiality of the concentration camp not to have been reaffirmed in the homes of the men responsible for the genocide. But today there is a new voice of enunciation, a collective force.

They, the former daughters, chose the Ni Una Menos march to make their public appearance as an act of defiliation. Each one of them had been personally and legally negotiating their situation in different ways. But the spatiality of the feminist streets is what enabled the defiance of the family history, understood as a mandate of complicity with the aberrant, based on a *collective* voice. Such spatiality has also created an atmosphere for further scenes of justice. The previous step had been organizing a repudiation, which wove them together as a collective, against the judicial attempt to grant impunity to military officers who had already been tried, known as the two-for-one law.[40]

Now we enter into, with the bravery of their narratives, the "domestic" horror. If the violence that was experienced in the homes of the men who committed genocide can be told in the first person, recounted and denounced by their former daughters, it is because violence analyzed in the heat of the feminist experience provides a new perception and makes that *continuum* audible. It is thus a first person that also becomes collective. Their testimonies are interlinked with the expansion of the field of trust for listening to abuses, inaugurated by the experiences of #YoTeCreo (#IBelieveYou) and others that created that form of speaking and narrating.[41] The former daughters' personal and collective story of defiliation establishes a new way of demanding justice and punishment, based on disobedience to patriarchy.

The second scene is also connected to the link between Ni Una Menos and the historical human rights struggles in Argentina. It is a trajectory that also has a militant, non-liberal genealogy, and is led by women: the Mothers and Grandmothers of the Plaza de Mayo. Thanks to the feminist movement, this genealogy has been revived, tracing new connections between the types of cruelty and torture that were inflicted in especially merciless ways on the bodies of politically active women. Today we know that sexual torture was intensified against women as a way of punishing their disobedience to a model of the family, which their practices questioned through the reinvention of other affective ties and other modes of life.[42] The intervention in this living memory by Ni Una Menos as the "daughters and granddaughters" of their rebellions in the recent anniversaries of the coup d'état (March 24) puts another form of filiation into play: rebellion as that which creates kinship.

This type of intervention into memory in the present tense also makes it possible for leaders of the Mothers and Grandmothers of the Plaza de Mayo, such as Nora Cortiñas, to now consider themselves feminists. This demonstrates a *temporality that emerges from the struggles that reopens history*, encompassing memories, archives, and narrations.

What I want to emphasize is that the feminist movement has harbored a double displacement, made by women and in a collective voice, in relation to the cruelty associated with the patriarchal mandate and its organic link with state terrorism. On the one hand, the former daughters of genociders, moved to defiliate from their parents, which is a way of imploding the image of the home and childhood as something protected from the concentration camp. On the other hand, the daughters of the militants of the 1970s invented a mode of nonfamily filiation, outlining kinship based on rebellion and, in that way, making visible the other families and bonds of love with which the militants sought to experiment. Both movements account for an anti-patriarchal register of the struggles for human rights and against the dictatorship that had not, until now, had to confront this strength or this feminist perspective.

The church hierarchy also condemned and attempted to invert this rebellion. In the midst of the debate about abortion, one of the most famous priests who work in the *villas* (slums) evoked the women who were detained-disappeared in ESMA to say that those women, even in that extreme situation, chose to give birth. With that image, not only does he neglect to mention the appropriation of their children, in which they were considered "spoils of war," where the Catholic Church played an important role; he also falsely recalls those women who were imprisoned and tortured as simply self-sacrificing mothers. The priest connected the kidnapped women forced into maternity in the concentration camp with the women of the villas who, according to him, also must give birth in extreme conditions, but should do so nevertheless.

Let's return to the question of contested spaces. What else does this analogy between the concentration camp (ESMA) and the villa say? That the villas are today's concentration camps? That the women in either space have no choice but to engage in maternity, at the cost of their own lives? What is clear is that the church, through its male spokespeople, is on a crusade against the rebellion of women and feminized bodies that are reinventing modes of autonomy and desire, and that are renarrating history (I will return to this in Chapter 7).

Excursus: A Materialism Based on the Body-Territory

We know from several references that Gilles Deleuze was preparing a book about Marx before he died. It seems that not much remains of that impulse, but the work of Deleuze—along with his and Félix Guattari's collaborations—is full of valuable references to Marx. To take one example that recalls the Spinozist question of what a body can do: the idea that bodies are not merely organic matter, but that life is a nonorganic phenomenon—one in which we can detect the presence of the virtual in the actual. At stake here is nothing less than the very idea of surplus value, where we can see the differential of a body that receives recompense for its actuality, but is taken advantage of in its virtuality, in its generic power of doing. Deleuze and Guattari's language of flows cannot be understood outside of the fact that these potencias refer to flows of desire and production (which allows for the situation of Marx and Freud on the same plane). But, Deleuze adds, what characterizes capitalism is that production is always attributed to a "sterile or unproductive instance": money.

This means that money, as a form of command, hides its condition as an abstract representative of what is created by bodies, through use of financial apparatuses. Thinking about money as command also reveals its concern for potencia, for what bodies can do—that is, for the foundation of all surplus value as the *indeterminate* element of bodies of labor, of desire, of vital potencia.

Today, resistance is confronted with a dynamic that constantly attempts to read and capture it due to the axiomatic functioning of capital. Capital's axiomatic dynamic, as Deleuze and Guattari theorized it in *A Thousand Plateaus*, highlights the tension that inheres in the flexibility (or versatility) of capture and exploitation by capital. At the same time, it demonstrates the need to distinguish operations through which that machine of capture subsumes social relations and inventions that also resist and exceed the diagram of capture/exploitation. When Deleuze refers to the axiomatic dynamic of capital, he makes his connection with Marx's *Grundrisse* explicit, referring to "economic-physical" processes that convert another body, that "sterile and unproductive body" of money, into something *more*. What this reference tells us is that the problem of the axiomatic dynamic is related to a question involving desire, economy, and politics. Here a question of the limit is also always in play: on the part of capital, in the expansion of scale, and in the expansion of the frontiers of valorization in the extractive register I have discussed. To do so, first capital must internalize the limit through an immanentization that works in the differential relation between flows—containing them, codifying them, recuperating their escape toward the outside. The role of the axiomatic, Deleuze says, is "to compensate the limit, to return things to their place,"[43] but in that operation of recuperation, it is forced into a new expansion each time. Additionally, there are always flows that escape: those that appear in the schizophrenic migrations of characters such as those in the plays of Samuel Beckett.

Particularly when Deleuze works with concepts of Michel Foucault's, it becomes clear that he placed importance on the articulation between the formation of territories, practices of desire, and diagrams of power (in their classic forms:

sovereignty, discipline, and control, and their co-functioning).
It is impossible to understand today, from a materialist point
of view, the economies that organize new forms of exploitation and value extraction—their assemblages, their financial
dispositions, their forms of obedience, and the proliferation
of forms of power that accompany them—without that architecture that is capable of identifying multiple dimensions that
converge on a single plane.

Let's turn to what we could propose as idea-forces of a materialism capable of creating existential territory—body-territory
—against the current forms of exploitation. That materialism
has two premises: First, there is the very idea that subjectivities
are expressed in practice, with structures that are articulated
practices and with discourses that are always a dimension of
practice ("foci of experience," Foucault would say), and that,
therefore, cannot be reduced to and do not privilege rational
spirituality or consciousness. Second, there is an understanding of the production of value as the production of existence,
which is seen in the concept of labor power, in its failed and
impossible conversion into a commodity, due to an impasse
that is impossible to surpass between the potencia of human
practice and the effective task. The materialism that concerns
us, that problematizes the diverse bodies of labor and common
goods (and their expression in different territories and conflicts), is one that combats a specific kind of abstraction—one
that operates through the conversion of body-territories into
the sterile and unproductive body of money.

Chapter 4

A Feminist Economics of Exploitation and Extraction

Feminist economics explains the specific ways that women are exploited in capitalist society. To do so, it expands the very notion of the economy, including everything from the sexual division of labor to modes of oppressing desire. Its first objective is to perceive, conceptualize, and measure a *differential* in the exploitation of women, lesbians, trans people, and travestis. But this is much more expansive than merely accounting for the activities carried out by women and feminized bodies. That is because the second objective of feminist economics— which is posited as a criticism of political economy, not as a demand for inclusion in the competitive neoliberal world— consists of defying, subverting, and transforming the capitalist, colonial, and patriarchal order.

The question of the differential of exploitation must be situated within this context as a task for feminist economics. The point of departure for this question is the *concrete place* where that differential starts: reproduction. Why? Because that differential is always relational. In other words, it reveals the unique position that the labor of women and feminized bodies holds in social relations; however, by visibilizing and understanding those specific dynamics, it sheds new light on exploitation in general. Making visible waged and precarious labor today, based on the feminist perspective that emerges from the analysis of historically non-remunerated labor and feminized tasks, thus enables a new analysis of the whole.

Furthermore, placing emphasis on the differential brings us to another central issue: it is not a matter of simply recognizing difference in order to demand *equality*. We do not want to decrease the gap in order to be equally exploited as men. What we are interested in, and what feminist economics allows us to value, is the struggle led by women, lesbians, trans people, and travestis for the reproduction of life against relations of exploitation and subordination.

Let me repeat that this is not merely a sectoral analysis, of interest only to a "minority" (a concept that is itself problematic), but rather a unique perspective from which to visualize the whole based on concrete conflicts. Methodologically, this means that women and feminized bodies are not a chapter to be tacked onto the end of an economic analysis, but present a perspective that reformulates economic analysis itself. It is a transversal political perspective, one that proposes another entryway into the critique of political economy, rather than a circumscribed agenda.

To cast feminist economics in political terms, as the organization of a critique, produces an ever-greater displacement. This is because feminist economics does not center its analysis on the ways the accumulation of capital is organized, but rather on how reproduction of collective life is organized and guaranteed as an a priori condition. Thus, the dynamic of social reproduction is revealed as the condition of possibility for capital accumulation. In philosophical language, we could say that reproduction is the transcendental condition of production.

This question, in turn, has two levels: on the one hand, it seeks to understand how this reproduction makes possible all the production from which capital benefits. In that sense, feminist economics asks why hiding reproduction is essential to processes of valorization in capitalist terms. But there is a second level. One of feminist economics' additional tasks is to discover in what forms, and in which experiences, social reproduction be can organized in non-extractivist and non-exploitative terms (which implies, as we will see below, fighting against its naturalization). With this, we go beyond opposing reproduction and production (as if they were antithetical terms) to instead think about reorganizing their relation. It is in this relation that we can situate the question of the differential of exploitation.

Several feminists have read Marx in this register. I would say that they carry out a two-part movement with a two-part objective. On one hand, they accompany Marx to the hidden places of his work; on the other, they radicalize Marx's method of investigation, of looking to the "hidden abode" of capitalist reality's production. As we will see, the first hidden dimension is reproduction: all of that which is made invisible, and at the same time is constitutive of social production organized in capitalist terms.

This is the perspective taken by Silvia Federici in speaking about the lacunae that feminists of the 1970s started to see in Marx's work, as they analyzed his perspective on gender and, later, reconstructed his categories themselves, based on their personal political experience of refusal. The feminist movement is, therefore, *another origin* of the critique of political economy. "The feminist movement had to start by critiquing Marx," writes Federici. And that "origin" was situated in political practice: "I maintain that the feminists of Wages for Housework found the foundations of a feminist theory in Marx that focused on women's struggle against unpaid domestic labor, because we read his analysis of capitalism from the perspective of politics, coming from a direct personal experience, in search of responses to our refusal of domestic relations."[1] More recently, taking up the category of the "hidden abode" (which is how Marx refers to production, in contrast to the "visible" sphere of circulation), Wendy Brown proposes that feminism must ally itself with critical theory (referring to the more radical contributions of the Frankfurt School), because that will allow it to include the invisible folds of the sphere of production. Here the "hidden abodes" that she highlights are language, the psyche, sexuality, aesthetics, reason, and thought itself.[2] And Nancy Fraser writes that feminism, ecological thought, and postcolonialism are three perspectives that reformulate Marxian analysis, precisely because they incorporate the "hidden abodes" of the production of social conflict in contemporary capitalism.[3]

In these approaches, each of three theorists takes up—from a different position—a reading of Marx that refers to how a feminist perspective makes visible the forces that *produce* capitalist power, not only through the subordination of labor to capital, but also via hierarchies that function within what we understand as labor. In this vein, they identify feminized labor as an example of that which capital must subordinate, discredit, and most of all *hide*.

This symptomatic reading of Marx has been a guiding line for feminist economics. First, because by taking up the Marxian thread of reproduction of labor power as a necessary activity for the accumulation of capital, it makes the class dimension of feminism clear. Then, because it detects the lacunae, abodes, and caverns that Marx left *unthought* precisely because his reading of capital as a social relation privileges the analysis of production, but not that of the production of production (or reproduction). If Marx debates neoclassical theories to defetishize the sphere of circulations, feminists dig deeper and defetishize the sphere of production. They get to the *underground* of reproduction. From there below, they see all the strata that finally make possible what we call capitalist production. This is how feminist economics inaugurates a true perspective "from below."

I am particularly interested in highlighting Federici's work because her reading of Marx emerges from struggles that used Marx and, in turn, *took Marx beyond Marx* in the concrete initiative of the Wages for Housework campaign.[4] In this sense, the feminist reading exhibits its own *constituent* character: it not only illuminates what is left invisible by Marx (replicating and expanding his method of looking to the "hidden abode" in the situation), but also explains the historical, political, and economic function of that invisibilization. The proposal of the domestic wage opens up a whole series of paradoxes and implosions within categories. Therefore, the perspective of feminist economics posits a theoretical and practical confrontation with the modes of capital valorization, that is, with both the concrete forms of subordination and the differential exploitation of feminized bodies.

This concern for the dynamics of capital valorization is, at the same time, tied together with feminist economics' insistence on thinking in terms of exploitation and domination. The sexual division of labor cannot be explained without the patriarchal mandates that sustain it. Thus, the "reproductive paradigm" capable of simultaneously analyzing both planes drives a feminist economics as "neo-materialism."[5]

From another perspective, the question of what feminist economics *is* can be answered affirmatively, as going beyond the critique of exploitation. In particular, I'm referring to the fundamental work of the feminist theorists J.K. Gibson-Graham (who share a single pen name) on "diverse economies." Gibson-Graham do so by also deriving a notion of *difference* from Marx, based on which they interpret those economies with a prefigurative, anticipatory capacity in their development in the present as *noncapitalist*. This perspective highlights the experimental character of community economies, which manage to both open up and decolonize the economic imagination of how we represent anti-capitalist alternatives, as well as deconstruct the hegemony of capital based on spaces that exist in the here and now. Difference serves to illuminate the actual reality of practices that negate capital, but at the same time, these practices also lend a processual and experimental character to the very notion of difference.

The strength of their approach—"to make a room of their own for new economic representations," they say at one point, paraphrasing Virginia Woolf—is also their perspective on becoming: they argue that the desire and subjectivities that inhabit such noncapitalist spaces must be "cultivated." In this way, they weave together a subjectivity that is still to come but that is made with the materiality of the desire for another life in the present.

Individual and collective subjects, Gibson-Graham argue, negotiate forms of interdependence and are reconstructed in that process. Diverse economies, as feminist economies, then include a politics of language that is capable of accommodating "the production of a language of economic difference to expand the imaginary of the economic, making visible and intelligible the diverse and proliferating practices that the concern for capitalist has obscured."[6] That language of economic difference is nourished by key counter-discourses: investigations about domestic labor as unpaid and invisibilized labor in countries' national accounting; research about informal economies and their imbrication in North–South transactions; and the language in *Capital* about economic difference (where it is not captured by stagism and developmentalism), according to a systematic conception of the economy.

The language of economic difference becomes a way of detecting other processes of becoming by placing special attention on their situated character. In diverse economies, the category of place serves as the concrete site and context where experimentation is rooted:

> In more broadly philosophical terms, place is that which is not fully yoked into a system of meaning, not entirely subsumed to a (global) order; it is that aspect of every site that exists as potentiality. Place is the "event in space," operating as a "dislocation" with respect to familiar structures and narratives. It is the unmapped and unmoored that allows for new moorings

and mappings. Place, like the subject, is the site and spur of becoming, the opening for politics.[7]

This question of place is critical because it does not strictly imply an anti-cosmopolitan "localism," but rather the construction of a transversal and situated ubiquity. As Gibson-Graham indicate, it nourishes the geographic imagination, in the sense that these are spaces that open up new mappings if they challenge the systematic invisibilization of those other economies. This logic of "difference" and "possibility" attempts to counteract the tendency to devalue these economic experimentations by classifying them as small, unreliable, or merely subsidiary to a regime of accumulation that presents itself as unchangeable. This question of place takes us to the discussion about the *scale* of experimentation: how we organize this confrontation at the global scale (of the world market), in which capital is organized as a global relation, without disregarding a politics of place.

Let's add another point: feminist economics, from a perspective such as that of Gibson-Graham, supposes a set of concrete experiments that include an element of "self-formation" or "self-education" (their sources range from worker-managed factories in Argentina to community-supported farms in the United States, from the anti-maquila movement to organizations of Filipina migrants). In other words, it is a moment of learning and of systematizing those diverse perspectives, which is simultaneously the experimental mode that can produce a new reality. There is a political and methodological premise operating here: the assumption of the instability of the reproduction of the social relation of obedience supposed by the capitalist social relation. Without challenging the automatic *reproduction* of the relation of obedience that makes exploitation possible, there can be no terrain of experimentation. As a methodological principle, there is a wager on the destabilization of those variable forms of obedience, but without the centrally planned control of the opposition and alternative. In other words, we are beyond a state-centric perspective.

In both approaches, there is an explicit double move, one that I think is central to feminist economics:

1) Feminist economics carries out a *diagnosis of the differential of exploitation* that takes reproduction as a central sphere from which to investigate and historicize the ways in which oppression, exploitation, and value extraction are combined.

2) Feminist economics encourages and places value on *experimentation in forms of economic difference,* in other words, experiences and processes that construct other economies here and now.

Women Workers of the World, Unite!

What does it mean to think about proletarian existence—that is, of all of us who use our labor power to relate to the world—from a feminist point of view? Marx and Engel's *Communist Manifesto* postulates the subject of communist politics by reading it against the backdrop of capital, establishing the fundamental antagonism: "The condition for capital is wage-labor."

We could say that certain feminist, Marxist, and anti-colonial perspectives make a similar move to Marx and Engel's statement, but do so within one of the poles of the capital–labor antagonism: *the condition of waged labor is non-waged labor or the condition of free labor is non-free labor.* What happens when one of the poles is opened up? It is the fundamental move with which difference (bringing feminist and anti-colonial struggles into play) intersects with class, but in a way that reconceptualizes the very idea of class.

This allows us to counter Marx and Engels' own reading of how difference functions in relation to women's labor. They argue that the development of modern industry through technical manual labor implies a simplification of tasks that allowed for men to be replaced by women and children. However, "differences of age and sex no longer have any distinctive social validity for the working class," they indicate. In this sense, we read that the incorporation of difference is carried out under the sign of its cancellation. Women and children are incorporated to the extent that they are homogenized as labor power (functioning as appendages of the machine).

Difference, in Marx and Engels' argument, is reduced to a question of costs. Age and sex are variables that make labor cheaper, but they are without social significance. They are, of course, elaborating capital's point of view. Marx would go on to say, in *Capital*, that machinery expands the exploited human material, to the extent that child and female labor is the watchword of mechanization. Again, this expansion takes place in terms of a homogenization dictated by the machine, but difference (of bodies, of materials) is annulled or reduced to an advantage that is also homogenized by the notion of cost. Then, a double abstraction of difference occurs: by machines (of the technical process of production), but also by the very concept of labor power.

If we rewrite the manifesto in a feminist register (precisely to highlight a perspective based on feminist economics), we carry out the inverse operation. We create a reading that includes all of us who produce value in order to think about how difference reconceptualizes the very idea of labor power. This means that the bodies that are in play account for different tasks in terms of a differential of intensity and recognition, which does not allow for fixating on a homogeneous figure of the working subject.

Labor, seen from a feminist lens, goes beyond those who receive a wage, because the common condition is not the measure of remuneration, but the experience of diverse situations of exploitation and oppression. This allows it to be both a more expansive and more situated category, and to go beyond the analytically privileged space of the factory. Labor, from a feminist lens, makes the body (as an indeterminate *potencia*) a measure that overflows the notion of labor power as merely associated with cost.

The feminist perspective emphasizes that the critique of this idea of the homogeneity of the labor force must start from the element that makes such a homogenization operational: it is not only machines (as stated in the *Manifesto*), but rather the "patriarchy of the wage" I discussed in Chapter 2.[8] This supposes two operations by capital: first, the recognition of only a part of labor (the waged part), and later, the legitimazation of its differential according to sex and age *only as* devalorization. Along these lines, we understand waged work as a specific form of the invisibilization of non-waged work that is produced in multiple geographies and that complicates our understanding of what constitutes work today.

Thanks to recent feminist theorizations and struggles, we can now make an argument based on a different reality: the expansion of exploited human material that Marx spoke about is carried out through the exploitation of its difference. This leads to its invisibilization, translation into hierarchy, political discrediting, and/or transformation into surplus for the market.

A feminist manifesto today is a map of the current heterogeneity of living labor that is capable of displaying, in practical terms, the differential of exploitation that, as a fractal geometry, captures all the difference that was abstracted by the hypothesis that universalized the waged proletariat. It was this hypothesis that gave rise to the classical form of the workers' political party. The perspective of feminist economics recognizes that the diversity of experiences of exploitation and extraction of value does not fit into the political party as the privileged and universalizing mode of organization.

The Crisis of the Wage

In the Argentinean crisis that exploded in 2001, it was women who made the inaugural gesture: they took charge of creating spaces for the reproduction of life in collective and community terms, in the face of the devastation caused by mass unemployment. This devastation was especially felt among men, whose numbers as "heads of household" declined; alcoholism and depression were recurring images for many of those suddenly cut loose from their jobs.

The formation of the movement of *piqueteros* (unemployed workers) implied, in this sense, two decisive things.

On the one hand, the politicization of reproductive tasks as they were extended to the neighborhood, jumping the barriers of domestic confinement. The work of reproduction was able to build the infrastructure necessary to maintain a series of roadblocks, providing meals, security details, and physical materials for the encampments on major routes, which would sometimes persist for weeks at a time. These roadblocks spatially displaced the picket from the factory gate to the routes of communication and commodity flows. On the other hand, those movements demonstrated the political nature of those tasks by producing a community value capable of organizing resources, experiences, and demands that challenged the categorization of "exclusion." In this gesture, they de-confined, in practice, reproduction from the household, understood as the "private" sphere.

These movements thus initiated a radical problematization of work and the meaning of a dignified life, understood as decoupled from the wage regime.[9] This is one of the fundamental political innovations that emerged from the crisis. What those movements invented—modes of self-management of a multiplicity of tasks without a boss (hundreds of worker-managed factories, self-managed food production and health care, and community organization of security and neighborhood infrastructure)—was maintained over the following decade's so-called economic recovery, in a way that allowed for the stabilization and systematization of a new proletarian landscape. That fabric, which we refer to as "*popular economies*," also involves a mode of managing the subsidies and benefits packages from the state, which were originally won by the piquetero movement.[10]

I want to emphasize that the *political* dimension of popular economies has to do with both a politicization of reproduction, and the refusal of the miserabilist management of its activities, that is, its reduction to pure survival. This dimension also has to do with a capacity to negotiate with the state for resources, the "origin" of which lies in the 2001 crisis as a moment-force that overturned the political legitimacy of neoliberalism in Argentina while also forming part of a regional sequence. However, it differs from that cycle of organization, in which there was a high level of participation by women, although they often did not occupy leadership positions or identify as feminist. Today, a new cycle of politicization is emerging, one that explicitly identifies as feminist and for which popular economies are a decisive terrain for its expansion. But this moment cannot be understood without reference to what came before.

Here we must point to another key element for understanding this politicization: the passage from the wage to the subsidy. We are referring to the situation in which, over the last twenty years, a large part of the population is no longer able to guarantee its reproduction through the wage as the principle source of income, but through state subsidies in the multiple forms of social welfare programs. This does not mean that the wage ceases to exist, but rather that there is a growing number of people who must achieve prosperity without taking the wage for granted as their principle income. That condition reached a mass level with the 2001 crisis, when it was "stabilized" by popular economies.

How does this new situation rework the idea of the "patriarchy of the wage" proposed by Federici? What are the effects of the destructuring of male authority produced by losing the wage as the "objective measure" of its power inside and outside of the home (and as the marker of that spatial-temporal boundary itself) and the decline of the figure of the male breadwinner? On the one hand, this destructuring is amplified and accelerated by the politicization of reproductive tasks that are *de-confined* from the home, spilling over onto a broader social terrain and achieving new social "prestige" that is embodied in feminized leadership. On the other hand, when male authority as the structuring element of relations of subordination falls into crisis, it leads to forms of "unmeasurable" violence, especially within the home.

Therefore, I want to propose that popular economies are a privileged prism for understanding the crisis of the patriarchy of the wage. This does not mean the end of patriarchy, of course, but the decomposition of a specific way of structuring the patriarchy. The intensification of sexist violence demonstrates that excess of violence that is no longer contained by the wage form.

However, it is also the role of such violence as a "productive force," as Marie Mies argues (to which I referred earlier, regarding the relation between patriarchy and accumulation), that brings the dynamization of illegal economies into play.[11] That is, violence as a productive resource is fundamental to the everyday prosperity of illegal economies. By this I mean that the proliferation of illegal economies in territories is fueled by the destructuring of the authority of the wage, which turns those territories into "quagmires" of new modalities of employment and spaces of competition for new regimes of territorial authority, which must constantly prove their validity.

Illegal economies provide new "authority" figures, especially as male "leaderships," which function by offering ways of replacing destructured masculinity in crisis. The same thing happens, legally, in the recruitment of young men to state security forces. Then, on the state side and the para-state side, these offer ways out of the crisis of male authority by recruitment into the new economies of violence over territories. This demonstrates, furthermore, a sort of competition and complementarity between state and para-state violence that are often deployed as dynamics exercised by the same subjects, combining and contesting instances, resources, and spaces. The question of commercialized drug trafficking is the most obvious, but not the only one.

Markedly different forms of managing and negotiating the decline of the "male breadwinner" emerge within the popular economies. Feminized leadership in the popular economies promotes new sources of social "prestige" that take on the challenge of making other principles of authority operational in the territories. We are left with a complex question: What sort of fabric is constructed by popular economies from the point of view of feminist economics?

The Daughters of the Piqueteras

The daughters of the piquetera women today are youth who were around five or seven years old when their mothers participated in the assemblies of the unemployed. Now they are part of the movements linked to the popular economy. Therefore, in practice, this generational element traces a genealogy between the current moment and those struggles. Their continuity becomes woven together because their mothers and grandmothers are still responsible for the initiatives of popular urbanization, community care, and domestic labor that, as I remarked earlier, are tasks that are scarcely limited to the home, but that spill out into the neighborhood.

Then, let's return to the question: What are these popular economies, from the point of view of feminist economics? Their reproductive dimension is central, thus the task of organizing everyday life is already registered as a productive dimension, in which the categories of *the street* and *the household* take on a practical indistinction for thinking about work. The historical affinity between feminist economics and the popular economy has to do with the politicization of social reproduction based on political practice within the crisis. In this sense, these activities of social reproduction appear to resolve and replace, while also critiquing, the plundering of public infrastructure. Today it is popular economies that are building common infrastructure for providing services that are called basic, even though they are fundamental: from health care to housing, from electricity to education, from security to food.

In this way, popular economies as a reproductive and productive fabric raise the issue of concrete forms of precarization of existence across different fields and demonstrate the degree of dispossession in urban and suburban territories, which is what enables new forms of exploitation. In turn, this implies the deployment of a concrete mode of conflict through understanding the territory as the new social factory.

Financial Extractivism

"In the same era in which they stopped burning witches in England, they began to hang the forgers of bank notes," Marx writes, commenting on the creation of the Bank of England, in his analysis of so-called primitive accumulation. What does this passage tell us about the disciplining of bodies: from the bodies of women-witches to the bodies of money forgers? In both cases, what is at stake is monopoly over the signifer of wealth; in other words, control over becoming.

Money functions by abstracting the body of labor. There is no abstraction without its synthesis in the abstract body of money. But for that synthesis to function as a "social nexus," as

Marx writes in the *Grundrisse*, it is necessary to have already burned the concrete bodies that are expressed in the figure of the witch (a "sentient, collective corporeality," or a "dreamlike materialism," in the philosopher León Rozitchner's words).[12] The abstraction of money consecrates, as Marx says, a social power defined by the relationship between the property owner and the nonowner. The counterfeiter endangers the command of abstraction as a property relation. The person who copies the bill (or marks it, or makes any other sign to distinguish it) puts the hierarchy that consecrates its exclusivity at risk. The difference between witches and forgers of banknotes is the existence of the banking institution, constructed after the stake.

I want to use this scene to highlight the relationship between bodies and finance, and to specify that relation in regard to the hegemony of finance in capital accumulation today. To put it in terms of a synthesizing question: How are finance and popular economies articulated, and why do they have a correspondence with sexist violence today?

It is necessary, first, to briefly historicize that relation, in reference to the crisis of the wage discussed above. A fundamental point of this articulation is the initiative taken by progressive governments following the plebeian revolt at the turn of the century, which caused neoliberalism's crisis of political legitimacy in Argentina and several other countries in the region.[13] It was the revolt that forced a new dynamic of negotiation with the political system, which was translated into a determined form of *inclusion*. This was carried out by the cycles of so-called progressive governments in the region through the financialization of popular life, shaping a landscape in which the production of rights and social inclusion are made effective through financial mediation.

This occurs in a context in which the wage ceases to be the privileged guarantee for debt, and is instead replaced by state benefits, which start to function as a state-backed guarantee for non-waged populations to take out credit. This occurs in two ways. First, benefits are distributed through debit cards that require recipients to open bank accounts; second, being a recipient of a benefits package is used as a guarantee to take out loans, instead of the traditional proof of the wage. That mutation is taken advantage of by banking and financial instruments to convert the subsidized population into subjects of credit.

Thus, the favored apparatus of financial mediation is mass indebtedness, which is carried out through the very subsidies that the state gives to so-called vulnerable sectors.[14] Consumption of nondurable and cheap goods—the main use of credit—was the engine of indebtedness in Argentina over the last decade, promoting what I have called *citizenship through consumption*. In this reformulation of the institution of citizenship, rights are no longer linked to waged labor, but rather to *banking inclusion*. Finance thus organizes the extraction of value directly from consumption, a key element to an expanded form of extractivism.[15]

It is important not to have a unilateral or moralizing perspective of this financialization of popular economies, which simultaneously involves a financialization of households and of access to goods. This allows us to recognize a historical change: debt is acquired while "skipping" the wage form. This is complemented with the earlier financialization of social rights.[16]

This reading of the phenomenon shows that finance "lands" in the economies that emerged in moments of crisis, which were fueled by modes of self-management and work without a boss, and that it exploits the modes in which subaltern fabrics reproduce life, which cannot be simply reduced to "survival." Finance recognizes this politicization of reproduction and translates it into potencia to be exploited. Thus, a multiplicity of forces, savings, and economies are "put to work" for finance. This means that finance becomes a code that manages to homogenize that plurality of activities, income sources, expectations, and temporalities.

This extractive mode, additionally, is assembled upon an earlier dispossession: state disinvestment in infrastructure. The popular sectors' consumption, by taking place through credit, implies the displacement of the state's obligation to provide public and free services, which are instead replaced by individual and private debt. On the other hand, class difference is renewed as these sectors are turned into debtors who are always at a disadvantage relative to other sectors of the population. The popular sectors go into debt in order to buy nondurable goods (such as household appliances and clothing) and to finance services that were defunded by the state (health care and transportation are prime examples) at particularly high interest rates. The forms of indebtedness vary according to social class. This difference is expressed in the interest rate that reintroduces the class differential in the seemingly homogenizing apparatus of debt. The lower classes, through credit cards and installment plans, pay an interest rate that is much higher than the credit offered to the middle and upper classes. This produces a differential in financial exploitation that falls especially on the popular sectors. In this way, the interest rate is not subsidiary to debt, but rather singularizes a differential in relation to the abstract form of exploitation.[17]

Thus, personal private debt, which is carried out with state mediation, with subsidies as a bank guarantee, turns into another form of the privatization of the provision of services (which were already privatized). But there is a third dispossession (after the double privatization): the exploitation of community labor (from health care centers to garbage collection, from soup kitchens to day cares) that replaces collective infrastructure in situations of extreme precarity.

This process expanded and deepened with the change of government in Argentina at the end of 2015, with the inauguration of the ultra-neoliberal Maurico Macri. Rising inflation meant that state benefits had ever less purchasing power, but ever more utility as a state guarantee backing the banks' operations. Here we must also note the intensification of compulsory banking, which was presented in terms of "financial inclusion."[18] The counterpart to this was the criminalization of certain popular economies that did not operate through banking institutions. The state's social programs orchestrated their accreditation through cell phones, which became "digital wallets." There was a widespread tendency, especially among the popular sectors, to allocate income and even loans for purchasing food, which became a key element of this new cycle of indebtedness.[19] Debt thus became a private form of managing poverty, inflation, and austerity; credit was offered as an individual platform for resolving issues of food consumption and paying for essential services.

This raises the question of how compulsory banking operated, over the span of a decade, to individualize and financialize the relationship with state benefits. Those same benefits, which were originally won as a result of roadblocks and other mobilizations, had been a source of community organization during the crisis, when social movements collectively managed them. We can thus ask: How has financial inclusion continued to expand, and to what effects, in the context of rising inflation and increasing poverty?

We Want to Be Debt Free

Following the call for the 2017 international feminist strike, the Ni Una Menos collective wrote another manifesto, entitled *Desendeudadas nos queremos!* (*We Want to be Debt Free*), showing how the antagonism between life and finance is also critical to understanding the strike. In that document, we declared ourselves in opposition to finance.[20] We presented the campaign with an act of "financial objection" in front of

133

the Central Bank of Argentina on June 2, 2017, which sought to embody that which domination attempts to abstract.

How and why did we identify finance as a target? In the action, we explained how we spend all day managing our accounts to ensure there is enough money, how we go into debt to finance daily life. We described our experience of ambivalence—of wanting to achieve economic autonomy and negate austerity in the here and now by using the promise of our future labor, at the same time as it imprisons us through the blackmail of debt. It is the contemporary feminist struggles that are driving a movement of the *politicization* and *collectivization* of the financial issue, proposing a specifically feminist reading of debt.[21]

Finance dramatizes the current moment, which claims to "revolutionize" production. We could say that "uninterrupted disturbance of all social conditions, everlasting uncertainty and agitation distinguish the bourgeois epoch from all earlier ones," to cite the *Communist Manifesto* again. Nevertheless, finance depersonifies the "bourgeois" of which Marx and Engels spoke, to the point that we must also rethink what both the means of production and the abolition of property mean today, from the perspective of the common.

We could say that from the Latin American perspective, there is also a *difference* when it comes to understanding the historical role of the bourgeoisie. As opposed to the revolutionary role that Marx and Engels attribute to them, what stands out in Latin America is the bourgeoisie's directly parasitic and rentier character. Therefore, the characterization of their role in the progressive development of societies is transformed from the start (from the foundation of republication states) due to its colonial character. Instead of the "discovery of America and the circumnavigation of Africa" serving as a revolutionary accelerator, as Marx and Engels posited, the modernization of the colonies at the hands of states claiming to be bourgeois takes another form, producing the predatory and archaic character of those elites, directly associated with global capital, as Silvia Rivera Cusicanqui argues in her characterization of the project of colonial, imperial, and capitalist modernity.[22]

Today, the patriarchal-financial apparatuses that renew the colonial pact in the present, combining it with forms of domination and exploitation,[23] are revealed to be fundamental for understanding the counterinsurgent dimension of the war against women and feminized bodies. It is in this sense that Latin American feminist positions today take on an anti-colonial, as well as class-based, dimension in the face of finance and predatory and neo-extractivist formulas. This is important both for thinking about what a relationship with the state means in our societies, and the state's complicity with projects that dispossess body-territories, as well as to account for the historical and lasting mis-encounters between a certain type of liberal feminism and popular struggles.

By making the connection between gender violence and economic, social, media, and colonial violence visible, we are able to build a feminism that puts forth a critique of capitalism based on demonstrating the rationality of the assemblages that link exploitation in the labor sphere with the implosion of misogynist violence in the home. In addition, it allows for accounting for the multiplication of forms of exploitation in the affective, communitarian, informal economies that go beyond the world of the wage, but that still play a central role, as dynamics of the feminization of labor, in the valorization of capital.

Therefore, one of the strategic tasks for the feminist movement is to make connections between the territories of the most precarious lives and the abstract apparatus of finance, in order to understand the new forms of exploitation and extraction of value and, in particular, the role of women's and feminized bodies in them. By challenging the distinction between the public and the private, the feminist analysis of labor also allows for a displacement and redefinition of the very idea of work, its zones and its tasks, based on a subjectivity that is supposedly "external" to or "expelled" from the central place of waged work.

As I discussed earlier, the genealogy of this displacement includes the movement of the unemployed, which, in the midst of the crisis at the turn of this century, managed to radically question what was meant by work, occupation, and remuneration and to resignify the traditional tool of the picket outside of the factory, using it to block the circulation of goods through the collective organization of roadblocks. Today, we see women, lesbians, trans people, and travestis questioning the porous borders—porous because they are being disputed politically, not because of an abstract fluidity—that have been elaborated for decades between domestic, reproductive, productive, affective, and care work, in the context of a crisis that turns feminized bodies into a key territory of dispute.

The return of that dynamic of crisis in Latin America today revitalizes the visibility of a type of expanded social cooperation in the territories of neighborhoods where popular economies proliferate in a non-temporary way and against which the violent offensive is especially strong. It is upon this social fabric that finance operates, through a mode that links the neo-extractivist advances in peasant and Indigenous, urban and suburban territories.

Overspill I: Popular Finance

Today finance captures, through mass indebtedness, the waged and non-waged incomes of popular sectors, which were traditionally excluded from the financial imagination. Debt functions by structuring a compulsion to accept any type of work in order to pay one's future obligation. This capture of the obligation to future work initiates the exploitation of creativity at any cost: it does not matter what type of work you do; what matters is paying your debt. The precarious, informal, and even illegal dynamic of jobs (or forms of income) is shown to be increasingly intermittent, while debt functions as a stable continuum. Advantage is also taken of that gap in time: debt becomes the mechanism of coercion to accept any employment conditions, due to the fact that the financial obligation ends up "commanding" one to work in the present time. Debt, then, drives a molecular diffusion of that extractive dynamic that, although it is of the future, conditions the here and now, over which it imposes greater velocity and violence.

There is a specificity to the general modus operandi of the debt apparatus when it is based on state subsidies to so-called vulnerable populations. That specificity lies in that while the state functions as a guarantor for sectors that are supposedly "excluded," including them through consumption, it also enables their rapid connection with informal, illegal, and popular economies, disputing its own limits and also putting them in competition among themselves.

These economies are all crucial, forming a polymorphic quarry of activities and income sources beyond the wage, extracting their dynamism and their capacity for political and territorial contestation from their entanglement with debt. This complex fabric, then, does not fit into the clichés that tend to associate informal economies with illegality and the absence of the state, or with poverty and financial disconnection. To the contrary: financial exploitation of popular sectors is situated within a modality of inclusion through consumption that legitimizes the financialization of less formal, structured, and routine activities. In turn, debt becomes the favored mechanism for laundering illegal money flows toward legal circuits, functioning as an artifact of the passage.

The affinity of this dynamic with the feminization of popular economies is fundamental for several reasons. First, the work of reproduction and production of the common forms part

of, and is directly interwoven with, labor in popular economies. This should not only be read in terms of the feminization
of poverty (although it also accounts for this), but also of a
capacity to redefine the production of value based on the
spheres of the reproduction of life. It should also be noted
that women play a central role as heads of households and
providers of resources within the fabrics of social cooperation,
in a context where banking has become mandatory in order to
receive welfare benefits, incorporating thousands of new users
into the financial system under the banner of "democratizing
banking." Therefore, looking at finance from a gender-based
perspective reveals specific uses of money, which also depend
on different modalities of indebtedness, as well as a flexible
relation to finance based on the way that, in the majority of
households, the reproduction of life depends on women and
their tactics of everyday management.

Various studies about debt note the preponderance of
women as debtors, generally classified as "exemplary payers."
Women's relationships of trust and kinship thus become a
value of which the financial system constantly takes advantage
—indeed, there is an entire body of work about microcredit
that discusses this in terms of "comparative advantage."[24] But
there is also a series of critical perspectives that emphasize
the exploitation of women's affective and solidarity networks.
In Bolivia, for instance, economist and sociologist Graciela
Toro's pioneering investigation analyzes the expansion of
microcredits especially designed for women, called "solidarity
credit," driven by a powerful social movement of debtors in
2001.[25] As Bolivian feminist activist María Galindo remarks in
her prologue to Toro's book, the bank exploits women's social
network, including their relationships of friendship and family,
to turn them into the guarantor for debt. Brazilian sociologist Nina Madsen, questioning the discourse of the formation
of a "new middle class" during the progressive governments
in Brazil, argues that the increased access to consumption

of an important portion of the populations was maintained through the massive indebtedness of households and the hyper-exploitation of the unpaid labor of women.[26]

We also know about the "moral" construction of the responsibility of the debtor figure and the risk evaluation that is tied to it. These classifications must be analyzed in relation to the way in which certain attributes—flexibility, ability to adapt to discontinuity, creating relations of trust—are considered to be feminine in nature and are linked to a certain financial training, a capacity to manage multiple flows of money and forms of debt. In the context of austerity and restrictions on consumption, these tasks become even more clear.

The notion of financial exploitation allows us to trace a connection between the increase in sexist violence and the financialization of popular economies by revealing the intimate relation between debt and subjection—that is to say, between indebtedness and the impossibility of economic autonomy.[27] It also shows how debt becomes a way of literally enclosing and subordinating women and feminized bodies in violent environments. In many cases, debt creates obstacles to fleeing. In others, it is multiplied in order to be able to escape.

Melinda Cooper, in her theorization of the notion of family responsibility, takes apart the widespread idea that neoliberalism is an amoral or even anti-normative regime, showing the affinity between the production of the heterosexual family as a basic unit of social life and the reification of the traditional role of women in that structure.[28] This is what makes it imperative for women to take on ever more tasks for the reproduction of life when faced with the privatization of public services. Targeted social assistance (as a favored form of neoliberal state intervention) also reinforces a hierarchy of merit in relation to women's obligation, according to their roles in the patriarchy family: having children, taking care of them, educating them, vaccinating them. This shows the clear importance of what I have pointed to as the *politicization of reproduction* that

makes those tasks spill over, out of the enclosure of the heteronormative family model.

Overspill II: Consumption and Finance

Finance has been able to skillfully and quickly detect the vitality from below that is woven into popular economies; that is
where it roots its extraction of value, which operates directly
over the labor force as living labor. This dynamic can be considered "extractive" since it does not have the wage as the
privileged mediator of the exploitation of labor power.[29] What
finance exploits in this mode of value extraction is a willing-
ness to work in the future that is no longer measured in the
form of the wage. As Marx indicated in the *Grundrisse*: "But
now, it is money which in itself is already capital; and, as such,
it is a claim on new labor."[30]

If there Marx was referring to capital's command over
"future labor" as the substance of "exchange" between capital
and labor, in the third volume of *Capital* he highlights the
same temporality—an expanded, multiplied, and accelerated form—in his analysis of "interest-bearing capital," that
is, financial capital. Underscoring its tendency to accumulate
"claims or titles" to "future production," Marx enables us to
discover the *expanded reproduction of control over labor to
come* (that is, the necessary labor to produce "future wealth")
that lies behind financial processes.[31]

Today, this demand for future labor is translated into the
compulsion to accept any type of work, even without the
guarantee of a stable or secure job. This type of compulsion
to work without the obligatory element of the wage setting
redefines the obligation to the future that debt produces. Thus,
there has been an important change in the way debt is understood; up to now, a system of debt for which the wage was the
horizon reinforced the obligation and commitment to one's

job and to the successive conditions of precarization that it may have imposed. It is something else entirely to go into debt without having a job: it structures a different relation between money and the future, since debt constrains people to accept any labor conditions, and even to invent forms of work that can quickly provide income.

The suppression of the mediation of the wage in contracting debt highlights how the apparatus of financial capture takes root in a vital force, making living labor visible in its dimension of pure potencia. I do not want to suggest a linear transition from the wage to debt, because there is a multiplicity of situations that continue being waged, due to which the dynamic of indebtedness has also been modified. However, the indebtedness of the non-waged is a prism that allows us to see how debt functions in general as a privileged apparatus of value extraction in contemporary capitalism, highlighting its key characteristics.

The compulsion to do any type work that debt enforces is what drives the versatility and labor opportunism appropriated by popular economies in their intersection with illegal economies, in a way that is analogous to how finance reads and captures that plebeian energy beyond the wage. This form of compulsion is, in turn, also codified by the dynamic of consumption encouraged by debt. Therefore, finance directly extracts value from consumption, an idea I will develop further below.

That is why it is so important to deepen investigations into the concept of *expanded extractivism* (as I began to do in Chapter 3). This term forces us *not* to disconnect the extractive question from the issue of the reconfiguration of labor, in all of its contemporary metamorphoses and mutations (which is also one of the methodological teachings from the anti-colonial archive). As I explained earlier, in popular economies, extraction is carried out over a labor force whose horizon is not strictly wage inclusion, and in that sense, it connects two terms that are frequently dissociated: *extraction* and *exploitation*. By highlighting the articulation between finance and popular economies, between debt and consumption, and their ties to state subsidies funded by extraordinary commodity rent and to sexist violence, we are drawing a map that connects the exploitation of a working class that is no longer exclusively waged with an extractive mode that is not only applied to so-called natural resources. In the process, this map redefines the very notion of "territory," as well as the "frontier" of valorization. Furthermore, it is precisely the feminist reading of these dynamics that is capable of making visible the type of war that capital unleashes against certain body-territories.

The Colonial Patriarchy of Finance

Let's return to the thesis from the beginning of this book: that the strike, as a feminist tool, carries out a radical critique of neoliberalism. The strike constitutes such a critique because it is a concrete and forceful refusal of the multiple types of dispossession and new forms of exploitation with which capitalism advances over our lives. And because it opens up a conversation about the provision of care, common resources, and infrastructure for everyday reproduction. The mass feminist movement is a response to the philanthropic and paternalistic ways that the state and capital have responded to precarity, by imposing conservative and reactionary forms of subjectivation fueled by fear. As I stated earlier, the tool of the strike managed to connect the brutality of violence against women, lesbians, trans people, and travestis to the forms of exploitation and oppression that turn that violence into the widespread symptom of a broader ensemble of capitalist, colonial, and patriarchal types of violence. This connection gives a materialist character to the critique of violence. And that connection is

142

also what opens up a perspective that gives concrete form to the movement's anti-capitalism and anti-colonialism.

In this chapter, I have shown what is entailed by the destructuring of the patriarchy of the wage and proposed that there is an attempt to restructure it through a colonial patriarchy of finance. This amounts to an attempt to replace command with a financial articulation that extracts value from the ambiguity between production and reproduction, which has emerged precisely as a result of ongoing struggles. That is, struggles gained their "visibility" by force, precisely by demonstrating the "central" character of social reproduction as a strategically denied and exploited dimension of capital accumulation. This displacement has been fundamental for rethinking the spatiality of the reproduction of the capital–labor relationship and, in particular, the division between the private-domestic and the public-waged. In Latin America, these struggles over social reproduction played a crucial role in the successive crises of the last two decades, which also revealed neoliberal perspectives on multiculturalism and gender technocracy as attempts to "metabolize" difference. This *politicization* of social reproduction through crisis is thus fundamental for expanding the perspective of social reproduction to an analysis of all the forms that production takes today. I must insist on this: feminist economics cannot be trapped in the sphere of reproduction (as the counterpoint to production), but such a perspective is necessary for rethinking social relations as a whole and their battles against the frontiers of capital valorization.

Today the feminist struggle—or, in other words, the question of difference—reconfigures the question of class. It is no longer an issue of a quality, or a supplement that remains relatively external to analysis or is added as a secondary variable. Instead, we encounter a diverse collective imaginary of what is called work, and of what it means to build a common form of collective action that is capable of accommodating the multiplicity that expresses class today as antagonism.

In this sense, financial exploitation, which I analyzed as a concrete apparatus of the extraction of value in feminized popular economies (and which is articulated with other extractive forms), reveals a mode of capturing social vitality beyond the limits of the wage and is strongly rooted in tasks of reproduction in a broad sense. Above all, it is a dispute over the temporality of exploitation: finance implicates obedience in the future and, therefore, functions as an "invisible" and homogenizing "boss" of the multiple tasks capable of producing value. But there is even more: in this modality, finance has a key relation with sexist violence and the management of the crisis.

Today, we see how finance—which has landed in popular, and once-peripheral, territories—has constructed a capillary network capable, on the one hand, of providing private, high-interest financing to resolve problems of everyday life caused by austerity and inflation; and, on the other hand, of structuring the temporality of an obedience to the future, casting blame and individualizing responsibility for the plunder that has emptied those territories of infrastructure (from health care to water, and even food access). Today, generalized debt is what pays for the crisis. It makes it so that each person has to individually confront the increase in service rates and must spend their time working ever-increasing hours for ever less money. Today, the very act of living "produces" debt, and that debt falls primarily on women and feminized bodies.[32]

We see, then, that debt is a way of *managing the crisis*: nothing explodes, but everything implodes. It implodes within families, in households, in workplaces, in neighborhoods; the financial obligation makes relations more fragile and more precarious because they are submitted to the permanent pressure of debt. The structure of mass indebtedness, which has been going on for over a decade, is what gives us clues to the shape the crisis takes today: as individual responsibility, as an increase in so-called domestic violence, as the growing precarization of existence.

Debt, we could say, using an image from the philosopher George Caffentzis, manages the "patience" of workers, housewives, students, migrants, and others.[33] The question regarding patience is: Up to what point do people tolerate the conditions of violence that capital needs to reproduce and valorize itself today? The subjective dimension that marks the limits of capital is a key element of mass indebtedness.

Today, it is the feminist movement, more than any other form of left politics, that raises a dispute precisely about that "subjective" dimension: about the modes of disobedience, contempt, and rejection of current forms of violence, which are intimately connected with exploitation and the extraction of value. Through the process of organizing the international feminist strike, we have pushed this point, which is also strategic: the strike visibilizes and draws connections between nonrecognized dynamics of work, rejects the hierarchy between the productive and the reproductive, and constructs a shared horizon of struggle that reformulates the very notions of body, conflict, and territory.

The colonial dimension is expressed, in this sense, by the colonization of new "territories," which are formed on the basis of an articulation of debt and consumption, since both function via the premise of collective dispossession. But here, "colonial" also refers, through this restructuring of patriarchy, to a way of bringing together finance and new forms of violence beyond measure that provides men with a principle of subjective stabilization based on their often-violent possession of feminized bodies and body-territories through transnational corporations. We can therefore understand the organic, and new, way in which violence and capital are tied together today. The colonial element of this patriarchy of finance is also a way of updating the division between governors and the governed under new coordinates, rendering the coordinates of institutional democracy somewhat anachronistic.

The organizational horizon of the strike replenishes the

class-based, anti-colonial, and mass dimension of feminism in a creative and defiant way because it does not provide a closed, ready-to-use tool; rather, it must be invented in the organizational process itself. At the same time, the strike allows us to understand why women and feminized bodies are constituted as a key element of capitalist exploitation, particularly in its moment of financial hegemony.

Excursus: Conquering Lands of Consumption

The Marxist geographer David Harvey's formula of "accumulation by dispossession" has been widely taken up in the debate about extractivism, especially in Latin America. Rosa Luxemburg's reflections on imperialism and the expansive dynamic of capitalism are a fundamental reference for Harvey. In fact, in her emphasis on the necessity of multiple "outsides" to enable that dynamic, Luxemburg is, among the classical Marxists, the theorist who can most contribute to our understanding of the issue of extractivism. Once her notion of the outside is separated from its exclusively geographic-territorial connotation, it becomes productive for thinking about the current moment.

Luxemburg's theory of imperialism allows us to characterize the dynamic of accumulation at a global scale and, in particular, signals some of the points we want to make about contemporary "extractive operations" of capital.[34] The imperialist question—as anthropologist Kaushik Sunder Rajan argues[35]—allows for a re-territorialization of value theory. From this point of view, it is fundamental to have a *joint* analysis of the constitution of labor markets (or forms of exploitation), the extraction of "raw materials" (and the debate about their content), and financialization (in terms of abstract and concrete operations). This final element (which Lenin also discussed in terms of imperialism) expresses an extension of the logic of capital accumulation in which its inherent contradiction is knotted (returning to Luxemburg): the spatial and temporal gap between the production of surplus value and its conversion into capital. But this implies a previous question: capital's relation with its "outsides."

This joint analysis of labor markets, raw materials, and finance provides us with an effective perspective for thinking about the different forms of extraction that are remapping its expanded meaning today. However, I propose returning to the issue of consumption in Rosa Luxemburg's work, since it plays a fundamental, and largely unrecognized, role in the debate. Consumption drives the social intensification of extractivism, which becomes a fundamental vector of its effective *expansion*. In other words, finance extracts value by boosting debt-driven consumption that constricts certain conditions of exploitation. Therefore, consumption becomes a strategic battlefield because that is where finance "recovers" monetary flows for the realization of commodities and because that is where its obligation "to the future" becomes "present." A quick reconstruction of Rosa Luxemburg's theory, focusing on her understanding of consumption as the field of the "realization" of surplus value, will allow us to further explore this issue.

In her 1913 *Accumulation of Capital*, which explains Marx's ideal theoretical framework for the production and the realization of surplus value between the figures of "capitalists" and "workers," Luxemburg proposes broadening those figures in an informal way, opening them up to a pluralization that seems to be revealed as inherent to consumption. "The decisive fact is that the surplus value cannot be realized by sale either to workers or to capitalists, but only if it is sold to such social organizations or strata whose own mode of production is not capitalistic."[36] She gives the example of the English cotton textile industry, which for two-thirds of the nineteenth century supplied India, America, and Africa, in addition to providing for peasants and the European petite bourgeoisie. She concludes: "The enormous expansion of the

English cotton industry was thus founded on consumption by non-capitalist strata and countries."[37]

The very elasticity of the accumulation process involves the immanent contradiction indicated previously. Capital's "revolutionary" effect operates in those displacements, capable of quickly resolving the discontinuity of the social process of accumulation. To that "magical art" of capital, Luxemburg adds the necessity of the noncapitalist: "Only on the pre-capitalist soil of more primitive social conditions can it develop the ascendancy necessary to achieve such miracles."[38] The violence of that appropriation by European capital requires a complementary political power that is identified only with non-European conditions: that is, the power exercised in American, Asian, and African "colonies." Here Luxemburg cites the exploitation of Indigenous peoples by the Peruvian Amazon Company, which supplied London with Amazon rubber, to demonstrate how capital manages to produce a situation bordering on slavery. "International trade" as a "prime necessity for the historical existence of capitalism" then appears as "an exchange between capitalistic and non-capitalistic modes of production."[39] But what emerges when the accumulation process is considered from the point of view of variable capital—that is, from the perspective of living labor (rather than that of surplus and fixed capital alone)?

The "natural" and "social" limits to the increase in exploitation of the labor force, Luxemburg says, mean that accumulation should increase the number of employed workers. Marx's quote about how capitalist production has been concerned with "establishing the working class as a class dependent on the wage" leads to the question of the "natural procreation of the working class," which does not follow the rhythms and movements of capital. But Luxemburg argues the "formation of the industrial reserve army" cannot depend on it to resolve the problem of expanded accumulation: "Labor for this army is recruited from social reservoirs outside the dominion of capital—it is drawn into the wage proletariat only if need arises. Only the existence of non-capitalist groups and countries can guarantee such a supply of additional labor power for capitalist production."[40]

Luxemburg adds the question of race to the sources of composition of the industrial reserve army specified by Marx, while an analysis such as that of Paolo Virno allows us to think in terms of how it is *expanded* in the contemporary moment as a condition that is virtual and transversal to all workers.[41] Capital needs to have access to "all territories and climes … nor can it function solely with the workers offered by the white race"; "It must be able to mobilize world labor power without restriction in order to utilize all productive forces of the globe—up to the limits imposed by a system of producing surplus value."[42] The point is that those workers of the nonwhite race "must first be 'set free' in order to be enrolled in the active army of capital." Recruitment, from this point of view, follows the *liberating* orientation that is attributed to the proletariat, understood as a "free" subject (Luxemburg cites the South African diamond mines as an example). The "labor problem in the colonies" is thus a mixture of work situations, ranging from the wage to other less "pure" modes of contraction. But we are interested in how Luxemburg highlights the "contemporary existence" of noncapitalist elements in capitalism as a key element for its expansion. This is the starting point for reevaluating the problem of the internal and external market, which she emphasizes are not only concepts of political geography, but primarily of social economy. The conversion of surplus value into capital, seen in this map of global dependency, is simultaneously revealed as "ever more urgent and precarious."[43]

But let's go a step further. Capital can use force, Luxemburg says, to appropriate the means of production and also force workers to become objects of capitalist exploitation. What it cannot do by violence is "force them to buy its commodities":

that is, it cannot force them to "realize its surplus value."[44] In other words, it cannot force them to become consumers.

There is a fundamental articulation between international credit, infrastructure, and commodity placement. Luxemburg analyzes this in detail in several passages: in her discussions of the struggle against all the "formations of the natural economy," and in particular of the dispossession of lands to put an end to the self-sufficiency of peasant economies, connecting it to the issue of debt, such as the mortgage debts of US farmers, as I discuss in Chapter 2.

Debt is that apparatus that puts the focus on the problem of the temporal and spatial gap between the realization and capitalization of surplus value; and, it follows, the necessity of *colonial* expansion. Luxemburg dedicates several emblematic paragraphs on this operation of debt to the relationship between England and the Argentine Republic, where lending, the English exportation of manufactured goods, and the construction of railways reached astronomical figures in merely a decade and a half. South American states, South African colonies, and other "exotic countries" (Turkey and Greece, for example) attracted similar capital flows, in cycles punctuated by bankruptcies and later restarted: "Realized surplus value, which cannot be capitalized and lies idle in England or Germany, is invested in railway construction, water works, etc. in the Argentine, Australia, the Cape Colony or Mesopotamia."[45] Its capacity for (temporal and spatial) dislocation, referring to where and when surplus value can be capitalized, allowed accumulation to function as an abstraction machine, albeit one that depended on the concrete circumstances that it attempted to homogenize time and again: "British capital which finds an outlet in Argentine railway construction might well in the past have been realized in China in the form of Indian opium."[46]

Abroad, however, a "new demand" had to be made to emerge, or else be "violently created": what was moved, Luxemburg says, was the "enjoyment" of the products. But how were the conditions produced so that this *enjoyment* took place? "The new consumers must indeed realize the products," she writes, "pay for their use, and for this they need money."[47] Today, the massification of indebtedness crowns the production of that enjoyment. This enjoyment is the translation of a desire that produces an *outside*. Of course, it is not strictly a literal or territorial outside.

What pre-announces the crisis, in Luxemburg's argument, is a catastrophic moment: the end of the noncapitalist world's appropriation through imperialist expansion. In the current permanent displacement of those limits (and constant management of the crisis), there is something under the surface that we should see: the creation of noncapitalist worlds (space-times of desire), toward which capital rushes with increasing voracity, velocity, and intensity. At the same time, we must also detect what type of extractive operations relaunch the *imperial* question, which now goes beyond national limits.

In this way, I want to underscore not only the axiomatic dynamic of capital—as Deleuze and Guattari call it—that is always capable of incorporating new segments and displaying an apparent multiform and infinite drive to annex, but also the moment *prior* to that. In other words, the production of those worlds where collective desire produces an outside, over which the frontiers of valorization are expanded through consumption and debt, in a way that links new modalities of exploitation and the extraction of value.

If Marx, as I already commented, says that machinery expands the human material of exploitation to include child and female labor, we can think about the broadened concept of extractivism as the expansion of exploited human and non-human material precisely through the dynamic of finance. We can project Marx's methodological premise that machines came to be used because of the limits imposed by labor: this moment of accumulation, defined by the so-called hegemony of finance, is also the result of the limits imposed by labor. Limits and expansion thus mark a dynamic that is not symmetrical but punctuated by conflict. The reading of an "outside" becomes a way of detecting how forms of resistance (in their historical difference) produce that limit over which capital later seeks to expand its frontier. It is a non-pure "outside," where the conflict that constitutes it takes on diffuse and multiple forms. The diverse financial apparatuses today (from consumer credit to derivatives, from mortgages to future bonds) transversalize capture across different sectors and activities, seeking to directly conquer *future* value, as opposed to work done in the past. The difference between this rent of extraction and the wage is that temporal difference, as well as a radical change in the measure of exploitation.

Consumption must also be understood along these lines: First, because there is a radicalization of its role in the current moment of capitalism. Second, because, as Federici argues, there is an aspect of consumption that is carried out beyond the limits of the wage, one that accounts for a refusal of austerity, as opposed to mere passive financial manipulation.[48]

Popular economies are spaces of the elaboration and contestation of those outsides, instances where extractivism is expanded in a more conflictive way. Identifying popular economies with forms of proletarian micro-economies highlights the fact that there is a dispute over social cooperation there. And it challenges the idea, which is so common in Latin America (and the global South more generally), that evokes the phantasmagoria of the lumpenproletariat: that class which does not manage to bring together the characteristics that would classify it as the proletariat. This idea, however, fits very well with the "naturalization" of wealth in the region, which is often identified as a continent of natural resources and raw materials. An analysis can be developed from those proletarian micro-economies of what Nancy Fraser calls "boundary struggles," through which capital constantly seeks to extract value from what she calls the "informal gray zones."[49] Fraser highlights the link between mass semi-proletarianization and neoliberalism as an accumulation strategy that is organized based on the expulsion of millions of people from the formal economy into those diffuse zones of informality.

Yet it is important to draw the connection between two elements that appear as separate in her argument: for Fraser, expropriation becomes a "nonofficial" mechanism of accumulation, while exploitation appears to remain the "official" mechanism. Instead, *exploitation and dispossession must be understood simultaneously*, as I attempt to do with the category of expanded extractivism. This highlights the importance of their interconnectedness under the extractive logic, as a form of valorization.

Saskia Sassen argues that extractive capitalism embodies a new geography of global power, composed of "frontier spaces" in which dynamics are produced that lead to decision making that operates as much on the transnational as on the national and local levels, revealing their interdependence. According to Sassen, a new international division of labor is at stake in that unfolding of national sovereignty over globally defined rules. She explains:

> It becomes clear that state sovereignty articulates both its own as well as external conditions and norms. Sovereignty remains as systematic property but its institutional insertion and its capacity to legitimize and absorb all power of legitimization, to be the source of law, has become unstable. The politics of contemporary sovereignties are much more complex than the notions of territorial exclusivity can capture.[50]

Expanded extractivism thus refers to a modality that functions over different "territories" (virtual, genetic, natural, social, urban, rural, of production and consumption), and finance concentrates its operation on that heterogeneity, redefining the very notion of territory as a sovereign unit. But it is in this sense that finance has raised the question about its "command" function: that is, its capacity to centralize and homogenize the different dynamics of valorization.

The concern about the political form of extractivism, as I have developed it here, leaves open questions about its particular form of sovereignty and how it takes root in specific territories, about the reformulation of the role of the state, and, even more, about how to think about the relationship between extractivism and violence. A feminist analysis enables us to understand the simultaneity of those planes of social conflict today, and in two very precise senses: namely, how extractivism operates both *on* and *against* body-territories.

Chapter 5

The Assembly as a Situated Apparatus of Collective Intelligence

The assembly has functioned as the specific site of the strike's formulation, time and again. It is the kitchen where it is prepared. That is the first thesis of this chapter: that the assemblies are constituted as a *situated apparatus of collective intelligence*. They are spaces for taking root and for projecting, where we experience the potencia of *thinking together*, of elaborating an idea (a slogan, a trajectory, a call, etc.) that does not precede the situation of the assembly itself. Even if assemblies have been held many times, the *situated evaluation* of each conjuncture creates a state of *newness*. Such evaluation means that it is right *there*, where its force, its functioning, its possible deployment, its difficulties are perceived.

The experience of thinking together is felt in the body as the potencia of an idea. It inaugurates a fundamental feature of the assemblies' intelligence: the deployment of a *pragmatism*. It ties together diverse elements, it evaluates tactics, it composes strategy. It is inscribed in the history of past struggles at the same time that it is experienced, I insist, as *new*. This mode of collective intelligence, additionally, weaves together the *time between* one event in the streets and the next; it puts them in a state of continuity and takes advantage of the discontinuities; it recognizes emergencies; and, at the same time, it provokes the unthinkable.

This leads to a second thesis: that assemblies produce the strike *in time, as a political process*, not as an isolated event on the calendar. The assembly is an instance that is updated. It is necessary to do so each time to create the swarm, the multiplicity of feminist struggles that are expanding, finding each other and narrating their own experiences. That is why it is an *apparatus for the temporalization of the process*: a repetition that produces difference each time.

The assembly is *simultaneously* situation *and* process.

The assembly produces a concrete situation: a space-time that is able to produce sovereignty over what is decided collectively. The assembly produces process: it gives continuity, it threads together moments, as markers of a flow that accumulates force. The assembly is where differences, in terms of experiences, expectations, and languages, mix. In doing so, it composes a common space of encounter, of debate, of misunderstanding, of discordance coming from bodies, gestures, schemes.

Therefore, both theses mutually reinforce one another. The assembly produces intelligence because it is collective and it is situated and, in this way, it *invents* historical time, *opens* it up under the question that it hosts: What do we do?

The assembly has three specific potencias: (1) the ability to evaluate the situation, (2) the strategic capacity to make political decisions, and (3) the skill to put those decisions into practice, to materialize them.

In the wake of the assembly for the first national women's strike in October 2016, the 2017–18 preparatory assemblies for the feminist strike in Buenos Aires tripled their attendance. They took place in the Asociación Mutual Sentimiento (Mutual feeling association) warehouse, a space where the memory still reverberates of its role as one of the biggest nodes of the barter clubs during the 2001 crisis, and one of the first experimental laboratories for generic medications.[1] The same thing happened in hundreds of assemblies that were multiplied around the country: in soup kitchens, in shantytowns, in workplaces, in schools, in unions, in plazas. It happened again in the December 2018 assembly, in which we condemned the abhorrent ruling that sought to absolve the men responsible for the femicide of Lucía Pérez. It also happened in the assemblies that took place in workplaces against layoffs over the course of the year, between the strikes, and in those that were called for other conflicts. I will return to this practice of the *situated assembly* later in the chapter.

Then a third thesis arises: that the assemblies function as a kitchen because that is where a *feminist diagnosis of the crisis is elaborated.* That diagnosis turns the strike into a practical formula and an effective mapping of working and living conditions today, from the point of view that we have woven together through the struggles of women, lesbians, travestis, and trans people. Therefore, a whole series of conflicts that redefine labor itself are connected and projected in each assembly.

The assembly's strength, then, comes from its capacity to function as a sounding board for a conflictiveness that continues growing in the face of systematic policies of austerity and layoffs. But in that sense, it broadens, based on a feminist diagnosis, what is understood by "labor": we are speaking of a dynamic that involves migrant labor, remunerated and non-remunerated labor, social subsidies and wages, contracted work and precarious work, temporary gigs and domestic labor. This dynamic extends to all of the current modes of exploitation of labor, which, when seen in their heterogeneity and complexity, can be read in relation to the diversity of contemporary forms of violence. Therefore, it also broadens what is understood by "conflict."

As Kathi Weeks argues in her Marxist-feminist scholarship, if in the 1970s the feminist reading of work focused on the tasks of reproduction, today this archive serves as a way to think in broader terms about a *general feminization of labor.*[2] It also provides us with hints for creating a radical imaginary of the refusal of its subordination. Today's feminist perspective that emerges from understanding nonpaid, badly paid, non-recognized, and hyper-exploited work gives rise to the most powerful clues for understanding the world of work in general. Therefore, the feminist perspective manages to visualize *the totality of the forms of exploitation* based on its particularity: it knows how to connect them, how the differential of exploitation is generated, and how value is produced by the political hierarchies that organize the waged and non-waged world of work. In this sense, as I have been arguing, it expands the notion of class.

Furthermore, the feminist perspective is able to produce a general understanding because, due to its historically *partial* position as devalorized subject, it is able to perceive how the very idea of "normal" work has imploded. Of course, such "normal" work, which is presented as the hegemonic image of a waged, male, formal job, still persists as an imaginary and even as an ideal. But, as it has become increasingly scarce, that imaginary can function in a reactionary way: those who have that type of job are limited to perceiving themselves as the privileged, as in danger, and as in need of defending themselves against the tide of the precarious, unemployed, migrant, and informal workers. Much of current union politics is also obligated to act as if it were "defending the privileged" and, therefore, to act in a reactionary register with respect to the situation of crisis in general and the multiplication of labor in particular.

To the contrary, the potencia of the *current feminist diagnosis* of the map of labor lies in its creation of *a non-fascist reading* of the end of a certain paradigm of inclusion—that which has operated through the system of waged work and the deployment of other images of what we call labor, among other formulas for recognition and retribution. This challenge directly interpellates the unions.

This is why the participation of compañeras from the unions has been so fundamental in the assemblies. It is not a coincidence that it was in the midst of the preparatory assemblies for the strike in March 2018 that the Feminist Intersindical emerged, an unprecedented joint initiative of women leaders from the five union federations of Argentina. Acts such as these have made it possible, for example, for the oldest federation, the General Confederation of Labor (CGT), founded in 1930, to use the word "feminist" in an official statement, announcing its compliance with the strike measure on March 8, 2018.

The strength of the dynamic of the assemblies and the strikes of women, lesbians, travestis, and trans people in Argentina lies in their capacity interrupt, convene, and energize the unions. This has directly impacted the visibility of many women leaders, in the conformation of a new type of leadership that took them out of the confines of their roles as secretaries of gender or social development into direct confrontation with the sexist hierarchies within unions and outside of them. That visibility has been produced both in the massive assemblies, where the unions are constantly called upon to convene the strike, as well as in the statements of many women union members who have utilized a reading and discourse of gender to interpret problems within their unions, their role in the internal structures, and the problems of work in general. It also had a generational impact: many young women leaders have been elected whose trajectories combine experiences in the women's movement and in unions, which have only recently begun complementing one another and are no longer experienced as dissociated.

The union question is transformed by this redefinition of the limits of the "world of work" and the incorporation of issues of reproduction into union "accounting." But this also occurs through a sharpened view of the differential impact that austerity and precarization have on women, lesbians, trans people, and travestis. At the same time, the force of the feminist movement has nourished union politics, particularly the women and sexual dissidents that comprise it, broadening its agenda and its vocabulary and giving a disobedient push to participation in the feminist strike. In the defiance displayed by the feminist movement in calling a strike, over and above the union monopoly on that tool, many women in the unions found a way to impose another relation of force, and also to reappropriate the strike *within* the union world, which has historically been organized by patriarchal hierarchies.

The transversality of the feminist movement finds a very important alliance in the union component, both in terms of mobilization as well as in massiveness and impact. In turn, the strength of the joint action turns union "unity" into a new question, because it exceeds the definition of who is a worker, since they have now achieved the interunion recognition of popular economy workers, as well as non-unionized workers. By the union's recognition of the production of value of reproductive, community, neighborhood, and precarious tasks, the union limit ceases to be a "fence" that confines work as something *exclusively* belonging to formal workers, to account for the concealment of other activities that the wage and precarization also exploit. The slogan that emerged from the strike in the midst of the Feminist Intersindical—#AllWomenAre Workers—synthesizes this movement.

Therefore, when we sing in an assembly "Unidad de las trabajadoras, y al que no le gusta, se jode, se jode," we are making a two-part gesture: one the hand, we are gendering that historical chant.[3] Thus, we account for a unity that does not need to be consecrated under the framework of the internal sexist hierarchies. The force of the movement within the unions denounces, in fact, the reality that this unity that subordinated women workers was one consecrated through forced obedience. On the other hand, on expanding the notion of workers—because all women are workers—that unity becomes a force of transversality: it is comprised of jobs and tasks that historically were not recognized, by unions, as labor.

Materialism of the Assembly

The assemblies are the *making of* the strike: its cauldron, to return to the witches' ambit. Women who have been laid off—from the transit company, from public institutions like the mint and the National Institute of Industrial Technology, from textile workshops, from food manufacturers, from hospitals, from graphics workshops, from supermarkets—find themselves in a *transversal* connection, again, with workers from the popular economy, with teachers in struggle, with sex workers and travestis, with agricultural producers in crisis, with housewives made desperate by the austerity measures that are attenuated by their everyday efforts to save and stretch their budgets.

I want to propose a fourth thesis related to the *materialism* of the assembly: that the assembly is the *concrete place where words cannot be detached from the body.* Where raising one's voice is to gesture, breathe, sweat, and feel that the words slip and are trapped in the bodies of others. Contrary to the idea that a strike is only organized virtually or by calls on the internet or social networks, the fabric of the assembly, its stubborn repetition at different scales, shows again how laborious body-to-body work is, the constant disagreement of the live encounter between divergent experiences and concrete and irreducible dissidence. The way of sharing a space, of patiently listening to the interventions, and, finally, of maintaining that tension that is thought provoking without necessarily producing consensus, demonstrates that heterogeneity is not only a question of discourses or stories.

Being together in assembly, as a laborious way of being with others, removes us from a passive or cynical relation with the relentless cruelty of sexist violence as it seeks to make itself into the everyday landscape. It also displaces us from the victimist mode of suffering the economic adjustment measures that make our existence precarious, with which they seek to make our lives austere and miserable, and confine us to a limited gender arena that codifies suffering and reparations. Because that is what is affirmed by the strike process: our capacity to remove ourselves from the victimization and state of permanent mourning to which they seek to submit us.

What occurs in the assembly is a patient and difficult elaboration. But in that effort, the everyday activity of many (union, political, educational, neighborhood, community, cultural, etc.) organizations is revitalized. The assemblies produce new images of counterpower, of a popular sovereignty that defies faith in the state as monopoly over the political, of insurgencies that have renewed dynamics of decision making and autonomy, of care and reproduction, of self-defense and collective knowledge.

These are intermittent and fragile moments, but to the extent that they are persistent and capable of producing new forms of *embodiment* and of power, we can say that *they are not only a moment, but a movement*—to borrow a characterization made of the Movement for Black Lives when its critics sought to confine it to its brief duration and untimely mode.[4] It is these types of *movements* that are putting into practice something that today is not only asked by high philosophy: What does it mean to act together when the conditions for doing so have been devastated?

The Sovereignty of the Assembly

I want to synthesize the above in the hypothesis that, in different places and at different scales (in this sense, the assembly is a very flexible, but also consistent, apparatus), assemblies produce a mode of collective intelligence via *three* acts: (1) an imaginary of common action, (2) an evaluation of the force needed to convene it, and (3) the development of the practical capacity required to make a collective decision operational.

But for this to happen, the assembly is also *produced*; it is *prepared*. It is constructed in a conversation that passes the news along; it grows into a rumor that takes shape in a meeting; and it amplifies a debate that makes the issue of the strike one question among many. It functions thanks to the gap that is opened in the union's agenda; as a comment during a conversation in school or in the line at the grocery store; it is expanded into an activity scheduled at a high school, and a whisper in a newsroom. A *call* is necessary for the assembly.

It is a call to *give ourselves time*—because it is in the assembly where *the political time is produced* to think also about our uses of time and to revise the distribution of work hours that we manage through constant juggling; because there we can complain about the abuses and lack of egalitarian opportunities, as well as dedicate ourselves to detailing our research and strategies. This appropriation of time is a way of anticipating, a way of stopping to think, stopping in order to imagine. It is a way of suspending our routine to open up another temporality; however, it is one that we do not want to be merely exceptional and momentary, but to have *lasting* effects after leaving the assembly. That is why the assembly is not evanescent: it does not simply last as long as it lasts (although it does that, too). It is prolonged in that the effects we intuit, think about, desire, and decide there are *embodied and put into practice* by a whole set of perceptions, actions, debates, and further calls.

The assembly (in its diverse versions) *transforms us* because it functions as a space for collectively processing the suffering caused by austerity measures and the crisis, by historical and more recent injustices. In this way, the narrative of a particular affect immediately takes on a political dimension. Thus it avoids the purely cynical or paternalistic inclinations: two registers into which the most realistic, and even the most lucid, diagnoses of the present are often translated.

The assembly is a machine of political decision making that establishes another *sovereign force*: it produces conditions of listening that are increasingly scarce in times of hyper-mediatization, and it produces *political decision making* by making listening a process of collective elaboration. It is also generates a mode of *accounting for the force* that allows us to put that decision into practice, to not remain limited to the recitation of our desires. *Power of evaluation* and *potencia of action* are two practical keys of subaltern knowledges, of the knowledges of assemblies.

Through the organization of the strike, the assembly form finds a revitalization through which the feminist movement, in all of its multiplicity, deliberates, theorizes, and organizes collective forms of decision making. It does so, furthermore, with the determination to take the streets. That orients the movement toward the streets as its horizon, allowing it to overflow each particular situation and, at the same time, to demonstrate that its strength comes from that multitudinous composition.

Knowing as Collective Rhythm

Knowing is a political practice. And one form of feminist knowing is trusting in collective intelligence (that is, something greater than the sum of individuals, and also beyond a consensus). Collective intelligence is what is experienced in an assembly, in a march, or in a strike, when we feel that we are part of a movement of thinking, which is practical know-how: putting assembled bodies into action. That intelligence is trained in a zone that moves between knowing and not knowing what to do. Or in other words: *when we don't know what to do, we call an assembly.* There is no preexisting *what to do* that is legitimized by the assembly. In any case, this is always a battle in the assembly—a battle to resist its transformation into mimicry, which would empty it of content and contention. Of course, there is a ritual, and a set of gestures that, in their repetition, *make* the assembly. But the challenge is for those to be the conditions of possibility for something to happen, not the bureaucratic simulation of a procedure.

In this sense, the production of the assembly as an encounter of diverse situations of conflict differs from the idea of the assembly as a clash between preexisting opinions and positions. Here the *disorder* of the male/patriarchal canon of doing things is also brought into play.

Then, to return to assembly-based knowledge: it is the *not-knowing what to do* that is the engine that sets collective intelligence in motion. This does not mean that there is not an accumulation of experiences, of repertories of action, of available vocabularies. But it is only the situation of *not knowing what to do* that opens up the space for a common thought and, I insist, leads to those three acts: the evaluation of forces, the capacity for political decision making, and the power to put into practice what is agreed upon.

That mode of knowing, as collective intelligence, supposes a *rhythm*. Silvia Rivera Cusicanqui situates this in two precious images: the hunger strike and the march. "The practice of the hunger strike and walking for days in a multitudinous march has the value of silence and the generation of a rhythm and collective breathing, which act as a true performance," she states, recalling the large protests in defense of the Indigenous Territory and National Park Isiboro Sécure (TIPNIS) in 2011. And she adds: "There are then, in those spaces of what is not said, a set of sounds, gestures, movements that carry the living traces of colonialism and that resist rationalization, because their rationalization is uncomfortable, it makes you fall out of the comfortable sleep of liberal society."[5]

What Rivera Cusicanqui signals about the distrust in those knowledges is fundamental. It is the historical contempt for gestures considered nonpolitical. We remember how movements are characterized as pre-political when they supposedly cannot articulate what they want in a certain grammar. It is a classic exercise of power: an indication that it does not understand what a collective or a movement wants, seeks, or attempts to conquer, if it does not enunciate them according to power's own rules of speech. The declaration of a movement's unintelligibility, on the basis that its discourse fails to display a certain kind of order, is a standard method for discrediting movements. It is also a favored mode of infantilization, a way of marking those who do not reach the maturity of verbal language, of the slogan, or of a proclamation legible within certain canons. In the case of the movement of women, lesbians, travestis, and trans people, we have seen how this reaches a fever pitch: "They do not know what they want," "Nobody understands what their demands are," "How can they know if they are progressing if their demands are unclear?" and so on.[6]

Perhaps some different strategies are possible when faced with such incomprehension. One is to vindicate failure, as postcolonial theorist Gayatri Chakravorty Spivak does when she speaks of "cognitive failure" as a politics and a method.[7] In her dedication to reading texts that inaugurate a new form of telling the history of subaltern subjects, those who are always devalued, she makes a political and methodological gesture: she shows the historiography of subalternity, to the extent that it manages to demonstrate relations of failure and to *read* in them a potencia of radicality and difference.

Spivak proposes a notion of history in which there are no transitions or progress in the linear sense, but rather displacements "woven as confrontations." In the revolts she comments on, those displacements manage to change meanings: from the religious to the militant, from crime to insurrection, from servants to workers. In a counter-reading of how the revolts are dismissed as irrational (e.g., as religious, criminal, or ancillary), she denounces that narrow way of classifying them that blocks their comprehension in terms of militancy, insurrection, or a new (non-European) proletarian class.

The fundamental point that allows for a realization and visualization of those displacements is that the initiative is situated in the insurgent, in the subaltern. From there emerges the force of displacement, of its epistemological and political capacity. It is not about an apparent rationality, imposed by the progressive transition, that would make the subjects "evolve." Here there is another twist: if we assume historians fail to access the consciousness of the subaltern—historical narratives, Spivak argues, always attempt to do so through the documents of the elites—what is revealed is merely a lateral, oblique trace: there is no complete, literal access to those rebellious practices and memories.

They are always recognized in a "non-originary" way. Spivak thus deploys a general theory of consciousness, which is always reached by traces and scraps. Against the progressive enlightenment of consciousness raising, there is another wager: that there is nothing to "raise." Of course, questioning the definitive "accessibility" of subaltern consciousness does not mean that it simply remains an impossibility. To the contrary, it provides an idea of consciousness that is effectively situated as "difference," rather than as identity.

This is taken up again in the negative, failed response to Spivak's famous question: "Can the subaltern speak?" By answering in the negative, the lateral, oblique dimension of consciousness and language is exposed. This negation is a mark of contempt with respect to the regime of enunciation that makes it so that only a certain grammar and a certain voice is audible as politics. But it also demonstrates that framing the expressive regime in terms of consciousness is always "subject" to a cathexis of the elite.

"I like the word 'subaltern' for one reason: it is truly situational," Spivak said in an interview prior to her arrival to Buenos Aires a few years ago. "'Subaltern' started as the description of a certain military rank. Later it was úsed by Gramsci to get around censorship: he called Marxism monism and was forced to call the 'proletariat' the subaltern. The word, used under coercion, was transformed into a description of all of that which does not fit into a strict class analysis. I like that because it does not have theoretical rigor."[8]

It is within these "scenes" of nonlinear translation and theoretical defiance, which are carried out in practice by the assemblies and feminist strikes, that I locate another hypothesis: that it is the situational appropriation of certain categories that gives that *displacement* strength. The lack of "theoretical rigor," or the fact that the words themselves seem "to be in question," is what forces us to use other languages, reinvent knowledges and their expressive regimes, which are, at the same time, organizational and political. I think, for example, about why the organization of migrant textile workers in Argentina, mostly migrants from Bolivia, constantly fails in certain "union" initiatives, and yet they never abandon that field; instead, they continue to question and challenge it from within. At the same time, that experience has been fundamental for the impulse that several women migrant workers from that sector gave to the Ni Una Migrante Menos collective,[9] which amount to a reservoir of struggles that support a new language. This language is anchored in an organizational, community, and vital experience that is very "illegible," for example, from the perspective of the narratives of slave labor (and this again refers to the discussion in Chapter 2 about what is hidden by totalizing narratives about trafficking).

When Spivak visited Bolivia, despite the fact that a list of official translators had been proposed, it was Silvia Rivera Cusicanqui who took up the simultaneous interpretation, and above all, who brought the indiscipline of the text and linear translation to the stage. "How to translate into Spanish the term 'double bind,' referring to the schizo that Spivak uses? In Aymara there is an exact word for that, and it does not exist in Spanish: it is *pä chuyma* and it means having the soul divided by two mandates that are impossible to fulfill." These exercises of translation, Rivera Cusicanqui says, reveal that today all words are in question: "That is the sign of the Pachakutik, of a time of change."[10] That is where we situate ourselves.

I will add another scene to this genealogy of defiance through language: the translation of the Subaltern Studies Group's work into Spanish, which was begun at the end of the 1980s in Bolivia. It was Silvia Rivera Cusicanqui and Rossana Barragán who edited the compilation, which was part of an effort to expand the field of theoretical arguments against the neoliberal multiculturalism that was imposed as state politics and that was proposed as the official solution to the problems of internal colonialism.[11] Raquel Gutiérrez Aguilar was another one of the translators who I also want to inscribe in this lineage of complainant and strategic language.[12] She carried out that work while she was incarcerated in the Obrajas women's prison in La Paz, for her activity in the Ejército Guerrillero Tupak Katari (EGTK). As it turned out, Gutiérrez Aguilar's involvement in the project afforded her the opportunity to translate historian Ranajit Guha's "The Prose of Counter-Insurgency," which provided her with new techniques for reading her own judicial file.[13] With this I highlight two questions: (1) a polemic with the academicist appropriation of the "decolonial," and (2) a subterranean line of failure of a political epistemology that accumulates another type of force.

Revolutionary Realpolitik

In Chapter 1, I spoke of a "realism of the assembly." I was referring to what I develop here, in accounting for the assembly as an apparatus that produces collective intelligence, as a sphere for the *evaluation of forces*, as *strategic practice to intervene in a historical process*. I now want to add another argument, concerning the *political realism* that can be practiced through feminism.

The assemblies amount to a form of doing politics that displaces the traditional choice between reform *or* revolution. That is how Rosa Luxemburg synthesized a historical polemic of Marxism in 1899 (in her debate with the social democratic thinker Eduard Bernstein). We can also call this displacement, which is *based on the assemblies'* capacity to go beyond the disjunctive (of the "or"), a *realism of the assembly*. How does another form of politics emerge that avoids that binary of reform *or* revolution?

The assemblies have a unique composition. They do not underestimate concrete claims—which emerge from situated research by different collectives—about budgets, laws, necessary changes to institutions, or specific demands that involve institutional and parliamentary activism. However, at the same time as this agenda of demands is registered, it is also overflowed by a distrust that that is the ultimate horizon of what the feminist movement is proposing. The revolution in bodies, bedrooms, and households comes to situate and project the reach expressed by the slogan "We want to change everything!" That desire for revolution, experienced based on the *realism* of a tremor in social relations, which are transformed in *all* spaces by forms of defiance, affirms that the time of revolution is now (and not a distant goal).

Therefore, the two planes are not experienced in opposition to one another. I insist: action is not divided between reform *or* revolution. There is a simultaneity of temporalities that do not function in disjunction. In the parliamentary dynamic that unfolded around the issue of abortion, as I analyzed in Chapter 3, this ability to simultaneously act on the two planes was demonstrated magisterially.

I want to highlight that double temporality because to the extent that it is simultaneous and not sequential-progressive, it enables a radical critique of neoliberalism. It is a concrete and forceful refusal of the multiple dispossessions and new forms of exploitation with which capital advances over our lives, doing battle in each frontier in which the dispute with capital takes place today. In that sense, it opens up a discussion about the ways that we organize the provision of care, common resources, and infrastructure for everyday reproduction. There are fights underway in all spaces of living and work. When it becomes mass feminism, the feminist movement is a response to philanthropic and paternalistic attempts to resolve precarity through the imposition of conservative and reactionary forms fueled by fear.

Now I will return to Rosa Luxemburg, turning to a concept that she herself put forth in order to use it in our present to displace the very distinction between reform and revolution. It is the idea of a "revolutionary realpolitik" of which she spoke in 1903, commemorating the twentieth anniversary of the death of Marx: "Only after Marx and due to him, is there a *socialist politics of the workers* that, at the same time and in the full sense of the words, is a *revolutionary realpolitik.*"[14] Luxemburg thus unifies two terms that would be opposed in principle, according to the line of "reform *or* revolution." "Realpolitik," in general, is used to characterize those who think and act in the plane of reformist possibility, in opposition to those who have a revolutionary expectation. But in a certain moment, Luxemburg starts to think about the combination of the parliamentary and extra-parliamentary struggle: a mode of linking everyday transformations with the horizon of radical change, in a movement *here and now*, of mutual imbrication. She finally connects reform *and* revolution as a political manifesto, describing her own way of being in the context of German social democracy. One of her most lucid analysts, Frigga Haug, comments: "The key for understanding that paradox resides in Luxemburg's idea of politics, that is, she conceives it as a politics 'from below.'"[15] Thus, the theology of the "final goal" is displaced, but not because it no longer exists or is weakened (that was the critique of Bernstein's reformism), but rather because it enters into another temporal relation with everyday politics, impregnating each concrete and specific action with the revolutionary dynamic. Therefore, opposition becomes complementary in terms of the radicalization of a concrete politics.

But there is even more: it creates a *strategic* temporality that is the deployment of the movement in the present tense. It manages to work within existing contradictions *without waiting* for the emergence of absolutely liberated subjects, neither in ideal conditions of struggles nor in the belief in a single space that totalizes all social transformation. In that sense, it appeals to the potencia of rupture of each action and does not limit the rupture to a spectacular final moment of strictly evolutionary accumulation.

This politics allows for engaging in revolutionary politics *in* the unions, for example, and, along these lines, challenges the distinction between economic and political struggles. Luxemburg's "art of politics," to cite the title of Haug's beautiful book, returns to Marx's thought about the crisis, and ruptures and projects it in relation to a politics of the everyday experience, of how the orientation of each crisis is determined based on concrete practices. That key element provides us with a precious clue for feminist politics. Politics cannot ignore a vitalist pragmatism, desiring to revolutionize everything and for that very reason able to reinvent realism. A revolutionary realpolitik.

There is a novel that seems to contain an inspiring image for Haug. It is a novel by the feminist writer Irmtraud Morgner, *Amanda: Ein Hexenroman*, in which two groups of witches divide up their tasks. Some do realpolitik, and during the day are busy with reforms; others instigate revolutionary disturbances. At night they meet in the "witches' mountain" and recount their successes. "In this way," Haug observes, "both groups are always at the level of what is really possible by both sides, which changes every day thanks to what has been done by the two groups. Could combining the two paths perhaps be a political objective in and of itself?"[16] Today, in their best moments, the assemblies function like that witches' mountain.

Situated Assemblies

What is achieved in the conjunction of these "popular," "community," "slum," "Black," "Indigenous," "campesino," and "Abya Yala" feminisms? I argue that such an expansive composition, named on the basis of these concrete situations, has managed to become more than a language for the few, but constitutes a common code: one that manages to express the discomfort and the desire of many women, and that does justice to very different stories. Here, another thesis emerges: that it is the composition of that diversity of feminisms (with their differences, tensions, and disagreements) that allows the movement to be *massive, inclusive, and radical*. It is in the assemblies that occur in each place where that composition is performed.

However, it is a particular type of inclusion in its combination with massiveness: *inclusion through radicalization*. It is a hackneyed political argument that in order to include more people in a movement, it must moderate and soften its slogans, its demands, its formulations. The current feminist movement is doing the opposite: it includes diverse struggles, narratives, dynamics, and conflicts precisely *because* they connect, they expand; and because they expand, starting from each conflict, they are able to map forms of violence and diagnose the crisis. Through its composition, which arises *from the conflicts and by tracing their connections*, the movement emphasizes radicality as a method of inclusion or composition. I mean

173

"radicality" in a very precise sense: that which puts in play a conflictiveness that both applies to each specific conflict and at the same time elaborates a *concrete and general* critique of the forms of exploitation and extraction of value, which today demand ever-greater levels of violence.

In the case of Argentina, we continued the strike beyond March 8 through *situated assemblies*. I will quickly mention two experiences. The first was with women workers who had been laid off from the transnational food corporation PepsiCo, who in the winter of 2017 installed a tent in front of Congress in Buenos Aires and inaugurated the slogan "Ni una trabajadora menos" (Not one woman worker less). Later, in September 2017, in the Patagonian city of El Bolsón, feminist organizations and compañeras from Mapuche communities gathered in opposition to the criminalization of Indigenous protest to recuperate their territories. There, the slogan was "Our bodies, our territories. Where is Santiago Maldonado?" in reference to the activist who at that time was disappeared following state repression.[17]

The assemblies manage to *map the conflicts in a dynamic that simultaneously displaces and situates them*. One of the ways in which violence is approached, worked on, and diagnosed by contemporary feminism is based on the production of links with social conflictiveness. What does it mean to be linked to conflictiveness?

This question presents several challenges. The first is to produce a *proximity* to the conflicts. Because the relation to conflicts is not evident or natural, this connection is neither automatic nor spontaneous. To the contrary, a *displacement that produces proximity* is needed. It is not about the traditional idea of "going" to a determined conflict, as if it were about simply "bringing" solidarity or running to take a photo. These formulas maintain feminism as something "exterior," as a rubric that does not intervene in the very definition of the conflict. The political challenge is something else: to open up the question about how feminism produces alliances, based on concrete conflicts that give those same conflicts new tools, ways of being defined, and, above all, ways of being connected with other conflicts.

By considering *displacement by conflict* as a feminist practice, I refer to the fact that the conflict itself becomes a situation from which to regroup and evaluate our forces, to diagnose what we call "conflict" in feminist terms, to narrate it, and, above all, to determine what it means to make it into a battlefield in which we can move (in opposition to the paralysis and cynicism that tend to accompany many ways of analyzing the conflict).

In our practice, the *situated assemblies* have been a mode of that displacement. At first glance it might sound contradictory: How can the ideas of *being situated* and *displacing ourselves* coexist?

The conflict is what produces the situation, the assembly is the apparatus of collective intelligence that diagnoses it, and displacement is what allows us to map what we call "forces in dispute" and to weave proximity.

Displacing one's self implies the construction of a sense of belonging to a conflict that, as it is opened up, makes it possible to be confronted because it *overflows* the confines of its definition. The assembly, insofar as it becomes an itinerant artifact, mobilized by conflicts, requires body-to-body work that is essential for the task of deploying a collective intelligence that speaks in multiple languages (that of demand and that of insurgency; that of everyday insubordination and that of the reformulation of public space; that of sabotage and that of mourning; that of the territory and that of the street).

If it does not want to be limited to questions defined by a narrow idea of gender, the horizon of that conflictiveness that finds a new space of political elaboration in feminism is one of weaving "unexpected alliances" that are uncomfortable and irreverent.

"Displacement" also implies a type of convening that is coproduced and that shows feminism as a sounding board for all struggles. It is this ability to function as a vector of radicalization that constructs its capacity to be immanent to conflicts: in other words, its possibility to exist within, as a force of definition of the conflict itself.

In her fantastic book *Living a Feminist Life*, theorist Sara Ahmed defines a structure as an assembly: "A structure is an arrangement, an order, a building; an assembly."[18] Thinking about assemblies as the mobile structuration of a political process led by a multiplicity of subjectivities that traverse different conflicts (in homes, in bed, in the streets, in places of study and work) also enables a composition that is not only *identitarian*.

Linking the question of identity to conflict allows for another interesting displacement: an avoidance of assemblage among certain identitarian politics that only cultivate a *victimist* enunciation and, therefore, a ranking of suffering. Often, when the enunciation occurs in this register, it organizes a hierarchy of victims that always allows some to have the power to blackmail and blame others. Thus it also restricts the conceptualization of violence that has been made more complex by the movement, in order to fall back on disconnected classifications.

The challenge is how to structure recognition of those differences, inequalities, and historical hierarchies without freezing them into an economy of victimization or erasing them in the name of a false equality. The assemblies manage, for moments, another type of efficacy. It is a composition, based on struggles and conflicts that structures a common plane—one that, without smoothing over differences, does not stage a testimonial of pure victims (that place where the patriarchy loves to situate us).

Excursus: Assemblies, Performative
Theory and Collective Leadership

Two important books have been published in recent years that carry the word *assembly* in their titles: *Notes Toward a Performative Theory of Assembly* by Judith Butler and *Assembly* by Michael Hardt and Antonio Negri.[19] I want to extract one question from each of them.

The question that Hardt and Negri raise is that of the duration of political dynamics: that is, the classic problem of organization that emerges when we consider that we have to go beyond the protest, the march, or a specific action. In other words, how can we ensure such permanence is not embodied in traditional apparatuses, whether that of the party, or of leadership concentrated in one person? How can we ensure that the critique of old structures does not trap us in an immediatist temporality of politics? According to Hardt and Negri, the valid critiques of leadership cannot completely do away with the question of duration. They seek to separate the traditional figure of the leader from the "political functions" of leadership. Their objective, then, is to find other methods of fulfilling those functions, which to them are key: decision making and assembly. To decouple them from "centralized" leadership supposes a deconstruction of the opposition between a horizontal social movement and a vertical leadership with decision-making capacity. Of course, this displacement implies another relationship between leadership and democracy.

Hardt and Negri clarify that they do not want to construct a theory of the assembly, nor analyze a particular assembly dynamic. Rather, they use the concept to review the political possibilities in different practices. But, above all, they do so in order to formulate an argument about why the political form of the assembly "corresponds" to or expresses enormous affinity with the circuits of production and reproduction that nourish social cooperation today. To do so, they explain the ambivalence of what they call the "entrepreneurship of the multitude": an expanded form that takes on primarily affective, cognitive, digital, and communicative labor, that delineates a new mode of production that neoliberal capitalism continuously exploits. The "entrepreneurial"—that is, neoliberal—conversion of community, self-managed, and cooperative modes of doing hinders the possibilities of converting those forces (of the *common*) into dynamics of self-organization and self-government.

Along this line, a "plural ontology of the social" requires political forms that do not reduce that plurality, but rather introduce modes of articulation of the multitudinous for making decisions. They conclude, "What begins as a coalition must, through processes of articulation and translation, undergo a sea change and assemble as a multitude of power new subjectivities."[20]

In a much less abstract register, Judith Butler uses the figure of the assembly to foreground the vulnerability of bodies: What is exposed when those bodies are revealed in their character of "interdependence"? It is precisely that which neoliberalism would want to combat under the "contradictory imperative" of showing us to be autonomous while destroying the social possibilities for autonomy, and expanding precarization as a generalized existential condition. Interdependence, in this argument, enters into antagonism with the morality of individual responsibility for risk and failure. It is, undoubtedly, another way to enter into the critique of neoliberal "entrepreneurship" as a mandate of the generalized privatization of existences. But it is also a way of redefining interdependence on the basis of vulnerability. This implies a consideration of vulnerability as part of the capacity for resistance, since it is to the extent that we have been affected by something that we have the capacity to respond. As Butler said in a presentation in Buenos Aires: "The point of resistance is not to overcome vulnerability to become part of a mass-subject (which is a very masculine idea). I think that we have to be capable of continuing to feel those affects to be able to face them." She thus proposes a decoupling of vulnerability from victimization. Putting one's body on the line, on the barricades, on the front, is not incompatible with maintaining vulnerability: we must simply put aside the male paternalism that opposes power to vulnerability.

But where does that interdependence, which Butler locates as the plane of production of a common fabric, have the opportunity to make itself visible? For the philosopher, it is in a space that challenges the distinction between the private sphere and the public sphere: the assembly of bodies. It would be that space where bodies function as a "referential force," and the situation that enables an alliance based on the assumption of precarity as a common condition that is politically imposed. The "right to appearance" that the assembly produces (Butler argues, in dialogue with Hannah Arendt) allows her to propose a political theory in relation to the assembly. However, it is an assembly form that is no longer that of the Greek polis, in which women and slaves were excluded.

The assembly is produced by occupying a space in corporeal terms, in a way that allows us to show that political performativity is not only discursive or pre-discursive. It can be a march, a vigil, the occupation of a plaza or a building, a public mourning or hunger strike, Butler says, referring to the assembly as a gathering of bodies. What matters is the materiality of the body that takes a risk and exhibits itself with others: that is, what it *says*. Another type of enunciation appears beyond linguistic enunciation. To put one's body on the line is to speak, but to speak in a different mode. "Performative" thus means putting a common force into action that one uses politically.

This form of foregrounding the body allows Butler to account for the corporealization involved in gender—that is, to situate the experience of those who do not live their gender in a way that is "understandable to the rest," as a way of connecting to struggles over precarization. On the other hand, this would be a way of failing to realize or experience autonomy in the mode demanded by neoliberal morality. Both experiences would allow for gender politics to make alliances with other populations affected by precarity. It is, I understand, both a "noncontractual politics" and a type of articulation that is not merely linguistic.

Then, we can highlight a turn in Butler's own theory: from a political theory of speech acts to a performative theory of gender; and from a performative theory of gender to a political theory of the transversal alliance of bodies that take on precarity in the assembly. This raises the question: Do we manage to practice and theorize the *transversality* of assemblary ensembles as potencia?

Chapter 6

The Feminist International

I'll begin this chapter by highlighting one of the most important innovations of the feminist movement in recent years: one that has not only become a genuinely global phenomenon, but also emerged from the global South. It has strong roots in Latin America—a region known to some by the Guna Indigenous people's term, Abya Yala—and it runs through multiple layers of history and struggle, connected to countless movements and organizations. Building from its Latin American roots, it has nurtured an *internationalism*—one that disrupts the scales, scope, and forms of coordination of a movement that nevertheless continues to expand, without losing its strength and anchor.

As an internationalism that challenges both the geographic imagination and the organizational imagination, it is infused with transborder alliances and does not have a centralized structure, or a party organization coordinating everything from some commanding heights. It is an internationalism that allows the current feminist movement to be projected onto the mass scale; an internationalism that finds inspiration in the autonomous struggles of Rojava and communitarian struggles in Guatemala, in the struggles of Chilean students and favela dwellers in Brazil, of campesinas in Paraguay and Afro-Colombian women. It is an internationalism that demonstrates the strength of Latin American migrant women in the United States and that feeds off the politicization of the domestic territory that they carry out with their movements, both literal and figurative.

It is an internationalism that requires alliances in every possible place: with strawberry-picking day laborers, Moroccan women working during harvest times in Andalusia, and the peasant unions and activist collectives of the towns and cities;[1] between women laid off from textile factories and students fighting against education cuts; between Indigenous women in rebellion and community organizers in each neighborhood of the urban peripheries. Therefore, what characterizes this feminist movement is that it is able to take root and territorialize itself in concrete struggles, and to produce links starting from those specific struggles.

It is internationalism as such because it is made up of alliances that defy the limits of nation-state geometry; because it challenges an abstract notion of class (in which shared "interests" are assumed a priori) or the people (in which an amalgam of homogeneous national affection is taken as a given).

We are talking about an already-existing internationalism. It is not something left for the future, to be designed and constructed as an evolutionary step for the movement of tomorrow. We proved its concrete working existence when we launched the third international strike in 2019: it is organized in each place, and the regional, global, plurinational fabric emerges *from there*. It also means that the very meaning of internationalism expands and is now interwoven with the plurinational question, which is a demand raised by different Indigenous movements in Latin America in order to go beyond the framework of the colonial nation-state and recognize the multiple nations that comprise any territory.

The internationalist dimension is also a method. As much was clear in the "plurinational" gathering of women, lesbians, trans people, and travestis in the Patagonian city of Trelew in 2018. A method was practiced in that gathering that connected struggles against mega-mining and other neo-extractivist enterprises that expropriate communal lands in Argentina to a regional map of struggles: against the militarization of the favelas in Brazil and repression in Nicaragua; against land grabs by transnational corporations using agro-toxins; against the advance of the church's moralization of our lives; and against the generalized impoverishment caused by austerity measures. The perspective of transborder feminism includes an analysis of the counteroffensive—a wide range of reactionary responses to the massive feminist rebellion—that complicates and exceeds the framework of the nation-state because it focuses on varied transnational institutions, such as the Vatican and media conglomerates, along with other transnational corporations that push free trade agreements, the advance of drug trafficking, state and para-state militarization, and the Women 20 (W20), a thematic group of the G20 that seeks to translate women's issues into a neoliberal frame.

How is internationalism expressed in the feminist movement? The internationalist dimension does not require struggles to become abstract and lose their specificity in the effort to coordinate a common feminist program, but builds a program based on that specificity. The internationalist dimension is not guaranteed by a hierarchical structure and therefore is not implemented from the top down. The internationalism that we are practicing qualifies each struggle: it makes them richer and more complex without having to abandon their rootedness in concrete situations; it makes them more cosmopolitan, without paying the price of abstraction. It broadens our political imagination at the same time that it creates a practical ubiquity; it is that feeling when we shout, "We are everywhere!"

The movement's ubiquity is its true strength. That ubiquity imprints an organizational dynamic on each particular space that has repercussions in others, ranging in scale from small meetings of five people to massive protests, from neighborhood assemblies with varying attendance to temporary collectives that come together for a specific action. The *international*, now tied together with the *plurinational*, becomes an adjective: it does not describe the state, but rather the encounter of different struggles. Therefore, it is not a progressive "integration" of demands, but a dynamic that is expanded in the organization of the international strikes; it is not merely a serialization of distinct struggles, a growing list of various identities, or a purely rhetorical gesture; rather, it is a constellation of struggles that empower each other as they are woven together to take on a new, expansive shape.

In this sense, the organization of the strike has asserted a politics of place, without succumbing to "localism." The movement is amplified through its dense connections to various conflicts and experiences, and it uses the strike as an occasion to hold meetings in places and neighborhoods and with people that often fall outside the boundaries of our struggle. It is an internationalism constructed *from* the territories in struggle. That is what, I insist, allows this internationalism to also expand toward the plurinational dimension as a key element of an anti-racist and anti-colonial politics. From the point of view of the March 8 date, it seems like an intermittent internationalism. However, to the extent that it is not only restricted to that date, it continues to be cultivated as multiple links. The effect, as Raquel Gutiérrez Aguilar charts, is "synchronous reverberation," a "seismic effect."[2] We have felt it: the earth trembles.

Therefore, the strike in 2020 is feminist, is international, and is plurinational; it brings together denominations, spatialities, and locations that turn this ubiquity into a truly heterogeneous and common composition. The current feminist internationalism does not have a structure; it has bodies and body-territories involved in concrete conflicts, arrayed across a differentiated terrain.

Territories of Internationalism

What are the territories of internationalism? I would like to highlight three of its privileged territories and show how their transnational dimension is a new element revealed by feminist struggles.

Consider, first, domestic territories. Historically enclosed between four walls, today they are spaces of practical internationalism where global care chains are assembled, where reproductive labor is negotiated, and where the costs of austerity and the lack of public infrastructure are felt most acutely. The domestic "scene" thus becomes a territory of forced internationalism.[3] This is due in part to the migrant composition of domestic workers in most households, because they use their transnational experience to weave networks and alliances that make internationalism into a force of denunciation, connection, and struggle. For example, compañeras from the Territorio Doméstico collective, made up of migrant domestic workers in Madrid, explain how they perform an "international catwalk" as a parade-performance and tool for public intervention. In those performance-interventions, they use costumes to represent figures such as "the transnational migrant," "the undocumented," and "the octopus" (the woman who needs eight hands to get all her work done). Thus, they highlight the conditions that weigh on the bodies of the international "models" who clean hotels, care for children, and inhabit the precarity of existing with a nonlegal residential status, while doubling as care workers in their country of origin, at a distance and in the home where they work, and, at the same time, organizing with other women to demand housing.[4]

Taking that forced internationalism as a point of departure and analysis of their own concrete situation, they propose "the work of finding each other" with other compañeras that, in turn, comprises a practical internationalism. We have seen the same thing in Argentina with the denunciation made by domestic workers in the gated communities of the Nordelta district. They were told that they smelled bad, that they talked too much. They were forbidden from traveling with their bosses or property owners, who did not want to share seats with them in the vans going to and from the gated communities, the only way that these women had of getting to their workplaces. Yet they do want those workers to clean for miserable wages and to silently suffer abuse. Like Territorio Doméstico, however, the women refused to remain silent. They forcefully intervened in the feminist assembly, insisting that their situation be taken into account in the strike call and organization. This domestic rebellion demonstrates how racism, classism, and patriarchy are articulated and become the basis for a public complaint and mobilization. Thus, the Feminist International emerges today, first of all, from what has historically been considered the most enclosed and confined place; it arises from domestic territories in revolt.

Second, let us consider Indigenous and communitarian territories. Long expropriated and considered as closed, even "backwards" economies, they are today spaces of borderless alliances, of communitarian embodiment, challenging extractive mega-projects and the new owners of the land who are in charge of agribusiness. A global diagram of capital's extractive dynamics emerges from those struggles where alliances, movements, and networks resist and reject these neocolonial advances. Thus, they vindicate resources (from land to water to knowledges about health) as common, while also updating the anti-colonial memories of internationalism. Thus, this Indigenous and communitarian feminism takes up anti-racism and anti-colonial practices, making them into a concrete component, a practical element, that structures the conflict.

Third, let us turn to the territories of precarization: from popular economies to migrant platform workers. Long considered to be "non-organized" sectors, today they are sites of experimentation with new union dynamics, as well as encampments and occupations of workshops and factories. Via virtual platforms, creative demands and complaints explicate the ways sexual abuse, discrimination against migrants, and exploitation always go hand in hand. In the United States, women working in restaurants—mostly migrants or daughters of migrants—explain that since the majority of one's wage generally comes from tips, sexual harassment is often understood as a condition of earning a good tip—and therefore a necessary part of earning a wage. Women who clean hotels and offices at night have also organized to confront the rapes to which they are subjected, under threat of having their immigration status reported to authorities.

In Argentina, trade unionism is being reinvented within labor dynamics that are directly connected to global platform capitalism and its modes of financial extractivism. These new forms include the Union of Workers of the Popular Economy (UTEP),[5] as well as the Association of Platform Personnel (APP), the first union in the region bringing together workers from digital transportation and delivery platforms such as Uber, Glovo, and Rappi. The jobs with the least recognition are the most exploited by the global structure, now condensed into algorithms. But they are also ones that demonstrate the brutality of that apparently "immaterial" valorization.

In turn, the three territories discussed above are interlinked in multiple ways. They are neither watertight compartments nor disconnected spaces. It is precisely their connection— through the broadening of demands, the growth of new language, and the threading together of geographies—that requires each space to be ever more expansive in how it enunciates problems, complaints, and conflicts, as well as strategies, alliances, and ways to accumulate common strength. Knowing that we are interconnected, with shared clues and hypotheses, weaving together resistances and inventions here and there, creates that "aquatic geography" of the strike (to use Rosa Luxemburg's term again), composed of rhythms, tributaries, velocities, and flows.

We Are Everywhere

I want to emphasize two points in relation to this internationalist form. First, that it is able to create an analysis that establishes new parameters and measures for thinking, visibilizing, and feeling different forms of oppression, based on collectively taking up this political word that combines very diverse scales. Second, that the feminist movement is notable for its ability to produce ubiquity without homogeneity. In other words, it has invented a way of being everywhere, without needing to become coherent under some ideological command or the orders of some hierarchical authority.

Both characteristics open up classic questions: What type of accumulation of forces does this internationalism achieve? How is its strength translated and expressed? What organizational horizon does it open up? Perhaps it is useful to displace the very image of linear accumulation, but without falling into a simplified notion of spontaneity or of a logic of events that melt into air. Expansion and complexification are the characteristics of a feminist program in construction.

Contemporary internationalism is expressed not as attachment to a representative structure but as the situated force of each struggle with a tremendous capacity to reverberate elsewhere. This ability to transform itself into a concrete presence in each conflict is what gives rise to its novel potencia. Unlike a process of universalization, which needs to make the concrete conditions of a situation abstract in order to make it fit and conform to a homogeneous parameter that provides recognition, the capacity of that international plane appears as the expansion of the horizon of possible connections and as immediate force in concrete struggles. Thus, this feminist internationalism that we are deploying has a body before it has a structure. It is that body, which is experienced as a common body, that allows for the generation of ubiquity through connection, without requiring a unitary synthesis.

Ubiquity: the capacity to be in many places at once. In the weeks leading up to the strike, compañeras from across Spain assembled a "road map," made up of dozens of actions across the country, that highlighted "a thousand" reasons for going on strike, including assemblies and large events and culminating in a "spider operation" in the Madrid subway, inspired by an action in Buenos Aires in 2018. Meanwhile, Ni Una Menos protests took place in Mexico. Thousands of women, lesbians, trans people, and travestis denounced femicide as a state crime, along with the constant threat of kidnapping attempts that have occurred in the subway, to which the state's only response has been more police. It was also in Mexico that we saw a long series of protests and strikes by women working in the maquilas of Tamaulipas. In the southeast of the country, Zapatista women released a letter explaining why they would not hold the Encuentro de Mujeres que Luchan in their territory on March 8, 2019, denouncing the military threat that lies behind the new government's touristic and neo-extractivist mega-projects, and instead delayed the gathering. This three-part scene, again, summarizes the stage initiated by the organizational horizon of the international strike: an interconnection of struggles and, based on that interconnection, an affirmation of the ways precarization and labor abuse are inseparable from femicides or from the exploitation of territory by transnational corporations.

Meanwhile, in Italy, compañeras from Non Una Di Meno launched the "countdown" to the international feminist strike with a series of posters that narrate scenes that substantiate the motive to strike: abusive bosses, ex-husbands who do not pay child support, and the use of welfare to manage poverty instead of enabling self-determination.

Chile's March 8 (8M) mobilization and coordinating body have continued to grow, following tremendous mobilizations in May 2019 for non-sexist education and the massive Encuentro Plurinacional de las que Luchan (Plurinational meeting of women in struggle) in December 2018, which was repeated during the January 2020 social uprising. Participants also carried out an operation in the subway, renaming each station from below with names taken from feminist history. Meanwhile in Brazil, compañeras in the northeast declared that fascism would not be allowed to pass, and Black feminists marched for justice for Marielle Franco and all those women who sustain the popular and favela economies against the criminalization of their work. In Bolivia, the #Bloqueo8M (8M Blockade) was prepared, denouncing the femicides that started off the year, but also accompanying women's resistance in the Tariquía Reserve, in Tarija, who blockaded the operations of Petrobras. Assemblies were carried out in Uruguay, organized by a coordinating body bringing together a wide range of feminist collectives and organizations and that was increasingly nourished by regional networks. In Ecuador, the strike and uprising were debated as tools with multiple histories of struggle, while in Colombia and Peru weekly meetings were held with 8M as their horizon.

Finally, another one of the strengths of feminist *internationalism* is its ability to produce a common diagnosis of the forms of counterinsurgency that seek to weaken and divide us (I will come back to this issue in the following chapter)—a diagnosis they are able to make in real time, rather than at the speed of academic publishing. It is the same advance that we see in several countries at once, with similar tactics and the shared aim of fragmenting the movement. One issue is clear: the counteroffensive seeks to attack the subversive potencia of the transversal and diverse anti-biological-determinist and anti-racist alliances that are created through the international and plurinational organization of the feminist strikes.

One experience that can be considered a clear precedent for this new form of internationalism is the Zapatista uprising. It is no coincidence that an *encuentro* was also convened in Chiapas on March 8, 2018, demonstrating Zapatismo's ability to form part of new internationalist resonances. Nevertheless, I will also try to point to some of the differences between earlier forms of internationalism and that being woven by the feminist movement today.

How has this expansive transnational form arisen from the feminism movement? As I have discussed throughout this book, the strike formula has been crucial for producing a diagnosis of violence that is able to overcome the moment of victimization, which is imposed on us as the only available reaction in the face of sexist violence, and femicide in particular. The strike is no longer representative only of a Eurocentric history of a white, male, waged working class; rather—like at other moments in history—it has become a way of highlighting other forms of blockade, sabotage, subtraction, and, also, connection with the historically denied element of feminized bodies: reproductive, communitarian, and migrant labor.

From the "general strike" of Black slaves depicted by W.E.B. Du Bois against the slave system of the plantations in the US South,[6] to the tenants' strike in Buenos Aires in 1907, the strikes of the rural workers during the "rebellion in Patagonia" of the 1920s, and the mythical strike of women in Iceland in 1975, to, more recently, the hunger strike of Central American migrants in the caravan on its way to the United States (coeval with teachers' strikes in several states of that country), and the peasant strike in India, we can reconstruct landmarks on an internationalist map of the strike that dislocates it from its traditional canon: namely, its composition as exclusively waged workers, with the factory scene as its central space.

In fact, we can historicize the role of reproduction and women's leadership in diverse forms of the strike to multiply the strike "from within" its own history.[7] But now there is a radicalization of the history of the strike, because the feminist strike has broken out of that history concentrated on the factory space and has opened up a new time. Over the past four years, the feminist strike has shifted to the terrain of reproduction, in order to make those tasks visible and even to propose abstaining from them. The feminist strike also identifies the spaces of production in an unprecedented way, because they are understood on the basis of their necessary connections and assemblages with reproductive tasks. In this way, the strike is not only the extension of an analytic of work that seeks to "laborize" tasks of care, affect, and social reproduction, but a perspective that emerges from those labors that reclassifies the notion of work in a general sense. To put it differently: the strike does not seek the recognition and incorporation of certain kinds of reproductive labor as a type of "work," in the prevailing ideologies of capitalist labor. Rather, its aim is to rethink the nature of labor itself.

This means that it broadens recognition of the sites of value production and that it highlights the reproductive dimension as key to a reconceptualization of what is historically considered work. To be more concrete: the free, non-recognized, fragile, intermittent—and, at the same time, permanent—dimension of reproductive labor today serves to explicate the components that make precarization into a transversal process. The forms of intensive exploitation of affective infrastructures, and, in turn, of the extensive lengthening of the working day in domestic spaces, reveal new forms of migrant labor and new hierarchies in service work. The superposition of tasks and the demand for availability—both primary subjective impositions of parenting—then allow us to understand the requirements of service jobs.

Therefore, the feminist strike has allowed for a rethinking, reclassification, and relaunch of another meaning of the general strike. The general strike becomes truly general when it becomes feminist—because, for the first time, it reaches all spaces, tasks, and forms of work. Therefore, it manages to embed itself in specific territories without leaving anything out, and, through that process, it produces *generality*. It covers every corner of unpaid and unrecognized work. At the same time, it affirms them as spaces that produce value, connecting them in their subordinated relation to other forms of labor. Thus, it makes visible the chain of efforts that trace a continuum between the household, the job, the street, and the community. In the face of attempts to confine feminism (to a particular sector, demand, or minoritarian politics), a demonstration that the strike is general *because it is feminist* is both a victory and historical vindication. It is a victory because we say that if we stop, we stop the world. It is to finally prove that there is no production without reproduction. And it is vindication with respect to the forms of the strike where the "general" was a synonym for a dominant partiality: waged, male, unionized, national labor that systematically excluded work not recognized by the wage (and its patriarchal order).

The feminist general strike reflects what we have learned through these years of assembling international strikes, taking the existential and labor multiplicity of our time into the organization of insurrection itself. Multiplicity is not dispersion, but a way of making the heterogeneity of tasks that we carry out correspond to the mandates that we disobey when we strike. The strike becomes general, and therefore becomes real and effective, only when it is broadened. That is why *the strike is general only because it is feminist.*

There is an intimate connection between generality and internationalism. With the feminist strike, we again *broaden* the strike: we make it leap over borders, we invent new geographies for it. We redefine the places themselves where work is done and value produced. The feminist mapping redefines the spatiality of labor, what we understand by the work "place," which is no more or less than the site where value is produced. That practice of reshaping spaces also outlines the new internationalism.

Let's go to the map. Women in Poland went on strike against the criminalization of abortion on October 3, 2016. Just sixteen days later, in Argentina, a strike wave launched with a strike, on October 19, in response to the femicide of Lucía Pérez. The action immediately ceased to be national and, in only one week, spread to twenty-two countries, including the United States, France, Spain, Mexico, Guatemala, Chile, and Uruguay, among others.

With the strike, we take charge of a global cartography that produces proximity from a new perspective. It consists of politicizing violence against women by displacing the status of victimhood. The strike enables an internationalist connection precisely because it creates a common horizon, a concrete action that situates us as political protagonists against the systematic attempt to reduce our pains to the position of a victim to be repaired by the state.

The strike also enables a new kind of internationalism because is starts from a research question in each life and each territory, opening up new forms of knowing by weaving together different knowledges from a multiplicity of concrete bodies and experiences. What does it mean to strike in each territory? What form does the strike take in each working and living situation? What are we striking against? Who recognizes that we strike? What hidden bosses are we striking from? It is these embodied and territorially embedded processes of investigation that produce new subjects, new practical understandings, and new internationalist and plurinational alliances.

On November 25, 2016, mobilizations expanded to more than fifty countries, politicizing the International Day for the Elimination of Violence against Women in a new way. On that date, Ni Una Menos launched a text titled #LaInternacional

Feminista (#FeministInternational), while the Non Una Di Meno movement simultaneously appeared publicly in Italy. At each one of the demonstrations around the world, there was a resounding call for an International Women's Strike on March 8, 2017, revitalizing a date laden with memories of workers' struggle.

There are two critical moments to the construction of this new internationalism: *resonance* and *coordination*. The first moment I refer to as one of resonance, due to its effect of diffusion, of echoes that have repercussions and that produce, as sound effects, amplifications of the body itself. The idea of resonance condenses an idea-force that could serve as a slogan, even if it does not seek to summarize an ideological consistency. It is the ability to open a shared meaning based on *affect*. But it is not an affect in the passive sense: the "affected by," as they tend to name those who suffer from catastrophes or the collateral effects of some phenomenon. Affection has to do with a capacity to be moved, not simply the reception of an effect.

The potencia of the resonance of the strike, as a process, has to do with the capacity to connect at a distance and with the mobilization of meanings instigated by the circulation of images, slogans, actions, and gestures. The strike, as it is broadened, opens up new spaces of enunciation, which are constantly being reinvented. But that capacity for resonance has to do with the subjective displacement that I have been talking about: a concrete action that enacts, puts in practice, the abandonment of the position of the victim; and at the same time it is taken up as an investigation-question in each place, asking what it means to strike in each territory.

After these resonances have sounded, the feminist movement develops a second moment: that of a coordination, a combination of virtual and material spaces of encounter between bodies, inaugurating circuits and reusing other already-existing ones. Networks form between groups in different countries, which begin calling themselves Ni Una Menos. There are exchanges of texts and action proposals, virtual meetings to coordinate global interventions on key dates, meetings between different activists traveling from one place to another.

Resonance and coordination weave together clues for feminisms' collective investigation; they mark differences and divergences; they accumulate a common language produced through practices.

From Solidarity to the New Intersectionality

What is new about the Feminist International? To put it briefly, the images that are evoked by the word "international" usually have to do with the formation the First International Workingmen's Association, and later, after its rupture, the Third International. Proletarian organization in Europe was the central axis of a project of class organization that had the capacity for coordinated action. The development of the strike as an instrument of struggle was one of its initiatives. The coronation of the Russian Revolution "successfully" condensed the revolutionary aspiration that was achieved by those initiatives but, as is well known, it also geographically defied Marx's predictions about revolution by taking place outside of Europe (a revolution against *Capital*, as Gramsci called it).

In the 1960s and '70s, a powerful Third Worldist internationalism woven by decolonization struggles, guerrilla organizations, and diverse insurrectionist movements sought to usher in another epochal shift, though this time one whose force originated from the global South. The amplifications of the revolutionary effects of that internationalism allowed it to overflow European and white confines, as well as to open up to issues not limited by a narrow sense of "class." Decades later, the Zapatista uprising, which began publicly on January 1, 1994, enabled us to talk about an international ("intergalactic," as they described it) network again. Due to its connection to a cycle of Indigenous struggles on the continent, as well as its capacity to interpellate struggles from around the world, the Zapatista struggle has been capable of denouncing injustices and providing new ways of thinking about how to weave together different forms of resistance. At the turn of the new century, the so-called anti-globalization movement also propelled a counterproposal to capital's global dimension, connecting struggles that were organized precisely against the organization of capital, and its calendar of gatherings.

As historian David Roediger indicates, the basic principle launched by Marx for the workers' international was "solidarity," even if such a concept did not figure into Marx's theoretical project, where the problem of "unity" was solved in advance by the homogenizing logic of capital.[8] Solidarity appears as the weapon against the permanent division of the working class practiced by capital, Roediger says, citing the works of the economist Michael Lebowitz. Therefore, workers' unity becomes a central problem when capital needs to produce and exploit "difference."

Some might say that a politics of solidarity is much simpler to cultivate among those who perceive themselves as similar, as opposed to those who see themselves as different, because they are constantly forced to differentiate themselves. Since it is their uniqueness that gives them value as workers in the precarious labor market, solidarity would be more difficult to cultivate there. There is, however, a mode of solidarity that does not appeal to similarity so much as to difference—but in a way that understands difference as "exteriority," something inherently foreign to our own experience. We often hear formulas of solidarity with different struggles that nevertheless leave us in a "safe" position, maintaining distance as evidence that we are in solidarity with something that is not "ours," thus reproducing a paternalistic or savior logic. Internationalism instead asks us to think about how to produce connections between trajectories, experiences, and struggles that unfold in different places. The question is how to produce a common plane without homogenizing differences and without falling into a paternalistic logic.

How can an accumulation of forces be synthesized? The notion of *intersectionality*, as it has been elaborated in the feminist movement, allows us to think about a logic of connection that globally maps, against the grain, capital's landings based on the imbrication of different forms of oppression. Even if the concept was systematized by civil rights advocate and lawyer Kimberlé Crenshaw in 1989,[9] to me it seems important to emphasize another political genealogy of its emergence, as scholar-activist Keeanga-Yamahtta Taylor indicates in *How We Get Free*.[10] There, she traces the concept to the practice of the Combahee River Collective (1974–80), even though they did not use the term. The collective's 1977 manifesto attained mythical status, Taylor observes, because it marked one of the first attempts to articulate "the analysis that animates the meaning of intersectionality, the idea that multiple oppressions reinforce each other to create new categories of suffering."[11] This way of drawing connections between different forms of oppression and showing how they overlap and act "simultaneously," she continues, was a fundamental political intervention by Black lesbians in the feminist movement, and served to generalize an analysis that would open up an entire mode of political radicalization to a new generation of Black feminists. Intersectionality thus becomes the key for understanding oppressions of sex, race, and class not as a sum of variables, but precisely on the basis of their mutual effects. The introduction of difference into the analysis of oppression thus achieves a particular political projection: it is capable of unraveling differences without thereby ceasing to problematize the convergence of struggles. Black feminism, in that sense, has been pioneering in its re-proposal of another idea of totality, one that starts from difference, and thus reconnects liberation from oppression to a liberation that is projected onto everyone.

In this sense, forms of *transversal* struggle put intersectionality into practice as a political and methodological principle, enacting a principle of composition and translation for new forms of transnational solidarity.

After the first International Women's Strike in 2017, Selma James—a North American feminist activist, and cofounder of the International Wages for Housework Campaign in the 1970s, stated that "Not one women less, we want ourselves alive" functioned as the feminist equivalent of "Black lives matter" in the United States, along with the feminist slogan "All women count."[12] I am interested in emphasizing how these connections prosper, forging links among us on the basis of our perspectives on struggles, and doing so in a way that goes beyond simple linguistic equivalences. Intersectionality is the promise of feminism in action, Angela Davis tells us, "against the pernicious powers of state violence." It is an "inclusive and intersectional" feminism" that "calls on us all to unite against racism, Islamophobia, anti-Semitism, misogyny, capitalist exploitation," she said in her speech at the January 2017 Women's March in Washington, DC.

These different territories of feminist internationalism show that feminism becomes more inclusive as it takes up a critical anti-capitalist practice. From there, we can hear a multiplicity of voices and weave that practical internationalism that already exists in the here and now.

Excursus: Neoliberalism and Internationalism

An analysis of neoliberalism has been a central feature of contemporary feminisms and therefore constitutes a crucial element of their internationalism. This is the case, first, because that analysis is a concrete interpretive key for identifying conflicts that were not previously understood as such, and mapping their connections. Second, it allows us to debate and challenge the ways neoliberalism translates and manages conflicts, through multiculturalism or subordinated inclusion that pacifies struggles. In Latin America, this also leads to a reconceptualization of the so-called progressive or populist governments of the last two decades and their relation to neoliberalism. Lastly, it enables a diagnosis of the conservative reaction that has been unleashed against feminism's transnational force.

I want to focus on the work of two theorists from the United States—Wendy Brown and Nancy Fraser—because their interventions are simultaneously philosophical, political, and epistemological, and because they raise the question of the definition of neoliberalism and link it to questions of feminism. I will attempt to outline a dialogue between them, based on the Latin American debate and, in particular, from the perspective that is enabled by mobilizations and struggles on this continent, in order to frame a critique of populism from a feminist viewpoint. My underlying hypothesis is that feminist struggles present an anti-neoliberal perspective capable of going beyond populist political articulation.

In her book *Undoing the Demos: Neoliberalism's Stealth Revolution*, Brown questions that notion of neoliberalism that seems to contain everything.[13] She does so by deepening "the antagonism between citizenship and neoliberalism" and by critiquing the model of neoliberal governance, which she understands as a process of the "de-democratization of democracy." In her argument, neoliberalism restricts democratic spaces not only at the macro-structural level but also on the plane of the organization of social relations; competition thus becomes the norm for any type of relation. She describes this process as an *economization* of social life that alters the very nature of what we call politics, reinforcing the contrast between the figures of *Homo economicus* and *Homo politicus*.

In this sense, she deviates from Michel Foucault, one of the original theorists of neoliberalism's subjective effects. For him, neoliberalism is not a total economization of society that closes off the political, but a new way of understanding the political that expands the idea of government and broadens the idea of the economy, beyond an economistic sense.

Brown, by contrast, emphasizes that in neoliberalism, citizenship is not only a set of rights, but also a sort of ceaseless activism in which we are obligated to participate in order to make ourselves valuable. The penetration of neoliberal rationality into modern institutions such as citizenship blurs the very concept of democracy, from Brown's point of view, who claims that "there are no citizens" in Foucault's genealogies. While her critique of neoliberalism as the neutralization of conflict is important, and her analysis very sharp, it remains within a *politicist* framework: it is based on a formalist definition of what is considered "political," leaving out other important fields and struggles that we would consider of a political nature.[14] The ability to analyze neoliberalism as governmentality is again restricted by her postulation of *neoliberal reason* as synonymous with the *disappearance of politics*. Therefore, the distinction between economy and politics (one foundational to capitalism) is recreated in a way that preserves an "autonomy of the political" as a field that is now colonized and must be defended. From a clearly Arendtian perspective, the "realm of rule" is the privileged space for the democratic deployment of *Homo politicus*.

Following this line of argumentation, Brown's explanation of Donald Trump's 2016 electoral victory—which she dubs as an "apocalyptic populism"—would be the consummation of neoliberalism's hijacking of the political. She writes:

> If this reproach to politics is one important strand of neo-liberalism's assault on democracy, equally important to generating support for plutocratic authoritarianism is what

I call neoliberalism's economization of everything, including democratic values, institutions, expectations and knowledge. The meaning and practice of democracy cannot be submitted to market semiotics and survive. Freedom becomes reduced to advancing in markets, keeping what one gets, hence legitimating growing inequality and indifference to all social effects. Exclusion is legitimate as strengthening competitiveness, secrecy rather than transparency or accountability is good business sense.[15]

For Brown, what is hollowed out by the economization of life is citizenship as a form of "popular sovereignty." The privatization of public goods and higher education contributes to weakening democratic culture, while the notion of "social justice" is consolidated as that which restricts private freedoms. In summary, "together, the open neoliberal disparagement of politics; the assault on democratic institutions, values and imaginaries; the neoliberal attack on public goods, public life, social justice and an educated citizenry generate a novel anti-democratic, anti-egalitarian, libertarian, authoritarian political formation." In Brown's perspective, that economized form of politics produces a type of subjectivity that is opposed to the stability and security of citizens: "This formation now burns on the fuel of ... fear and anxiety, sliding socioeconomic status and rancorous wounded whiteness." Fear, anxiety, precarity, and "rancorous whiteness" are the *affects* that are *liberated* when the confines of citizenship do not produce or regulate democratic subjectivity. Thus, for Brown the equation looks like this: freedoms are increased to the extent that politics is reduced, while pernicious energies are freed to the extent that there is no citizen contention. The result is a politics that, in Trump's case, is not anti-state but rather the business management of the state.

There are three problems with the understanding of "the political" proposed by this vision. On one hand, I think that the right-wing vote, considered in very broad terms, cannot be simplified as plainly anti-democratic spirit. Here I am thinking not only of Trump's victory, but also the so-called turn to the right in Latin America. This "turn to the right," since it coincided with Trump's victory, has driven a similar search for explanations about such a shift in electoral preferences. In other words, a simple analogy is made between Trump's victory following Barack Obama and Mauricio Macri's win after Néstor Kirchner. However, we can complicate this analysis. If it is not an abrupt turn to the right by the masses, what is it? I consider it, instead, a form of "realism" with respect to the nondemocratic element of (liberal and progressive) democracy, which right-wing governments, using the words of the vernacular right, "make sincere" through a cynicism that accepts the status quo as a given. With this I want to say that there is a double *idealization of democracy* at work in Brown's argument (which is the source of her politicism). This is the case, first, because it erases the violence that gave birth to neoliberalism, both in its origins (the coup d'états and state terrorism in Latin America, as well as the racism legitimized by democracy) and in its prolongation by post-dictatorship democracies in diverse but constitutive ways. Second, a conception of democracy as the reign of rule, accompanied by its projection onto citizens, prevents us from seeing its repressive violence in terms of the ways social conflicts are structured today. These conflicts perceive that understanding politics as a field of rules is a discursive privilege of the elites with the freedom to assume that those rules do not function for everyone, as was made explicit by the Movement for Black Lives and the murders of poor youth in Latin American metropoles.[16]

This type of analysis returns to the unilaterally reactionary psyches of the masses, based on an understanding of the "psychic" energies that these regimes mobilize (taking up lines of Frankfurt School analysis on the "authoritarian personality") and that point to the "apocalyptic" nature of populism in the North American case. Populism, then, returns to the side of the nonrational, since its drift can only be explained in terms of an unconscious neoliberal desire expressed by the masses. As a counterpoint, I do believe we need to think about that psychic and affective dimension, because there is an unavoidable materiality to it. But I believe that it is more productive to do so in terms of feelings that are direct qualities —again, "realistic" qualities—of contemporary labor power, as the Italian philosopher Paolo Virno has long argued, rather than mere degradation in the face of the breakdown of citizen habitus.[17]

The discussions around the political defeat of progressive governments in Latin America involve a series of issues related to the political subjectivity expressed at the polls. These are summarized by the bewilderment expressed by those progressive forces when the people who they claimed to favor and benefit "betrayed" them at the ballot boxes. In other words, why do the poor "vote against their interests"? Ernesto Laclau's theory has been among the most widely used for this form of narrating defeat, in a way that reinforces an understanding of the heterogeneity of "the people" in terms of *lack*, and thus requiring a totalizing articulation from above.[18]

However, I want to return to the question of the materiality of psychic energies, since their discussion in the contemporary moment brings us to one of the Frankfurt School's major themes: mass consumption. This was a fundamental element of progressive governments' programs in the region, based on increasing access to consumer goods, particularly among the popular classes. But there was a particular feature to it: it is consumption that is already "detached" from its connection with employment, meaning that debt is what makes it possible. Progressive populism cannot be understood without recognizing the articulation that it produced between neoliberalism and neo-developmentalism under the command of finance (as I discussed in Chapter 4).

Lastly, I think that the critique of neoliberalism is weakened when neoliberalism is considered nonpolitical. Under this idea of politics, the properly political moments of neoliberalism are denied, and, in particular, the immediately political efficacy of "operations of capital" remain unrecognized.[19] The arduous political work of constructing norms and spatiality, as well as of producing subjectivity, is occluded from our analysis. Again, it is not economics versus politics, but rather the politicization of every action that makes it possible to sustain capitalist valorization. In relation to this, it seems fundamental to think about political practices capable of questioning neoliberalism without considering it the nadir of politics. If there is something challenging and complex about neoliberalism, it is that its constitution is *already* directly political and, as such, can be understood as a battlefield. If Brown highlights the apocalyptic features of Trump's populism and its perverse continuity with the undemocratic character of neoliberalism, Nancy Fraser speaks of Trump's victory as an "electoral mutiny" against neoliberal hegemony, or more specifically as a "revolt against global finance."[20] She also located Brexit, Bernie Sanders's campaign, the popularity of the National Front in France, and the rejection of Matteo Renzi's reforms in Italy within this narrative. In these diverse events, she saw the same will to reject "financialized capitalism." This reading is tied to her analysis of the contemporary crisis as one of "progressive neoliberalism." As she wrote in her article on the conjuncture at the beginning of 2017:

> In its U.S. form, progressive neoliberalism is an alliance of mainstream currents of new social movements (feminism, anti-racism, multiculturalism, and LGBTQ rights), on the one side, and high-end "symbolic" and service-based business sectors (Wall Street, Silicon Valley, and Hollywood), on the other. In this alliance, progressive forces are effectively joined with the forces of cognitive capitalism, especially financialization. However unwittingly, the former lends their charisma to the

latter. Ideals like diversity and "empowerment," which could in principle serve different ends, now gloss policies that have devastated manufacturing and what were once middle-class lives.

This argument was already present in her essay "Contradictions of Capital and Care," where she argued that the mainstream imagination of gender equality both was premised on and reinforced a liberal individualism in which the privatization and commodification of social protection was capable of imbibing a "feminist aura."[21] Such a feminism entails the presentation of reproductive tasks as simply obstacles to women's individual professional careers, but also as tasks that neoliberalism, fortunately, frees us from via new markets for waged reproductive labor. A certain sort of feminist emancipation takes on a reactionary character, Fraser argues, by reformulating the division between reproduction and production. Thus, it normalizes the field where today many of the deepest contradictions of capital are found. In this sense, "progressive neoliberalism" would be the counterrevolution to the feminist hypotheses of the 1970s. Now it seems that emancipation is produced because we are pushed into the labor market, establishing the model of the "two-income household" as a perverse metabolization of the feminist critique of the family wage. Of course, this situation is sustained by an ever more classist and racist hierarchicalization of the global division of labor, in which poor migrant women from the South fill the "care gap" of women in the North, who are dedicated to their careers.

From this perspective, "progressive neoliberalism" is the response to a series of struggles against the disciplining hegemony of waged, masculine labor. Those struggles converged in social movements that politicized and challenged sexist and racist hierarchies. The strength of neoliberalism, understood as reaction and counterrevolution, would be to convert those struggles into a sort of multicultural cosmetics for policies of austerity, unemployment, and social disinvestment, while managing to express them in the language of minority rights. Melinda Cooper, in this sense, warns of the risk in Fraser's argument: "In her most recent work, Fraser accuses second-wave feminism of having colluded with neoliberalism in its efforts to destroy the family wage. 'Was it mere coincidence that second-wave feminism and neoliberalism prospered in tandem? Or was there some perverse, subterranean, elective affinity between them?'"²² The suspicion that Cooper raises in regard to Fraser's questions is important for building a critique that does not rely on nostalgia or the restoration of the family (even if in more egalitarian ways) in the name of a lost security.

The passage from hard neoliberalism (that of Thatcher or Reagan) to a more progressive one (that of Blair or Obama) involved the defeat of multiple struggles, which had varying levels of intensity. Their intensity can be measured in relation to the radicality of the response: this functions as a political and methodological principle for understanding neoliberal rationality, starting from revolt. The dilemma lies in ensuring that this reading does not turn into a rationalization of an always-anticipated defeat. In other words, the question is how not to assume—through an a priori logic that is ratified as an a posteriori analytic—neoliberalism's capacity to metabolize and neutralize all practices and critiques, thus guaranteeing its success in advance.

This power of capital, which we could also name as the *immanentization of capital's logic of capture,* is what is accounted for by Gilles Deleuze and Félix Guattari's notion of the axiomatic of capital.²³ This notion makes explicit the tension between a flexibility and versatility of capture and exploitation by capital, on one hand, and, on the other, the necessity of distinguishing between operations through which that machine of capture subsumes social relations and interventions that also resist and overflow the diagram of capture/exploitation.

Finally, one last point of debate with Fraser: the moment of articulation. For Fraser, the type of "articulation" that this progressive neoliberalism carries out is superficial and counterproductive: "Progressive neoliberalism," she writes, "superficially articulates immigrants, people of color, Muslims, LGTBIQ as the 'we' and turns the white man into a 'them.' This is a horrible way of dividing us, a form that only benefits capital." According to Fraser, it is precisely this "superficial" articulation that Sanders tried to contest: "For Sanders, the idea was to mix an anti-racist, anti-sexist and pro-immigrant 'recognition policy' alongside a 'distributive' anti–Wall Street policy in favor of the working-class." What I want to challenge is Fraser's consideration that Laclau's populism proposes a different type of articulation. In her words, "I feel much closer to someone like Ernesto Laclau, who saw populism as a logic that could be articulated in many different ways." I want to debate this notion precisely by taking seriously a problem that Fraser herself raises in thinking about the radical left: how an "effective critique of financialization" is combined with an "anti-racist, anti-sexist, and anti-hierarchical vision of emancipation."

There are two points to make here. First, Laclau's notion of "populist reason" disregards any "destituent" effect originating from the social dynamic "from below" that is not inscribed in "demands" that are acceptable to the political system,[24] discrediting any force of overflow that makes it necessary to rethink (as frequently happens) the game of the political institution in terms of the common-multiple.[25] Second, progressive populisms abrogate any effective critique of financialization. In both dimensions, once again, a division and hierarchization are at work between the so-called social and political, where the instance of representation of the political system functions as a moment of "truth" for struggles that supposedly do not achieve their own political agency and thus are permanently infantilized.

Contending with Fraser's reference to populist articulation is fundamental today if we are to understand the types of assumptions that are in tension within the collective formulation of the call for a "feminism for the 99 percent" made in the United States.[26] On the one hand, this formulation is very interesting because it directly opposes corporate ("lean-in") feminism; on the other hand, two lines are problematically inscribed within it: a *populist articulation* and an *intersectionality of struggles*. This premise opens up a discussion about the political practice itself through which a feminism of the majority is produced.

If there is a possibility of rethinking the category of "popular sovereignty" (to take up Brown's term), it is indeed within the feminist register: that is, to make the distinction between "the popular" and "populism." From this point of view, we can also interpret the tension that inheres in a "feminism for the 99 percent," as Fraser discusses.[27]

The mass feminism practiced and theorized in Argentina fundamentally differs from a populism based on an abstract notion of the people. It does so, first, because it does not suggest an equivalence between political desire and personal leadership condensed in a presidential figure (the condensation of Laclau's theory). Second, our movement takes responsibility for changing the material living conditions of the majorities, where the dynamics of dispossession and financialization have transversally upset the thresholds of violence in social relations. Third, it distinguishes itself by creating space for political composition based on a feminist diagnosis of the crisis, simultaneously projecting a practical internationalism and thus defying the methodological nationalism of populism. And lastly, this mass feminism concretely generates a new sovereign dynamic (not confined to the rhetoric of the nation-state), forming and sustaining new spaces for the production of political decisions and creating the conditions to make those decisions operative.

I am speaking of an assembly-based dynamic that turned the international feminist strike into a process and converted that collective action into a common plane and organizational horizon. The dynamic of the assembly was maintained between the 2017 and 2018 strikes, not only as a preparatory and organizational apparatus with a predetermined goal, but also as a mode of mapping social conflict (layoffs and Mapuche land struggles, to name a few) and of reactivating the democratic, everyday practices of organizations (unions; political, educational, and cultural organizations; etc.) that produce new images of anti-neoliberal popular sovereignty in practice. These are intermittent and fragile sovereign forms, yet they are persistent and capable of producing new forms of power from below. This dynamic puts a body—a body that is extensive, a body-territory—to the question asked by high philosophy today: What does political action mean in conditions of extreme neoliberalism?

Like the formulation of "feminism for the 99 percent," the "feminism of the masses" confirms that the feminism that is emerging is newly expansive. On this point, the mobilizations in Argentina—including the growth in organization from one strike to another, in relation to the internationalist web in which the movement unfolds—brings together the relation between the mass scale and vectors of minoritarian struggles in a new way. By this I mean that we have enacted a shift from the neoliberal language of *recognition* of minorities, to now submerge the vectors (and not the identities) of struggles that were long qualified as minoritarian, accounting for the protagonism of their "difference" on a mass scale.

Now, this massiveness foregrounds the question of the *transversality* of political composition, that which makes its anti-neoliberal character effective. Here there is not naivete, nor is there restitution of the depoliticized character of the "social" as an infantilized stage of political representation. Massiveness, then, is inscribed in a popular horizon, and even a popular-community horizon, because it is what allows feminism to connect with social conflict (as opposed to its populist abstraction), and because it allows us to understand the web of violence that enables neoliberalism to persist.

Chapter 7

Counteroffensive:
The Specter of Feminism

We are experiencing a counteroffensive: that is, a reaction to the force deployed by feminist movements. It is important to emphasize the precise sequence: the counteroffensive *responds* to an offensive, a *prior* movement. In other words, the resurgence of feminisms precedes a later fascist turn in the region and at the global level. This has two implications. First, in methodological terms, it means starting from the force of feminism, *as a constituent force*. Second, in political terms, it means affirming that feminisms are a threat to the established power, activating a *dynamic of disobedience* that reactionary forces attempt to contain, counteracting it with repression, discipline, and control at various scales. The counteroffensive is a call to order, one whose aggressiveness can be measured in relation to the perception of threat to which it is responding. Therefore, the ferocious counteroffensive that has been unleashed against feminism provides us with a counter-reading of the force of insubordination that has been perceived as already happening and, at the same time, as a possibility of radicalization.

Feminism has been constructed as the new "internal enemy" that endangers the family, sexual, moral, and political order. Statements from heads of state and church officials, direct provision of economic and repressive resources for fighting feminist demands, and the attempt to construct a counter "movement" (for example, in mobilizations against abortion rights) shape the contours of this counteroffensive. Let's look at each of these in more detail and then return to a characterization of what is defined as a "threat," since that will allow us to understand why different powers seek to conjure feminism as a threatening specter.

The Ecclesiastic Counteroffensive

The concept of "gender ideology" synthesizes an authentic crusade led by the Catholic Church today against what it considers feminist destabilization of the family and traditional gender roles. "Gender ideology is a discursive strategy devised by the Vatican and adopted by numerous Catholic and Christian intellectuals and activists to counterattack the rhetoric of equality for women and LGBTI people," argues anthropologist Mara Viveros Vigoya.[1] Sociologist Éric Fassin points out that the attack on the term *gender* by North American Catholic and right-wing groups began openly in the mid 1990s in connection to the 1994 UN International Conference on Population and Development, held in Cairo, and during the preparatory meetings for the UN World Conference on Women, which were held in New York in 1995.[2] Several chronicles consider the Vatican's most active lobbyist during this period to be Dale O'Leary, a conservative North American Catholic journalist who developed this argument in her 1997 book *The Gender Agenda*. There she argued that gender was presented as "a neocolonial tool of an international feminist conspiracy." According to legal scholar Mary Anne Case,[3] the attack first emerged against laws and policies, and later focused on theory, singling out Judith Butler as the "pope of gender."[4]

Joseph Ratzinger, before he was anointed as Pope Benedict XVI, had pursued such an attack in doctrinal terms as far back as the 1980s, when he was head of the Congregation for the Doctrine of the Faith. His arguments against "gender ideology" were perhaps best crystallized in his 1997 book *Salt of the Earth* and were further developed in a series of ecclesiastic documents and publications that, starting in 2003, systematically took on the question of gender, which Ratzinger himself made a focal point for the Vatican following his election in 2005. These texts sustain campaigns driven from above, as Brazilian researcher Sonia Corrêa argues: "They have not been developed from the base of our societies, but rather in the top spheres of international negotiations and theological reflection."[5]

One of the most emblematic texts of this crusade is *Lexicon: Ambiguous and Debatable Terms regarding Family Life and Ethical Questions*.[6] In the book's preface, the cardinal and president of the Pontifical Council for the Family, Alfonso López Trujillo, expresses his fear over the ambiguity of contemporary language, recalling the relation between language, authenticity, and truth in Heidegger. For that reason, he postulates the need for this lexicon. The lexicon itself lists seventy-eight terms with the greatest danger of slippage, in which the concern over meaninglessness and the slippery "ambiguity" that we must battle is concentrated. They are, in short, words that must be rectified. Here he dedicates a special aside to the use of "gender" as a concept installed by the UN's Beijing Conference on Women. He argues: "The family and life are being literally bombarded by a deceptive language that does not encourage but complicates dialogue between individuals and peoples." He also denounces the concept of discrimination against women sustained by the CEDAW (Convention on the Elimination of All Forms of Discrimination against Women), along with debates about abortion, free love, the idea of rights, and so on. The entry on gender in the *Lexicon* was written by the German Catholic theologian Jutta Burggraf. She outlines the coordinates of the discussion to point to Butler as responsible for decoupling biological sex from the "cultural" category of gender and for enabling its indiscriminate proliferation. As she also argues in many other ecclesiastic texts, Burggraf shows concern for the reception of the word "gender" by international organizations such as the UN and the resources implicated by those agencies. But what I am most interested in highlighting is the affinity that she traces between gender ideology and an "individualist anthropology of radical neoliberalism."

Before Butler, the theoretical lineage described in these sorts of publications goes back to Friedrich Engels and Simone de Beauvoir. In particular, however, the precedents to "gender ideology" are traced to the theorizations of the Frankfurt School in the 1930s and, especially, to the way its concepts were disseminated in the revolts of the radical movements of the 1960s. The "cultural Marxism" of the Frankfurt School would be the enemy of Western Christianity. These sorts of diatribes are familiar to us in Latin America; the same arguments were advanced by the dictatorships against political radicalization in the 1970s, at that time directed particularly toward the guerrilla but also more broadly at any countercultural expression. Now the conversion of the vocabulary of gender into an anathema, into a curse, re-creates and updates a whole fable of the threat to Christian and Western civilization, but with an added dimension: it also underscores feminism's capacity for ideological "transversality" and, therefore, its capacity to spread beyond what is recognizable as "the left." Case argues:

> Over the course of the same half century, the Vatican and those operating under its influence around the world came to view the English word "gender" as anathema and to associate the word with what it terms an "ideology of gender" it sees as linking feminism and gay rights in a worldwide effort to redefine, not only secular laws governing the sexes, sexuality, reproduction, and the family, but human nature itself.[7]

The dispute is enormous. According to the Catholic Church, human nature itself is at stake because of the questioning of the gender binary, which constitutes the basic building blocks of heteronormative reproduction and the family. Therefore, in that crusade, trans identities and bodies, as well as reproductive technologies, also take on increasing importance. Both issues are represented as an advanced stage of "gender ideology," the consecration of the decoupling of sex from gender and, therefore, a threat to the Christian anthropological-theological theory of the complementarity between the male and the female. To summarize it in the words of researchers Sarah Bracke and David Paternotte: "The Vatican considers the analytical notion of gender as a threat to Divine Creation."[8] The notion of gender then usurps—and therefore threatens—the divine power of creation. Creating diverse genders—or "troubling gender," to play with Butler's most famous title—appears, to the church, as a direct dispute with God. It is striking how some arguments, following that same reasoning, speak of defending "sexual difference," but, of course, in relation to the precise framework of binarism. Understood this way, "sexual difference" would be annulled by a sort of equality extremism that would make roles, identities, and even natures malleable and interchangeable. The question of the unregulated difference of the binary mandate, understood as a "divine" mandate, opens up the potencia of gender variation as a human attribution.

Why do they characterize gender as an "ideology"? According to those ecclesiastic texts, the gender question has a latent capacity throughout all social spheres and is particularly skilled at "concealment," in order to promote the objectives of social dissolution with greater efficacy. That is how Juan Varela summarizes it in a document of the Spanish Evangelical Alliance titled "Origin and Development of Gender Ideology: Theological Foundations of Marriage and the Family." He argues:

> Within this confabulation of factors, we highlight the astute conversion of gender ideology as a sort of Marxist vindication, whose origin in communist ideology is denied, disguising it to

convert it into a transversal question, in such a way that without any apparent type of politically defined ideology it encompasses and cuts across all political spectrums and colors, driven additionally by women's victimization, defense of human rights, freedom of expression, and the inclusion of the most socially disadvantaged groups, elements with which any party which seeks to be "politically correct" must align itself with.[9]

With that characterization, the campaign against gender ideology had to expand its spokespeople, beyond cassock wearers. It must be remembered, for example, that even the former president of Ecuador and oft-vaunted "progressive" figure of the so-called pink tide, Rafael Correa, spoke of the threat of "gender ideology" on his public television programs.

In 2017, researchers Roman Patternotte and David Kuhar compiled the volume *Anti-gender Campaigns in Europe: Mobilizing against Equality*.[10] They ask a fundamental question: How has a theoretical concept been translated into religious discourse and, especially, how do those discourses then go on to convene mobilizations at the global level? They explore the question in the European context, of its intersection with nationalism and right-wing forms of populism. With the same concern about its political articulation with the right, feminist scholars Agnieszka Graff and Elżbieta Korolczuk use the Polish case to demonstrate how the right-wing attack on "gender" identifies those who propagate the "ideology" as liberals and members of the elite. Meanwhile, the religious crusade claims to defend the working classes, who are supposedly naturally conservative due to their condition as "victims" of globalization.[11] Graff and Korolczuk argue that "'Genderists' are viewed as well-funded and well-connected to global elites; common people are viewed as paying the price of globalization." The association between neoliberalism and gender is insisted upon through several means, preparing the terrain to argue—as we will see in relation to the Argentinian debate—that anti-neoliberalism can only come from the conservation of "family values" and work discipline to which they are intimately associated. In the case of Argentina, researchers Mario Pecheny, Daniel Jones, and Lucía Ariza say that up until 2016, the vocabulary of "gender ideology" was not widely used:

> The expression "gender ideology" occupies a relatively marginal place in the discursive field framed by the religious actors who oppose sexual and reproductive rights. Theirs are usually isolated voices, coming mainly from intellectuals who are part of a minority ultra-conservative stream within the Argentine Catholic Church, and whose public interventions do not have major repercussions on public discourse by the ecclesial hierarchy or on wider societal debates.[12]

One of its Argentine spokesmen, however, boasts of being at the vanguard of this theorization. The Catholic lawyer Jorge Scala, from the city of Córdoba, published a remarkably successful book in 2010 entitled *La Ideología de Género: O, el Género como Herramienta de Poder* (Gender ideology: or, gender as a tool of power) (the book has already seen more than ten editions in Spain). Its main argument is that "gender ideology seeks to impose itself in a totalitarian way, through the exercise of absolute power, especially at the supranational level—and from there to spread to different peoples and nations—by controlling the means of propaganda and cultural elaboration." He claims to detect three paths through which "gender ideology" is propagated: the formal education system, the media, and human rights. He defines the "totalitarian" as a closed system, a system of a "global brainwashing." "An ideology is a doctrinal body that is coherent and closed upon itself—in the style of mathematics—from which, upon entering the system of thought, one cannot escape," he clarifies. In 2012, the book was translated into Portuguese and published in Brazil. In March 2013, before the Argentinian cardinal Jorge Mario Bergoglio's consecration as Pope Francis, Scala wrote:

> There is a coincidence that seems particularly important to me: on March 13, 2012, the Supreme Court of Justice of the Republic of Argentina issued an unfair ruling seeking to legalize abortion on request in that country. Exactly one year later, on March 13, 2013, the College of Cardinals elevates the Cardinal Primate of Argentina to the See of Peter. It is like a caress from the Holy Spirit.[13]

According to Mary Anne Case, the two popes who have embodied "the Vatican's war against gender ideology" are Benedict XVI and Francis. Their origins from Germany and Argentina do not go unnoticed:

> In ways not previously analyzed, Ratzinger seems to have been reacting directly to then-recent events in Germany, including, on the one hand, the presence of books by feminists highlighting the social construction of gender roles (e.g., Scheu 1977; Beauvoir and Schwarzer 1983) on local best-seller lists and, on the other hand, the constitutionally mandated German federal legislation guaranteeing individuals an opportunity legally to change their sex. Trans rights claims were, together with feminist claims, thus a foundational component, not a recent addition, to the Vatican's sphere of concern around "gender" and to the focusing of that concern on developments in secular law. Just as Ratzinger may have carried his memory of events in Germany with him to Rome, so Jorge Mario Bergoglio, as he traveled to Rome in 2013 to become Pope Francis, left behind an Argentina that had only the year before passed, with opposition from Bergoglio but none within the legislature, a law on gender identity that is among the most generous in the world toward people who wish legally to change their sex.[14]

In Case's analysis, however, what Francis synthesizes is having found a tactical twist to the dispute: with the Argentine pope, "gender ideology" becomes associated with a "colonizing ideology," driven by nongovernmental organizations and international agencies. In this way, the pope who comes from the "Third World" mobilizes a pseudo-anti-imperialist rhetoric in the battle against the rights of women and LGTBQ+ people.

Case credits Francis with a second achievement: successfully uniting different creeds (especially Evangelicals and Mormons) in the crusade against "gender ideology," brought together by the spread of the "threat." The Evangelical proliferation is not in competition with the Catholic Church; rather, the two reinforce each other and find "unity" against a common enemy.

It is over the past few years that the ecclesiastic doctrine has turned into a multi-use hashtag and mobilization tool for disputing in the streets: #NoALaIdeologíaDeGénero (#NoTo GenderIdeology). The March 4, 2017, protest in Peru of the collective Con Mis Hijos No Te Metas (Don't mess with my children) is exemplary in this regard. "Gender ideology," in this case, would refer to the content of a new school curriculum that incorporates notions such as "gender equality" and "gender identity," which, according to the protesters, would promote "homosexuality and sexual debauchery in school children." In Argentina, we can point to the offensive against National Law 26.150, which creates the right to comprehensive sexual education from the beginning of schooling, a law defended by organizations that popularized the slogan "La educación es una causa feminista" (Education is a feminist cause) and included age-appropriate discussions of consent, abuse, sexual difference, and desire. Meanwhile, Monsignor Aguer (the archbishop of La Plata) declared that "the increase in femicides has to do with the disappearance of marriage."[15] This was the same Aguer who had already stated in 2009, in regard to comprehensive sexual education, that "feminist thought is hegemonic there." In Colombia, the attack on "gender ideology" played a key role in the campaign that incited the "gender threat" in favor of the triumph of the *no* vote to the Havana peace accords in 2016. Sonia Corrêa draws up a balance sheet of these struggles across Latin America:

> At the beginning of 2017, anti-gender campaigns took off in the context of the Constitutional Reform of the Federal District of Mexico and shortly after an "anti-gender" bus began circulating all around the country. Two months later that same bus was traveling around Chile, right after the final vote to reform the law that changed the prohibition of the termination of pregnancy put in place by the Pinochet regime in the 1980s. There was also a campaign against "gender ideology" in the public education curriculum in Uruguay, a country known for its secularism. In Ecuador, a legal disposition that tried to limit gender violence was attacked by conservative anti-gender religious groups. The Bolivian Constitutional Court overturned the recently approved gender identity law, arguing that a person's dignity is founded on the sexual binary of the human.[16]

2019 opened with the debut of right-wing extremist Jair Bolsonaro's mandate in Brazil, whose first presidential speech referenced the combat against "gender ideology."[17] A few weeks later, the young businessman Nayib Bukele won the presidency in El Salvador under the same banner. The war of the twenty-first century is thus being fought on multiple fronts. There is a red thread among these contexts—a struggle and war between reaction and autonomy—but its precise framing mutates according to the local situation, according to the construction of the landscape of the neo-fascist turn in the region.

It is impossible to understand this becoming-slogan of the mobilization of the fundamentalist religious crusade—that is, its fabrication as a "social movement"—without taking into account the rise of the mass and radical feminisms that I have been narrating and to which this crusade is reacting.

In Argentina, there is a tipping point: it is the "green tide" in favor of the legalization of abortion that, throughout 2018, flooded the streets and spread its impact around the world.

As I argued in Chapter 3, the broadening of the debate over abortion—in terms of sovereignty, autonomy, and class, its militant radicalization by new generations, and the political projection of its demands in the feminist atmosphere—unleashed a new virulence in the ecclesiastic counteroffensive. We saw a series of street protests in which sky-blue handkerchiefs were waved, against the green of abortion rights, phrases in defense of "the two lives," and calls to hatred in religious schools and pulpits. But above all, there has been an inflamed militancy in hospitals, in courts, and in the media against abortion. This culminated in 2019, in the aberration of cases of eleven- and twelve-year-old girls in the provinces of Jujuy and Tucumán who had been raped and were denied abortions. The rape and forced maternity of minors was then vindicated in an editorial in the country's principle newspaper, *La Nación*.[18]

Political spirituality

Michel Foucault uses the notion of "political spirituality" in a posthumously published interview with Farès Sassine.[19] Following an accident, Foucault spent several weeks during the summer prior to the 1978 Iranian Revolution recuperating and reading *The Principle of Hope* by Ernst Bloch, which includes his descriptions of a teleological hope as an engine of social and political transformations in Europe in the sixteenth and seventeenth centuries. The possibility of a hope oriented by a teleology typical of a certain spirituality, on the one hand, and the uprising as a form of social and political transformation of a present situation, on the other, share a certain political *potencia*. Foucault believes he detects a theoretical (and "anti"-strategic) wager from the Iranians he meets on his travels. An effort to trace the magnitude of this "political spirituality" was a focus of his interest that led him not so much to pledge his fidelity the Iranian Revolution—he affirms, there at least, his "skepticism"—but rather recommits him to some suspicion of a Western, and particularly French, position that ruled out the revolutionary potentiality of a "political spirituality" in action.[20]

Feminism speaks of bodies at the same time that it contests the meaning of political spirituality. As a multiform movement, feminism disputes the prevailing understanding of bodily sovereignty and of feminized bodies in terms of their differentiated hierarchy. They are bodies that were historically declared non-sovereign, sentenced as incapable of deciding for themselves—that is, designated as bodies under guardianship or tutelage. For feminism, it is a political spirituality precisely because it does not separate the body from the spirit, nor flesh from fantasies, nor skin from ideas. There is a mystical dimension to feminism (as a multifaceted movement). It works from affects and passions. It opens that thorny field of desire, of relationships of love, of erotic swarms, of ritual and celebration, of longings beyond their sanctioned borders. Feminism, unlike other politics that are considered leftist, does not deprive bodies of their indeterminacy, of their not-knowing, of their embodied dreaming, of their dark potencia. And therefore, it operates on the field of the pliable, the fragile, while at the same time mobilizing the plane of spirituality.

Feminism does not believe there is an opium of the people; it believes, to the contrary, that spirituality is a force of rebellion. Feminism holds that the gesture of rebellion is inexplicable and, at the same time, the only rationality that liberates us. And it liberates us without requiring that we be turned into pure, heroic, or even good subjects.

The church has always understood this. We can refer once again to Silvia Federici's classic *Caliban and the Witch* to remember why the burning of witches, heretics, and healers was used to discredit feminine knowledge about bodies and to terrorize its healing effervescence, its strength as a technology of friendship between women.[21] We could also turn to the even more classic *Witches, Midwives, and Nurses: A History of*

Women Healers by Barbara Ehrenreich and Deirdre English.[22] There, they analyze the fifteenth-century witch-burning guide *Malleus Maleficarum*, which that assured, "Nothing does more harm to the Catholic Church than midwives," who of course are also the abortionists.

Today we see a battle for political spirituality in the streets, in homes, in bedrooms, and in schools (which, as a mass movement, dyes everything green, as a principle of hope). Once again, the Catholic Church, through its male representatives and spokespeople, feels that it has a mission to complete, that its task is the salvation of souls, which is translated into a war for monopoly of tutelage over feminine bodies. Pope Francis plays a special role in this crusade due to his connection to various social movements in Argentina.

The church of the "poor"

This dispute over bodies takes on a particular intensity when it comes to battles over the exercise of tutelage and guardianship over "poor" women.[23] This happens precisely in the moment in which feminism is gaining strength in working-class neighborhoods, often starting with the youth but, at the same time, through a new alliance between mothers and children. This is reinforced by the ongoing debate in Argentina, which emphasizes the class-based differential of risks that abortion implies. As a young woman from the organization Orilleres de la Villa 21–24 y Zavaleta (Poor people of Villa 21–24 and Zavaleta) declared in Congress: "In our neighborhoods, there are interventions by institutions such as the churches that are responsible for moralizing our bodies, our decisions, and that operate so that we women do not have access to legal abortion. Without rights over our bodies and our lives, we are condemned to continue being violated."[24]

A few days before, a well-known priest from the villa slum had insisted on saying that abortion is not a working-class demand. He argued that "the IMF is abortion" (the title under which his speech circulated in the media), claiming that the demand for abortion is an imposition from the global North, much like the International Monetary Fund's austerity measures. With this, the church seeks to establish women's self-determination, the right to decide over our bodies, as a neoliberal issue, which is only of interest to the elites and disconnected from working-class concerns. *They ignore and falsify both the historical struggles for abortion and the current state of the feminist movement, where the demand is associated with the desire for a dignified life against neoliberal austerity, and in whose amalgam pañuelazos* (protests waving the green handkerchiefs) *were carried out in many neighborhoods and slums.*

In their pretension to be seen as the only anti-liberals, the church spokesmen direct their argument particularly at "poor women": those whom they feel a particular compulsion to direct, whose decision-making ability they take away in the name of their social condition, whom they only make visible as resistant if they are mothers. In this way, the trap that they lay claims to be "class-based," but in reality it is precisely the opposite: they attempt to draw a class distinction that would justify the idea that poor women have no other choice than to be poor and Catholic, because maternity is their only option. In this way, they attempt to reduce abortion (that is, a decision about desire, maternity, and one's own life) to an eccentric gesture of the middle and upper classes who clearly have different economic resources. The "class-based" argument, which of course exists in terms of differentiated possibilities of access to a safe abortion, is reversed: it becomes a justification for its clandestine condition. The right to decide, for the church, must therefore be kept away from popular neighborhoods. This crusade to infantilize "poor" women is the spearhead, because if it is disarmed, the church itself will be left without any "faithful." What is most brutal is how, to sustain this, they have to turn a deaf ear to—ignore and deny—what the women of the slums themselves and the organizations who work with them are saying. Even when those women emphatically insist on using the slogan "Stop speaking for us."

It is clear that the church, through its male spokespeople, does not want to stop legislating over women's bodies, and that it sees the feminist movement as a direct threat to its power, built upon control of feminized bodies and spiritualities. Indeed, it is a form of control over life and modes of life (a whole war unfolds over the very meaning of "life") that are at stake in making spirituality into a synonym of obedience and renewed forms of guardianship.

With considerable effort and urgency, the church has tried to create a vision of feminism and neoliberalism as indissoluble. For example, the church does this by arguing that abortion is synonymous with "throwaway culture." But it is precisely an anti-neoliberal feminism, which has been gaining strength in recent years, that shows the falsity of that argument from the ecclesiastic institution.

The Moral *and* Economic Counteroffensive

At its core, this is a dispute over the meaning of neoliberalism and the shape of a meaningful opposition to it. Additionally, it is a debate that asks what the well-worn concept of "the popular" implies in its strategic capacity to construct a critique of and an alternative to neoliberalism. That is the heart of the debate. The critique of the concept of "gender ideology" proposes that neoliberalism must be combated through a return to the family, to disciplined work as the only source of dignity, and to forced maternity as the reassurance of women's place.

For the church along with other allied forces, both progressive and conservative, neoliberalism is thus defined as a form of politics and a mode of subjectivation that involves the pure disintegration of the family and labor order, that is, of the patriarchal order. The fact that this order is patriarchal, of course, is not problematized. We arrive at a sort of contradictory logic: Can an anti-neoliberal politics be based on a patriarchal order whose biologistic and colonial structure is indisputable? This is precisely what feminism, in its diversification and massive radicalization, has made clear: there can be no neoliberal capitalism without the patriarchal and colonial order.

Pope Francis's doctrine attempts to make the argument that "gender ideology" is "colonial" and "liberal." But it seems paradoxical that the institution that owes its foundations in our hemisphere to the bloodiest iteration of colonialism would deploy an "anti-colonial" discourse. It seems paradoxical that in a moment when the Catholic Church hierarchy faces denunciations of sexual abuse of minors by its own members, it would take up the banner of anti-neoliberalism, of a miserabilist and patriarchal type, from above, in order to point to feminism as the internal enemy. And it seems paradoxical that in a moment in which the "colonial unconscious," as Suely Rolnik calls it, or the "decolonizing practices" of which Silvia Rivera Cusicanqui speaks, have found an enormous space of problematization and resonance in feminisms, the Roman Catholic Apostolic Church wants to present itself as anti-colonial.

How is the ecclesiastic counteroffensive articulated with the economic counteroffensive? The economic adjustment measures in recent years, which are translated into inflation and rate increases for basic services, and into layoffs and cuts to public services, especially impact women and, in a more generalized way, feminized economies. Those economies absorb the costs of austerity measures, building community infrastructure with dwindling resources and women's extra labor.

Many women from social organizations already confess to skipping meals in order to feed their own children. Technically, this is called "food insecurity." Politically, it shows how women put their bodies on the line in a differential way, in the face of crisis. This is reinforced by the bankarization of food through "food cards" (part of the compulsory bankarization of social aid over the last decade, which I described in Chapter 4) that are only redeemable in certain businesses and that are tied to the speculation that some supermarkets engage in when setting prices. The specter of "looting" of food businesses is incited as a threat of repression, motivating the persecution of protests in name of "security."

Confinement, debt, and biology

The economic counteroffensive demonstrates a fundamental feature of contemporary neoliberalism: the deepening of the crisis of social reproduction that is sustained by an increase in feminized labor that replaces public infrastructure and is implicated in dynamics of super-exploitation. The privatization of public services, or the restriction of their scope, means that those tasks (be they health, care, food, or otherwise) must be supplemented by women and feminized bodies as non-remunerated and mandatory tasks. This reproductive crisis is taken advantage of by conservative forces to discipline and moralize certain bodies and their behaviors. Here, the basis of a convergence between neoliberalism and conservativism becomes clear.

As Melinda Cooper argues, we need to locate the moments when neoliberalism, in order to justify its structural adjustment policies, revives the tradition of private family responsibility and does so in the name of "domestic debt."[25] Putting households into debt is part of its call for neoliberal responsibilization, but at the same time it reinforces the conservative goal of folding social reproduction into the confines of the cisheteropatriarchal household.

Confinement, debt, and biology: that is the formula of the neoliberal–conservative alliance. It is the strategic reinvention of family responsibility in the face of the looting of public infrastructure that enables this more profound convergence between neoliberals and conservatives. ,

We see this clearly in the ways the economic counteroffensive is also a *moralizing counteroffensive*. It draws its strength from accelerated impoverishment that expands through the financialization of family economies, in which the poorest sectors (and now, not only those sectors) go into debt to pay for food and medicine and to finance payment for basic services through installment plans with exorbitant interest rates. If everyday subsistence on its own generates debt, what we see are seeing is an intensive and extensive form of exploitation that, as I analyzed in Chapter 4, uses feminized popular economies as its laboratory.

Yet the conservative element adds a new twist. On one hand, by encouraging women to meet the work requirement for social assistance with family demands, deploying a logic of care and responsibility, it reinforces ideas about women's traditional roles and positions. On the other hand, it makes it so that churches are today the privileged channels for the redistribution of resources, fomenting the church's social and economic power in peripheral neighborhoods. Thus it consolidates a structure of obedience that operates over the everyday and the future, forcing people to individually and privately take responsibility for the costs of austerity, and to receive moral conditions in exchange for scarce resources.

That is why the economic counteroffensive can be characterized as financial terror: because it unfolds as an everyday "counterrevolution."[26] It does so in two ways: first, it tries to make us desire stability at any cost; and second, it operates over the fabric of the day to day, precisely that space which feminisms have opened up to questioning because it is where all forms of obedience are micropolitically structured.

It is not a coincidence, then, that political activists close to the Vatican attempt to construct a false antagonism between feminism and hunger, arguing that feminism is at best a distraction from, and at worst directly antithetical to, anti-hunger activism. Once again, they infantilize feminism as a trivial and middle-class politics, especially as compared to the popular urgency of hunger.

Of course, it is the opposite that is true: there is no opposition between the urgency of hunger caused by the crisis and a feminist politics. It is the feminist movement, in all its diversity, that has politicized, in a new and radical way, the crisis of social reproduction as both a civilizational crisis and a crisis of the patriarchal structure of society. The state responds to that crisis with targeted social assistance (the favored form of neoliberal state intervention) that seeks to reinforce a hierarchy of who deserves aid, based on women's obligations according to their roles in the patriarchal family: having children, caring for them, educating them, vaccinating them.

What the religious counteroffensive cannot bear is that in confronting hunger, one also defies the patriarchal mandate to reproduce the family norm, domestic confinement, and the obligation to give birth. The religious counteroffensive thus seeks to use the economic counteroffensive as an opportunity to exchange the image of the popular for the conservative, and that of the conservative for the genuine; in so doing, it creates an idea of the "anti-neoliberal" that does nothing other than obscure the alliance between neoliberalism and conservativism that we see today in the regional and global neofascist turn.

The feminist movement grows within diverse organizations and therefore is present in the most defiant movements of the current moment. That is what allows it to produce non-fascist diagnoses of the crisis of social reproduction. Hunger is not defined by biology. Women heads of households take their pots onto the streets, cooking collective meals in a public display of defiance, and put their bodies on the line to denounce austerity, inflation, and debt. Young women and girls living on the street discuss the specific forms of violence of illegal economies.

Incarcerated women, trans and non-binary people denounce the prison machine as a privileged site of humiliation. In order to sustain the false antagonism between feminism and hunger, it is necessary to ignore these powerful places of enunciation.

But there is another element to the current link between neoliberalism and conservatism. Why are they amalgamated into economies of obedience driven by religious morality and financial morality? Why does this alliance find a parallel, and at the same time an exploitable flow of arms and money, in illegal economies (as I discussed in Chapter 4)?

We can turn to an earlier question that Luci Cavallero and I have developed in our elaboration of a feminist reading of debt:[27] What happens when workers' morality is not produced in the factory and through the habits of discipline tied to repetitive mechanical work? How does debt function as an apparatus of moralization that replaces that factory discipline? How does moralization operate over a flexible, precarious, and, from a certain point of view, undisciplined labor force? What does debt as an economy of obedience have to do with the crisis of the heteropatriarchal family? What type of moral education is necessary for indebted and precarious youth?

As Cavallero and I wrote:

> We do not think it is a coincidence that they seek to impose financial education in schools at the same time as they reject the implementation of Comprehensive Sexual Education (ESI), which means budget cuts, its outsourcing to religious NGOs, and in its restriction to a preventative norm. The ESI is limited and redirected to restrict its capacity to open up imaginaries and legitimize practices of relations and desires, beyond the heteronormative family. Combating it in the name of #Don'tMessWithMyChildren (#ConMisHijosNoTeMetas) is a "crusade" for the remoralization of youth, while they seek to complement it with "financial education from an early age."[28]

The ecclesiastic response to the economic counteroffensive is to fortify the work of reproduction in the family, reinforcing obedience in exchange for resources, the depoliticization of feminist networks for confronting hunger and destructuring families as the norm, and an attempt to remoralize desire. The economic response to the religious counteroffensive has been to unify debtor morality with family morality.

The Military Counteroffensive

In recent years, there has been a notable uptick in the assassination of women territorial leaders, the criminalization of the struggles of Indigenous communities, and the legal persecution and selective repression of protests. The assassination of Brazilian human rights activist and politician Marielle Franco in 2018 is one of many examples that points to the targeting of Black women and sexual dissidents as the new and principle "enemy."

There is another piece of information that must be connected to the above: the increase in femicides by personnel from the security forces. What is verified is precisely the intersection of femicidal, state, and institutional forms of violence, but also their ramifications in para-state repressive dynamics that handle arms obtained from the state. As the anti-repression organization CORREPI explains in its 2019 report:

> What is notable is the increase in cases of femicide and relational femicides [cases in which the aggressor not only kills the woman but also other family members] committed by members of the security forces, especially in recent years, which led us to compare our data with the general statistics on femicides. We estimate, based on existing records at the national level, that until the end of 2018, one in five women murdered in a context of gendered violence was the victim of state violence, usually

embodied in the service weapon. But in 2019, that 20 percent increased to almost 30 percent, since of the first 15 femicides of the month of January, four were committed by members of the repressive state apparatus. This demonstrates how when repressive state violence and sexist and patriarchal violence intersect one another, they are enhanced.[29]

The deregulation of weapons and the fight against "gender ideology," two of Bolsonaro's first declarations after taking office, suggest an intimate relationship between punishment and state terror.

Then, how can the current alliance between neoliberalism and neo-fascism be explained? For one, contemporary fascism is a politics that constructs an "internal" enemy. That internal enemy is embodied by those who have historically been considered strangers in the "public" sphere of politics. Today, the internal enemies to which fascism points are the feminist movement (in all its diversity) and migrants, as subjects that are also feminized. Contemporary fascism detects and responds to our force as a feminist, anti-racist, anti-biologistic, anti-neoliberal, and, therefore, anti-patriarchal movement.

The aggressiveness of contemporary fascism, however, should not distract us from another important point: it expresses an attempt to stabilize neoliberalism's continuous crisis of political legitimacy. That crisis is being produced by the deployment of forces by the transnational and pluri-national feminist movement, which is currently inventing a radical mass politics precisely on the basis of to its ability to weave unexpected alliances that concretely put in practice its anti-capitalist, anti-colonial, and anti-patriarchal character. Those alliances, as a political fabric patiently constructed in temporalities and spaces that do not tend to be recognized as strategic, formulate a new strategy of insurrection among those who have historically been considered noncitizens of the world.

I want to end with a question recently put forth by Judith Butler, because it allows us to situate the investigation that lies ahead of us even more precisely: "So can we now ask how the anti-gender-ideology movement is part of fascism, whether we can say that it shares some attributes, it contributes to emerging fascisms, or that it is in some sense symptomatic of new fascism?"[30]

Chapter 8

Eight Theses on the Feminist Revolution

Let the Chicago Boys tremble. Long live the feminist movement.
Graffiti in front of the Catholic University of Chile, 2018

In what sense does the contemporary feminist movement—in the multiplicity of struggles that it participates in and leads today—express an opposition to neoliberalism from below? How does the movement initiate political forms that, while bearing the traces of discontinuous temporalities and longer genealogies of struggle, are nevertheless something radically new? I want to propose eight theses about that novelty.

1. **The feminist strike is a tool that maps new forms of the exploitation of bodies and territories, with the aim of making such an exploitation visible and insubordination to it formidable. The strike reveals the diverse composition of labor in a feminist register, by recognizing historically disregarded tasks, by showing its current imbrication with generalized precarious conditions, and by appropriating a traditional tool of struggle to reinvent what it means to strike.**

The international strike opened up a feminist perspective on labor. Because the feminist perspective recognizes territorial, domestic, reproductive, and migrant labor, it broadens the very notion of the working class, from below. It starts from the recognition that 40 percent of the workers in our country are involved in diverse modes of the so-called informal economy, vindicated as the popular economy. Because it makes visible and values work that has historically been ignored and devalued, it affirms that #AllWomenAreWorkers.

We could take this further and say that the strike opens up a whole program for collective research. What do we call labor from the perspective of the living and working experiences of women, lesbians, trans people, and travestis? When our movement faces the question of what it means to go on strike from reproductive labor, we are, in a practical way, mapping the multiplicity of tasks we take on, the intensive and extensive working days that are not paid, or are badly paid, or are remunerated in a way that always expresses the hierarchy of the sexual division of labor. Some of those tasks have gone almost unrecognized as work; others have been called names that only belittle them.

The feminist strike is strengthened because of its impossibility: it is comprised of the women who cannot strike but desire to do so; of those who cannot stop working for even one day and want to rebel against that exhaustion; of those who believed that it would be impossible to strike with the union leadership's authorization, and yet called the strike anyway; and of those who were audacious enough to imagine a strike against forces as nebulous as agrotoxins and finance. All of those women pushed the frontiers of the strike. From the conjunction between impossibility and desire, a radical imaginary emerges about the multiple forms of the feminist strike, taking our movement to unsuspected places, prying it open in order to include vital experiences, and reinventing it based on bodies that are disobedient to what is recognized as labor.

With the strike, we made visible the *differential of exploitation* that characterizes feminized labor: that is, the specific subordination involved in community, neighborhood, migrant, and reproductive labor. We showed how its subordination is an integral and necessary part of all forms of work. We also indicated that there is a concrete place where the stratification of labor starts: in the reproduction of life, from its meticulous and constant organization, which is exploited by capital at the cost of it being obligatory, free, or poorly paid. But we went even further and found that when we take seriously the work of reproduction, and its ties to domestication and colonization, it becomes possible to rethink waged labor, which is itself traversed by ever-greater levels of precarization.

With this way of connecting all the modes of value production (and exploitation and extraction), we also mapped the concrete imbrication between patriarchal, colonial, and capitalist violence. This made clear, yet again, that the feminist movement is not something external to the question of class and working-class politics, even if it is often presented as such. Nor can it be separated from the question of race. There is no possibility of isolating feminism from those terrains where the combat against renewed forms of exploitation, extraction, oppression, and domination is situated. The feminist movement exhibits the historical character of a class marked by the systematic exclusion of all of those not considered to be white waged workers. Thus, this feminism also shows that there can be no class without understanding its racialization. In this way, the feminist movement makes clear the extent to which the historical narratives and organizational formulas of the labor movement were modes of systematic subordination of feminized and migrant labor and, as such, the cornerstone of the sexual and racial division of labor.

2. With the strike, we produced a new understanding of violence: we escaped the silo of domestic-violence activism by connecting it to economic, labor, institutional, police, racist, and colonial violence. In this way, the organic relationship between sexist and femicidal violence and the current form of capital accumulation becomes clear. The anti-capitalist, anti-colonial, and anti-patriarchal character of the feminist movement comes from the establishment and dissemination of that analysis through our political practice.

The strike produces a perspective simultaneously based on resistance to expropriation, insubordination to labor, and financial disobedience. This creates a unique lens for investigating the relationship between territorial struggles against neo-extractive initiatives and sexual violence; the nexus between harassment and power relations in workplaces; the articulation between the exploitation of migrant and feminized labor and the extraction of value by finance; the plundering of public infrastructure in neighborhoods and (formal and informal) real estate speculation; and the clandestine condition of abortion and the criminalization of Indigenous and Black communities. All of these forms of violence take feminized bodies as spoils of war. The strike not only connects gender-based violence to the violence of dispossession in an analytical way, but through a collective practice that seeks to understand the relations of subordination and exploitation in which femicides are made intelligible, and to chart a strategy of organization and self-defense. Through the assemblies, strikes, *encuentros*, and demonstrations, the feminist movement practices a popular pedagogy that connects violence and oppression, and does so based on a contempt for both. Its capacity to escape from the totalizing narrative of victimization is what enables the diagnostic of violence to avoid translation into a language of pacification or pure mourning and lament. It is also rejects the institutional responses that reinforce the isolation of the problem and that seek to resolve it through a new government agency or program. These institutional instruments can be important, as long as they are not part of a regime of guardianship that codifies victimization and encloses violence as exclusively domestic. The strike has made it possible to diagnose the intersectionality of violence, and to construct and expand another place of enunciation and organizational horizon of the movement. This broad map widens our view and goes to the roots of the connection between patriarchy, capitalism, and colonialism, building a new shared common sense.

3. The current feminist movement is at once massive and radical. It achieves this rare conjunction because it builds bridges between very different struggles and, in this way, invents and cultivates a mode of political transversality.

Feminism makes explicit something that is not always obvious: that nobody lacks a territory. Thus, it disproves the metaphysical illusion of the isolated individual. Since we are all situated someplace, we can also think of the body not as something isolated and hermetically sealed, but instead as a body-territory. Following this analysis, feminism is no longer an external practice or thought in relation to "others." Rather, feminism becomes an interpretive key for understanding the conflict in each territory (domestic, affective, labor, migrant, artistic, campesino, urban, popular, community, and so on). This enables the unfurling of an intergenerational mass feminism, because it is taken up as their own by the most diverse spaces and experiences.

How is this transversal composition of movements produced? We start from the interconnection of diverse struggles. This is neither spontaneous nor natural. To the contrary, in relation to feminism, the opposite was true for a long time: it was understood in its institutional and/or academic variants, but historically dissociated from processes of popular confluence. There are fundamental genealogical lines that have made the current expansion possible. We can point to four such lines in Argentina: the history of the human rights struggle since the 1970s, led by the Mothers and Grandmothers of the Plaza de Mayo; the more than three decades of the Encuentro Nacional de Mujeres (now the Encuentro Plurinacional de Mujeres, Lesbianas, Trans, Travestis, y No Binaries); the emergence of the *piquetero* movement, which also had a feminized protagonism when it came to confronting the social crisis at the beginning of the century; and a long history of the movement of sexual dissidences, ranging from the legacy of the Frente de

Liberación Homosexual (Homosexual liberation front) of the 1970s, to lesbian militancy for autonomous access to abortion, to trans, travesti, and intersex activism that revolutionized the bodies and subjectivities of feminism against biologicist limits.

The form of the strike's organization produces transversality. In so doing, it updates those historical lines of struggle and projects them onto a feminism of the masses. This feminism is rooted in concrete struggles of popular economy workers, migrants, cooperative workers, precarious workers, women defending their territories, new generations of sexual dissidents, housewives who refuse enclosure, those fighting for the right to abortion in a broad struggle for bodily autonomy, mobilized students, women denouncing agrotoxins, and sex workers, among others. In organizational terms, it creates a common horizon that functions as a practical catalyst.

By weaving together this multiplicity of different conflicts, each rooted in particular relationships of domination and exploitation, the meaning of mass politics is redefined. Now, it is based on practices and struggles that have historically been defined as "minoritarian," and therefore as anathema to mass politics. The confluence of struggles undoes the presumed opposition between the "minoritarian" and the "majoritarian": the "minoritarian" takes up the mass scale as a vector of radicalization within a composition that is ever expanding. Therefore, it challenges the neoliberal machinery of minority recognition (as an isolated identity politics) and the pacification of difference (in the register of multicultural neoliberalism).

This political transversality is nourished by the diverse territories of conflict, and it constructs a common affect concerning problems that tend to be experienced as individual, as well as a political diagnosis of the various forms of violence that tend to be encapsulated as "domestic." This complicates a certain idea of solidarity: that which supposes a level of exteriority that confirms distance in respect to others, refers to forms of political activism via a paternalistic premise, and thus avoids problematizing its own situation while reinforcing a savior logic. Transversality, in contrast, prioritizes a politics of the construction of proximity and alliances, without ignoring the differences of intensity between conflicts.

4. **The feminist movement has launched a new critique of political economy. It includes a radical denunciation of the contemporary operations of capitalism, and, in turn, it furnishes an updated concept of exploitation. Crucially, it does all this by broadening what is usually understood as "the economy."**

In Argentina, the intersection of a new branch of feminist economics and the explosion of popular economies has provided us with a new critique of the contemporary conditions of capitalist valorization. The material fabric of these economies is composed of *cartoneros* (informal trash pickers) and sewing workers, market vendors and care workers, cooks and community health practitioners, cleaners and small agrarian producers, all of whom emerged from social mobilizations at different moments of crisis. Popular economies, as reproductive and productive webs, express an accumulation of struggles that opens up the imagination of the feminist strike. That is why in Argentina the feminist strike manages to deploy, problematize, and valorize a multiplicity of tasks based on a map of work in a feminist register, since it is connected to a *piquetero* genealogy and its problematization of waged labor and forms of "inclusion." It is these experiences that are at the origin of popular economies and that persist as an insurgent element that is summoned once again by popular feminisms.

Two processes take place in popular economies with the organization of the feminist strikes. On one hand, there is a politicization of reproductive spheres beyond the home, which become the concrete spaces for expanding the definition of labor that is recognized and valued by the strike. On the other hand, a feminist perspective highlights the patriarchal and colonial mandates that naturalize those tasks as "women's work," enabling them to be exploited and value to be extracted from them.

By defying the inscription and enclosure of reproductive tasks in the family, the feminist strikes challenge the permanent moral augmentation imposed by social welfare benefits. This creates an intersection between feminist economics and the popular economy that radicalizes both experiences. Through the strike, the feminist movement also produces figures of subjectivation (be they vital trajectories, forms of cooperation, or modes of life) that escape the neoliberal binary that opposes victims to entrepreneurs of the self (even using the pseudolanguage of "gender liberation" that speaks of entrepreneurial "empowerment"). In this sense, feminisms are anti-neoliberal because they take on the task of collective organization against individual suffering, and because they denounce systematic policies of dispossession.

The current feminist movement puts forth a precise characterization of neoliberalism and, therefore, expands the horizon of what we call anti-neoliberal politics. Due to the types of conflicts that it maps, visibilizes, and mobilizes, a complex notion of neoliberalism unfolds that cannot be reduced to the binary of "the state versus the market." On the contrary, its struggles point to the connection between the extractive logic of capital and its imbrication with state policies, determining why value is exploited and extracted from certain body-territories. The perspective of feminist economics is therefore anti-capitalist.

5. The feminist movement takes to the streets and constructs itself in assemblies; it weaves together its potencia in territories and elaborates a comprehensive analysis of the conjuncture; it produces a counter-power that is able to win new rights while retaining its focus on a more radical horizon. In short:

our movement dismantles the binary between reform and revolution.

Through the strike, the feminist movement constructs a common force against precarity, austerity, layoffs, and their related violence. It highlights an *anti-neoliberal* element (that is, it challenges business rationality as the order of the world), affirming its class-based nature (that is, it does not naturalize or minimize the issue of exploitation) and its anti-colonial and anti-patriarchal character (because it denounces and defies the specific exploitation of capitalism against women as well as feminized and racialized bodies). This dynamic is key: it produces a practical intersection between race, class, and gender, and it generates another *rationality* for reading the situation. Both the parliamentary debates (affirming that there is no right or force of law that is not first formulated in social protest) and the radicalization of the popular organization of feminisms resist being reduced to a "quota," "sector," or "theme."

This dynamic of the movement is twofold: it constructs its own institutionality in the form of autonomous networks, while it simultaneously reorients existing institutions. In turn, it creates a strategic temporality that simultaneously acts in the present—both with what *exists*, and with what also *exists but still as a virtuality*, as a latent possibility yet to be realized. The feminist movement does not exhaust its demands nor its struggles in the horizon of the state, even if it does not ignore that field of action. It decidedly does not presume that the state is a place where violence can be ameliorated. Its utopian dimension, nevertheless, is not only a distant final objective, postponed to an unknown future, but something that retains an active and practical effectiveness in the present. Therefore, the utopian dimension also manages to operate within the existing contradictions, without waiting for the appearance of absolutely liberated subjects or ideal conditions of struggles, nor trusting in a sole space that totalizes social transformation.

In that sense, it appeals to the potencia of rupture of each action, and it does not limit the rupture to a spectacular, final moment of a strictly evolutionary political accumulation.

The feminist revolution of our time challenges the proclamation of the end of revolution that, with pure faith in defeat, ends up pacifying and disqualifying what exist as concrete dynamics of disobedience, revolt, and radical change. What revolution are we talking about? The revolution that takes place in bodies, the streets, beds, workplaces, and homes comes to situate and project the reach expressed by the slogan "We want to change everything!" The desire for revolution emerges from the *realism* of the change that is already taking place everywhere, affirming that the time of revolution is now (and not a distant final objective).

This, again, is connected with the potencia of *transversality*, that which grows due to the way in which feminist activism has turned into an available force that is put into play in different spaces of struggle and life. In this way, it protests against the "sectorization" of the so-called gender agenda and against the infantilization of its political practices, which seek to minimize and/or postpone feminist demands. In other words, transversality is not only a form of coordination, but also a capacity to make feminism into its own force in each place, while avoiding its circumscription as a logic of specific demands. This is not easy to sustain, because it involves a daily work of weaving, of conversation, of translation, of the expansion of discussion, of trial and error. But what is most powerful about this movement today is that the form of its composition is felt as a need and a desire to open up a temporality of revolution here and now.

6. Contemporary feminism weaves together a new internationalism. It is not a structure that abstracts struggles and makes them homogeneous in order to take them to a "higher" plane. It is perceived, on the contrary, as a concrete force in

each place. It drives a dynamic that is made transnational based on situated trajectories and bodies. Therefore, the feminist movement is expressed as a coordinated force of global destabilization whose potencia arises from Southern soil.

Ours is an internationalism based on territories in struggle. That is what makes its construction more complex and polyphonic: it incorporates ever more territories and languages. It does not adhere to the framework of the nation-state; therefore, it already overflows the name "internationalism." Rather than international, it is transnational and plurinational. This is because it recognizes other geographies and draws other maps of alliance, encounter, and convergence than those between nations-states; and because it entails a radical critique of the national enclosure that seeks to limit our struggles. Its connections are based on migrant trajectories, and it approaches landscapes that recombine urban, suburban, campesino, Indigenous, slum, and community elements. Thus, multiple temporalities are folded into it.

Feminist transnationalism and plurinationalism involve a critique of the neocolonial advances against body-territories. They denounce different forms of extractivism and demonstrate their connection with increasing sexist violence and forms of labor exploitation that take the maquila as their emblematic scene on this continent.

The feminist strike constructs an unstoppable transnational web because it maps, against the grain, the world market that organizes the accumulation of capital. However, this transnational link is not organized according to the calendar of meetings of large agencies at the service of capital. Based on the feminist strike, the movement adopts the role of a coordinator, on the one hand, and of a committee, on the other, in its encounter with struggles in the here and now: they are all initiatives that break boundaries and cross borders. The movement reflects a transnationalism that made the strike a global watchword, thus forging a new form of coordination: "If we stop, we stop the world."

The force of destabilization is global, then, because it first exists in every home, in every relationship, in every territory, in every assembly, in every university, in every factory, in every market. In this sense, it is the inverse of a long internationalist tradition that organizes from above, unifying and giving "coherence" to struggles based on their inscription into a program.

The transnational dimension composes the collective as an investigation: it is presented both as self-education and as a desire of articulation with experiences that at first are not close. This is quite different from assuming collective coordination as a moral a priori or an abstract requirement. Feminism in neighborhoods, in bedrooms, or in households is not less internationalist than feminism in the streets or in regional encounters, and that gives it its powerful politics of place. It comes from its non-disjunction, its way of *making* internationalism as a politics of rootedness and of opening territories to unexpected connections.

7. **The global response to the transnational feminist force is organized as a tripartite counteroffensive: military, economic, and religious. Neoliberalism now requires conservative policies to stabilize its mode of government.**

The fascism that we are seeing as a Latin American and global scenario is fueled by a reactionary response to the force deployed by the transnational feminist movement. The feminisms that have taken the streets in recent years, that form a capillary, concrete force in all social relations and spheres, have called into question the subordination of reproductive and feminized labor, the persecution of migrant economies, the naturalization of sexual abuse as a way of disciplining the precarious labor force, the norm of the heteropatriarchal family as a refuge against that same precarity, domestic confinement as a site of submission and invisibility, the criminalization of abortion and of practices of sovereignty over one's body, and the poisoning and dispossession of communities by corporations in cooperation with the state. Each one of these practices has made the normality of obedience tremble, shaking up its everyday and routinized reproduction.

The feminist strike, woven as a political process, opened up another sense of time, interrupting and subverting the normality of the temporality of capital. But it extends beyond the day of the strike. It expands as a revolutionary desire, changing our experience of time. It has left no place untouched by the tide of insubordination and questioning.

Now, neoliberalism needs to ally itself with reactionary conservative forces because the destabilization of patriarchal authorities puts capital accumulation itself at risk. We could put it like this: capital is extremely aware of its need for articulation with colonialism and patriarchy in order to reproduce itself as a relation of obedience. Once the factory and the heteropatriarchal family no longer manage to maintain discipline, and once securitized control is defied by feminist forms of managing interdependence in eras of existential precarity, the counteroffensive intensifies. And we very clearly see why neoliberalism and conservativism share strategic objectives of normalization.

Since the feminist movement politicizes the crisis of social reproduction in a new and radical way—as a crisis that is in turn civilizational and a crisis of the patriarchal structure of society—the fascist impulse that is launched to counteract it proposes economies of obedience to channel the crisis. Whether by religious fundamentalisms or the paranoid construction of a new internal enemy, what we are witnessing is the attempt to terrorize the forces of destabilization rooted in a feminism that has crossed borders.

8. The feminist movement today confronts capital's most abstract image: financial capital, precisely that form of domination that seems to make direct, person-to-person antagonism impossible. By confronting the financialization of life, which occurs when the very act of living "produces" debt, the feminist movement initiates a struggle against these new forms of exploitation and extraction of value.

An "inverted" image of the very productivity of our labor power, of our vital potencia, and of the politicization (or valorization) of reproductive tasks appears in the form of debt. The feminist strike that shouts, "We want ourselves alive, free, and debt free!" manages to make finance visible in terms of conflict and, therefore, as a direct threat to our autonomy. It is necessary to understand the mass indebtedness that lands in the feminized popular economies and in domestic economies as an everyday "counterrevolution" because of the ways that debt constraints our choices, binds us to search for work, extracts our wealth and value, and commands from a distance the way we spend our days. Thus, it is an operation of capital in the very terrain where feminisms have shaken up everything.

When the feminist movement takes finance as a terrain of struggle against generalized impoverishment, it practices a counter-pedagogy in respect to financial violence and concretely explains the new forms of exploitation of bodies and territories.

The addition of the financial dimension to our struggles allows us to map flows of debt and to complete the map of exploitation in its most dynamic, versatile, and apparently "invisible" forms. An understanding of how debt extracts value from domestic economies, non-waged economies, and economies historically considered not to be productive enables us to see financial apparatuses as true mechanisms of the colonization of the reproduction of life. It also allows us to understand debt as a privileged apparatus for laundering illicit flows and, therefore, to understand the connection between legal and illegal economies as a way of increasing direct violence against territories. What it seeks is precisely an "economy of obedience" that serves the most concentrated sectors of capital, and charity as a way of depoliticizing access to resources.

All of this gives us, once again, broader and more complex possibilities for diagnosing the different forms of violence that take feminized bodies as new territories of conquest. We must recognize debt and guilt as a fatal coupling, whereby the latter is maintained by a heteropatriarchal morality and further reinforced by the differential exploitation of our vital forces. A feminist response to the machinery of debt is necessary because it also means acting against the machinery of guilt.

Acknowledgments

First, I would like to express my thanks to Sebastian Budgen and Ben Mabie, the editors at Verso who have worked rigorously and enthusiastically from the beginning to get this book published, and to the final observations of Duncan Ranslem. I am especially grateful for the committed and loving work of Liz Mason-Deese. Her translation fed into the writing process itself, which, through our long friendship, has brought us to exercise and share many twists and turns in language. And to Alicia Balsells, for her suggestion to *dwell in possibility.*

In the whirlpool of everything that has happened and that is narrated here, I am infinitely grateful to Iván, the daring accomplice of all becomings. To Natalia Fontana, my sister. To Luci Cavallero for love in permanent revolution and for the most ruthless intelligence.

To Marta Dillon and Cecilia Palmeiro for a journey that still continues. To Virginia Giannoni for her sharp friendship. To my compañeras from the Ni Una Menos collective, together we have cultivated a political friendship.

To Silvia Federici and Raquel Gutiérrez Aguilar for serving as elder witches and for their advice and strength. To Silvia Rivera Cusicanqui, the ultimate teacher of irreverence and complex thought. To Suely Rolnik, for the schizoanalysis at a distance and in proximity. To Marta Malo, for her impassioned complicity throughout so many different eras. To Alida Díaz for building us a house everywhere. To Rita Segato for the continuous conversation. To Dora Barrancos for her trust. To Marie Bardet for her thinking-in-movement.

To my mom and my amigas-compañeras over so many years: Andrea Barberi, Clarisa Gambera, Susana Draper, Charo Golder, Mariela Denegris, Alejandra Rodríguez, María Medrano, Lili Cabrera, Delia Colque, Maisa Bascuas, Neka Jara, Maba Jara, Silvio Lang, Ana Julia Bustos and Cecilia Abdo Ferez.

To Sandro Mezzadra for his intelligent and generous dialogue.

To Natalia Brizuela, Judith Butler, and Wendy Brown for the stimulating invitation.

To the constellation of compañeras from Bolivia, Peru, Uruguay, Brazil, Ecuador, Chile, Mexico, Colombia, Paraguay, Guatemala, the United States, France, Germany, Italy, and Spain with whom I have conversed, debated, and shared questions, across different moments and trajectories, that nourish this book. In particular, Gladys Tzul, Ita del Cielo, Dunia Mokrani, Claudia López, Carmen Arriaga, Eli Qu, Lopo Gutiérrez, Mariana Menéndez, Betty Ruth Lozano, Anahí Durand, Camila Rojas, Daniela López, Pierina Feretti, Cristina Vega, Cristina Cielo, Helena Silvestre, Graciela Rodríguez, Analba Texeira, Josy Panão, Florence Oppen, Nazaret Castro, Beatriz García, Eva García, Lotta Meri Pirita Tenhunen, Alejandra Estigarribia, Pilar García, Inés Gutiérrez, Alioscia Castronovo, Marina Montanelli, Giuliana Visco, Tatiana Montella, Isabell Lorey, Caro Kim, Mila Ivanovic, Begoña Santa Cecilia, Rafaela Pimentel, Pastora Filigrana and Sara Buraya.

For the delicate readings of parts of the manuscript: Gaby Mendoza, Florencia Lance, Mariana Dopazo, and Amador Savater; and especially the editorial comments of Diego Picotto and Josefina Payró. To my dad and brothers for their network of care. To my compañer*s at Tinta Limón, especially Andrés Bracony and Ignacio Gago, who continue making books into a militant craft.

Notes

Foreword and Introduction

1 Lohana Berkins, "Travestis: Una identidad política," *Emisférica* 4:2, hemisphericinstitute.org.

2 An English translation of that document, as well as other texts from the movement, can be found in *Critical Times* 1:1 (April 2018), 158–77.

3 In Spanish, there are two words for "power": *poder* and *potencia*, which derive from the Latin *potestas* and *potentia*. A Spinozist understanding of that difference underscores that while "potencia" has a dynamic, constituent dimension, "poder" is static, constituted. "Potencia" defines our power to do, to affect, and be affected, while the mechanism of representation that constitutes "poder" separates "potencia" from the bodies that are being represented. To preserve the emphasis of this distinction, the Spanish word "potencia" is used, where appropriate, throughout this book. For the matter of this philosophical translation, see Michael Hardt, "Translator's Forward: The Anatomy of Power" in *The Savage Anomaly: The Power of Spinoza's Metaphysics and Politics*, Antonio Negri (Minneapolis: University of Minnesota Press, 1991).

1. #WeStrike

1 The formulation "women, lesbians, travestis, and trans people" is the result of years of debate within the feminist movement, and is meant to demonstrate the diverse political subjectivities and collectives involved in the movement and to highlight its inclusive character, beyond a limited category of "woman." In this translation, we keep the term "travesti" to recognize it as a political category built through years of struggle against marginalization and violence, often related to struggles for recognition of sex work.

2 See Precarias a la Deriva, "A Very Careful Strike: Four Hypotheses," Franco Ingrassia and Nate Holdren, trans., *The Commoner* 11 (Spring 2006), 33–45.

3 I take this phrase from Sergio González Rodríguez, *The Femicide Machine* (Los Angeles: Semiotex(e), 2012).

4 See Julia Monárrez's pioneering investigations into what she calls "systemic sexual feminicide" in that city: "Elementos de análisis del feminicidio sexual sistémico en Ciudad Juárez para su viabilidad jurídica," presented at the international seminar Femicidio, Ley y Justicia, Mexico, 2004.

5 This is synthesized in Rita Segato's seminal work, *Las estructuras elementales de la violencia* (Buenos Aires: Prometeo, 2003).

6 See Susana Draper, "Strike as Process: Building the Poetics of a New Feminism," Liz Mason-Deese, trans., *South Atlantic Quarterly* 117:3 (July 2018), 682–91.

7 See Raquel Gutiérrez Aguilar, *¡A desordenar! Por una historia abierta de la lucha social* (Buenos Aires: Tinta Limón, 2016).

8 See Ernesto Laclau, *On Populist Reason* (London and New York: Verso, 2007). I expand on the relation between populism and feminism in Chapter 5, debating some of Nancy Fraser's formulations.

9 See Suely Rolnik, *Cartografia sentimental: Transformações contemporâneas do desejo* (Porto Alegre: Sulina, 2006).

10 On November 25, 2018, those responsible for her femicide were acquitted, leading to a massive repudiation, assemblies, and a call to strike across the country on December 5. Judges Facundo Gómez Urso, Aldo Carnevale, and Pablo Viñas of the Oral Federal Criminal Court of Mar del Plata argued that she died from intoxication. As of this writing, the ruling is being appealed in the provincial chamber.

11 In 2017, the perpetrator was sentenced to life in prison using the legal category of "travesticide" for the first time: "Perpetua por el travesticidio de Diana Sacayán," *Cosecha Roja*, June 18, 2018, cosecharoja.org.

12 The CTEP, formed in 2011, is a coalition of various social organizations coming out of the piquetero experience. It proposes to be a new type of union tool, linked to the popular economies composed of diverse forms of self-managed work without a boss and collective enterprises that are connected, also in different ways, to social subsidies from the state.

13 A whole debate about how to reread the "measure of value," and the crisis of the value form in Marx himself, has been driven by feminist theorizations of "unmeasurable excess," incorporating notions such as "affect value" and "community value." These are other components of value and other economies, which express the crisis of the measure of the wage itself as quantitative retribution for a certain quantity of work hours. We could synthesize it as a feminist perspective that destabilizes calculation according to the rationality of capital and whose origin demonstrates the unmeasurable and excessive quality of the potencia of labor. I will return to this discussion in Chapter 4.

14 First published in English in 2004 by Autonomedia, *Caliban and the Witch* was translated and published in Argentina in 2011 by Tinta Limón

and subsequently reprinted by publishing houses in Bolivia, Mexico, and Spain, among others.

15 Silvia Federici, *Patriarchy of the Wage: Notes on Marx, Gender, and Feminism* (Oakland: PM Press, 2020).

16 Angela Davis, *Women, Race, and Class* (New York : Random House, 1981).

17 These benefits packages were a central demand of the movements of the unemployed in the late 1990s and 2000s and now include a variety of programs. In many cases, those movements also won the right to determine what activities fulfill the work requirements to receive benefits, providing a pathway to effectively remunerate many reproductive tasks. Today, many of these programs either explicitly or implicitly target women, such as the Universal Child Allowance, which provides benefits to unemployed heads of households with children, or Ellas Hacen, which provides work and training opportunities to women. In April 2015, in an activist meeting with Silvia Federici at the Villa 31, the conversation focused on the relationship between Wages for Housework and these new social programs. See Verónica Gago, "El caldero de las nuevas brujas," *Las12*, May 3, 2015, pagina12.com.ar.

18 Rosa Luxemburg, *The Mass Strike, the Political Party and the Trade Unions*, Patrick Lavin, trans. (Detroit, MI: Marxist Educational Society of Detroit, 1925), 32.

19 See Mujeres Creando, *La virgen de los deseos* (Buenos Aires: Tinta Limón, 2005).

20 For an exquisite elaboration of the notion of a catalyst, see Deleuze's analysis of Foucault's conception of power in his *Foucault* (Minneapolis: University of Minnesota Press, 1988).

21 See Colectivo Situaciones and MTD de Solano, *Hipótesis 891: Más allá de los piquetes* (Buenos Aires: Tinta Limón, 2002).

22 See, for example, E.P. Thompson, *The Making of the English Working Class* (New York: Pantheon, 1970); Mario Tronti, *Operai e capitale* (Turin: Einaudi, 1966); Antonio Negri, *Marx beyond Marx: Lessons on the Grundrisse* (New York: Autonomedia, 1991).

23 See Silvia Federici, *Wages against Housework* (Bristol and London: Power of Women Collective and Falling Wall Press, 1975).

24 Davis, *Women, Race, and Class*; Peter Linebaugh, *The Incomplete, True, Authentic, and Wonderful History of May Day* (Oakland: PM Press, 2016).

25 Raquel Gutiérrez Aguilar, "Women's Struggle against All Violence in Mexico: Gathering Fragments to Find Meaning," Liz Mason-Deese, trans., *South Atlantic Quarterly* 117:3 (July 2018), 670–81.

26 Susan Buck-Morss, *Hegel, Haiti, and Universal History* (Pittsburgh: University of Pittsburgh Press, 2009).

27 Carole Pateman, *The Sexual Contract* (Stanford: Stanford University Press, 1988).

28 Jacques Rancière, *The Ignorant Schoolmaster: Five Lessons in Intellectual Emancipation* (Stanford: Stanford University Press, 1991).

29 Michel Foucault, *The Punitive Society: Lectures at the Collège de France, 1972–1973*, Bernard E. Harcourt and Graham Burchell, eds. (New York: Picador, 2018), 3.

2. Violence

1   See Silvia Federici, *Patriarchy of the Wage: Notes on Marx, Gender, and Feminism* (Oakland: PM Press, 2020).

2   See Section 3 of Rosa Luxemburg's "The Historical Conditions of Accumulation," *The Accumulation of Capital*, Agnes Schwarzchild, trans. (New York: Routledge, 1951 [1913]).

3   Berta Cáceres was an environmental activist, feminist, and Indigenous leader, cofounder of the Council of Popular and Indigenous Organizations of Honduras (COPINH), and winner of the Goldman Environmental Prize. She was assassinated in 2016, with investigations pointing to the involvement of military officials who received training at the School of the Americas in Fort Benning, Georgia.

4   See Verónica Gago and Sandro Mezzadra, "A Critique of the Extractive Operations of Capital: Toward an Expanded Concept of Extractivism," Liz Mason-Deese, trans., *Rethinking Marxism* 29:4 (October 2017), 574–91.

5   See the position of the jurist Raúl Zaffaroni in his article "Femicide," *Página 12*, May 18, 2017, pagina12.com.ar.

6   See "El efecto contagio de Ni Una Menos," *Revista Noticias*, February 15, 2017, noticias.perfil.com.

7   See Amarela Varela, "La trinidad perversa de la que huyen las fugitivas centroamericanas: Violencia feminicida, violencia de estado y violencia de mercado," *Debate Feminista* 53 (2018), 1–17; Varela, "Notes for Antiracist Feminism in the Wake of the Migrant Caravans," *South Atlantic Quarterly* 119:3 (July 2020).

8   See Verónica Gago, "The Strategy of Flight: Problematizing the Figure of Trafficking," Liz Mason-Deese, trans., *South Atlantic Quarterly* 117:2 (April 2018), 333–56.

9   See Michel Foucault, *"Society Must Be Defended": Lectures at the Collège de France, 1975–1976*, David Macey, trans. (New York: Picador, 2003), 44–51.

10 Maria Mies, *Patriarchy and Accumulation on a World Scale: Women in the International Division of Labour*, 2nd ed. (London: Zed Books, 1999).

11 Silvia Federici, *Caliban and the Witch: Women, the Body, and Primitive Accumulation* (New York: Autonomedia, 2004), 184.

12 See Rita Segato, "Patriarchy from Margin to Center: Discipline,

Territoriality, and Cruelty in the Apocalyptic Phase of Capital," Liz Mason-Deese, trans., *South Atlantic Quarterly* 115:3 (July 2016), 615–24.

13 Suely Rolnik, *Esferas de insurrección. Apuntes para descolonizar el inconciente* (Buenos Aires: Tinta Limón, 2019).

14 These could also be thought about in relation to Cameroonian theorist Achille Mbembe's use of Frantz Fanon in *Critique of Black Reason* (Durham, NC: Duke University Press, 2017).

15 For the concept of "expressive violence," see Segato's *Las estructuras elementales de la violencia: Ensayos sobre género entre la antropología, el psicoanálisis y los derechos humanos* (Buenos Aires: Prometeo, 2003). For her analysis of Ciudad Juárez, see *La escritura en el cuerpo de las mujeres asesinadas en Ciudad Juárez: Territorio, soberanía y crímenes de segundo estado* (Buenos Aires: Tinta Limón, 2013).

16 Rita Segato, *Las nuevas formas de la guerra y el cuerpo de las mujeres* (Puebla: Pez en el árbol, 2014), 5–13.

17 See Dawn Paley, *Drug War Capitalism* (Oakland: AK Press, 2014).

18 Gilles Deleuze and Félix Guattari, *A Thousand Plateaus: Capitalism and Schizophrenia*, Brian Massumi, trans. (Minneapolis: University of Minnesota Press, 1987).

19 Lou Andreas Salomé, *Friedrich Nietzsche en sus obras* (Barcelona: Minúscula, 2005).

20 Audre Lorde, *The Cancer Journals* (San Francisco: Aunt Lute Books, 2006).

3. Body-Territory

1 Maria Mies, Veronika Bennholdt-Thomsen, and Claudia von Werlhof, *Women: The Last Colony* (London: Zed Books, 1988).

2 Maria Mies, *Patriarchy and Accumulation on a World Scale: Women in the International Division of Labour* (London: Zed Books, 1986).

3 See Marie Mies and Vandana Shiva, *Ecofeminism* (London: Zed Books, 2014); Laura Junka-Aikio and Catalina Cortes-Severino, "Cultural Studies of Extraction," *Cultural Studies* 31: 2–3 (2017), 175–84; Alberto Acosta and Ulrich Brand, *Salidas del laberinto capitalista: Decrecimiento y postextractivismo* (Buenos Aires: Tinta Limón and Fundación Rosa Luxemburgo, 2017).

4 The political theory of the possessive individual that Macpherson traces in British political thought between the seventeenth and nineteenth centuries conceives of society as a set of relations of individual commercial exchange. Each individual is thus understood as "free and equal" to others and relates to them as the owner of their own person or capabilities without owing society anything for them. See C.B. Macpherson, *The Political Theory of Possessive Individualism: Hobbes to Locke* (Toronto: Oxford University Press, 1962).

5   Judith Butler and Athena Athanasiou, *Dispossession: The Performative in the Political* (Malden, MA: Polity, 2013).

6   See Claudia Korol, *Las revoluciones de Berta* (Buenos Aires: América libre, 2018).

7   Cited in Francesca Gargallo Calentani, *Feminismos desde Abya Yala: Ideas y proposiciones de las mujeres de 607 pueblos de nuestra América* (Bogotá: Desde Abajo, 2017).

8   Verónica Gago, *Neoliberalism from Below: Popular Pragmatics and Baroque Economies*, Liz Mason-Deese, trans. (Durham: Duke University Press, 2017).

9   Marxa Chávez and Claudia López, "Women Rebel in Tariquía in Southern Bolivia: The Fight for Dignity and against Oil Interests begins with Women," *NACLA Report on the Americas* 50:4 (2018).

10 María Galindo, *No se puede descolonizar sin despatriarcalizar* (La Paz: Mujeres Creando, 2013).

11 Mina Navarro, "Luchas por lo común contra el renovado cercamiento de bienes naturales en México," *Bajo el Volcán* 13:21 (2013), 161–69.

12 Silvia Rivera Cusicanqui, "La larga marcha por nuestra dignidad," *Cuestión Agraria*, vol. 4 (La Paz: Tierra, 2017), 7–38.

13 Paola Bolados and Alejandra Sánchez, "Una ecología política feminista en construcción: El caso de las mujeres de zonas de sacrificio en resistencia, Región de Valparaíso, Chile," *Psicoperspectivas* 16:2 (2017), 1–13.

14 Rocío Silva Santisteban, *Mujeres y conflictos ecoterritoriales: Impactos, estrategias, resistencias* (Lima: AECI, 2017).

15 Cristina Cielo and Cristina Vega Solis, "Reproducción, mujeres y comunes: Leer a Silvia Federici desde el Ecuador actual," *Revista Nueva Sociedad* 256 (2015).

16 Astrid Ulloa, "Feminismos territoriales en América Latina: Defensas de la vida frente a los extractivismos," *Nómadas* 45 (2016), 123–39.

17 Lorena Cabnal, "Defender un territorio de la minería sin defender a las mujeres de la violencia sexual es incoherencia," *Periódico Diagonal*, May 23, 2016.

18 Silvia Rivera Cusicanqui, *Un mundo ch'ixi es posible: Ensayos desde un presente en crisis* (Buenos Aires: Tinta Limón, 2018).

19 Silvia Federici, *Witches, Witch-Hunting, and Women* (Oakland: PM Press, 2018).

20 Keeanga-Yamahtta Taylor's book *From #BlackLivesMatter to Black Liberation* (Chicago: Haymarket Books, 2016) deserves special mention in the discussion about empire, for its analysis of the relationship between Obama's government and the blaming of the Black population following the subprime mortgage crisis that massively destroyed "the treasured wealth of African Americans."

21 For more on the commodity boom hypothesis, see Maristella Svampa, "Commodities Consensus: Neoextractivism and Enclosure of the Commons in Latin America," Liz Mason-Deese, trans., *South Atlantic*

Quarterly 114:1 (January 2015), 65–82; Eduardo Gudynas, "Beyond Variaties of Development: Disputes and Alternatives," *Third World Quarterly* 37 (2016), 721–32; Edgardo Lander, "La implosión de la Venezuela rentista," *Cuadernos de la Nueva Política* 1 (September 2016); Pablo Ospina Peralta, "¿Por quién doblan las campanas?," Centro Ecuménico de Proyectos, www.cepecuador.org.

22 For the case of Brazil see, for example, Celia Kerstenetzky and Christiane Uchôa, "Moradia inadequada, escolaridade insuficiente, crédito limitado: Em busca da nova classe média," in A *"Nova classe média" no Brasil como conceito e projeto político,* Dawid Danilo Bartelt, ed. (Río de Janeiro: Fundação Heinrich Böll, 2013).

23 See Saskia Sassen, *Territory, Authority, Rights: From Medieval to Global Assemblages* (Princeton, NJ: Princeton University Press, 2006).

24 Nazareth Castro, Aurora Moreno, and Laura Villadiego, "De Colombia a Indonesia: Estas mujeres están en pie contra el aceite de palma," *El Diario,* January 20, 2018, eldiario.es.

25 Verónica Gago and Sandro Mezzadra, "A Critique of the Extractive Operations of Capital: Toward an Expanded Concept of Extractivism," Liz Mason-Deese, trans., *Rethinking Marxism* 29:4 (October 2017), 574–91.

26 See also Michael Hardt and Antonio Negri, *Assembly* (New York: Oxford University Press, 2017); and Saskia Sassen, *Expulsions: Brutality and Complexity in the Global Economy* (Cambridge, MA: Harvard University Press, 2014).

27 James Ferguson, *Global Shadows: Africa in the Neoliberal World Order* (Durham, NC: Duke University Press, 2006).

28 Achille Mbembe, *Critique of Black Reason* (Durham, NC: Duke University Press, 2017).

29 Giorgio Agamben, *Homo Sacer: Sovereign Power and Bare Life* (Stanford: Stanford University Press, 1998).

30 Carole Pateman, *The Disorder of Women: Democracy, Feminism, and Political Theory* (Stanford: Stanford University Press, 1990).

31 Félix Guattari, *Chaosmosis: An Ethico-aesthetic Paradigm,* Paul Bains and Julian Pefanis, trans. (Bloomington: Indiana University Press, 1995).

32 Colectivo Situaciones, *19 and 20: Notes for a New Social Protagonism,* Nate Holdren and Sebastián Touza, trans. (New York: Minor Compositions, 2012).

33 Carole Pateman, *The Sexual Contract* (Stanford: Stanford University Press, 1988).

34 The laws granting immunity to those responsible for the human rights abuses under the dictatorship were finally overturned in 2005, and since then more than 500 people have been indicted for those crimes. However, Articles 178 and 242 of the Argentine Legal Code impede a person from "denouncing or declaring against a spouse, an ascendant, descendant, or sibling, unless the crime appears to have been carried

out to the detriment of the complainant." The collective of the former daughters of genociders presented an amendment in 2017 for those prohibitions to be removed "in the case of crimes against humanity, thus enabling the sons, daughters, and family members of genociders, who voluntarily wish to testify, to be able to contribute to the legal case in that way." Ultimately, that modification was not approved.

35 The "death flights" were a system of extermination during the military dictatorship that consisted of anesthetizing and throwing into the river or ocean from airplanes more than 4,000 detained-disappeared people who had been previously kidnapped. Those responsible were condemned to life sentences for the first time by the Argentine justice system in 2017.

36 Florencia Lance, "Soy hija de un aviador de los vuelos de la muerte," *El cohete a la luna*, March 25, 2018, elcohetealaluna.com.

37 During the dictatorship, ESMA served as a concentration camp where over 5,000 people were illegally detained, tortured, and killed. Task Group 3.3.2 was the operational unit responsible for running the camp. For Krichmar's account, see "La nena que jugaba en la ESMA," *Revista Anfibia* (2018), revistaanfibia.com.

38 Mariana Dopazo, "Este será mi primer 24 de marzo," *El cohete a la luna*, March 25, 2018, elcohetealaluna.com.

39 Quoted in Alejandra Dandon, "No le permito más ser mi padre," *Página12*, August 13, 2017, pagina12.com.ar.

40 In 2017, an Argentine court ruled that Luis Muiña, convicted of human rights violations, had the right to benefit from the two-for-one law, in which each day of preventative detention without conviction counts twice, opening the door to early release for many of the dictatorship's worst criminals. Millions of people took to the streets against the ruling and, ultimately, the Supreme Court overturned it.

41 The #YoTeCreo (#IBelieveYou) campaign arose in 2016 when several young women denounced famous rock musicians for sexual abuse against girls and teenagers. In 2017, the #MeToo campaign resonated with what had already been happening in Argentina, and the thread continued with #MiraComoNosPonemos, a collective denunciation of sexual abuse and harassment made by actresses. In Argentina, these campaigns took place in the context of the massiveness of the Ni Una Menos movement, the feminist strikes, and the mobilizations for abortion rights. The actresses showed how sexist violence, abuse, and rapes in the entertainment industry are directly linked to precarity, and they used a collective enunciation to do so.

42 Marta Dillon, "Huellas rebeldes," *Página12*, March 25, 2018, pagina12.com.ar; Natalia Fontana, "Hijas y nietas de sus rebeldías," personal correspondence, 2018.

43 Gilles Deleuze and Félix Guattari, *A Thousand Plateaus* (Minneapolis: University of Minnesota Press, 1987), 105.

4. A Feminist Economics of Exploitation and Extraction

1 Silvia Federici, *El patriarcado del salario* (Buenos Aires: Tinta Limón), 45.

2 Wendy Brown, "Feminist Theory and the Frankfurt School: An Introduction," *Differences: A Journal of Feminist Cultural Studies* 17:1 (May 2006), 3.

3 Nancy Fraser, "Behind Marx's 'Hidden Abode': Toward an Expanded Conception of Capitalism," *New Left Review* SII, 86 (April 2014), 55–72.

4 Silvia Federici and Arlen Austin, eds., *Wages for Housework: The New York Committee, 1972–77; History, Theory, Documents* (New York: Autonomedia, 2018).

5 Federica Giardini, *Dominio e sfruttamento: Un ritorno neomaterialista sull'economia politica* (Rome: Roma Tre-Press, 2017); Federica Giardini and Anna Simone, "Reproduction as Paradigm: Elements Toward a Feminist Political Economy," *Viewpoint Magazine*, October 31, 2015, viewpointmag.com.

6 J.K. Gibson-Graham, "Building Community Economies: Women and the Politics of Place," in *Women and the Politics of Place*, Wendy Harcourt and Arturo Escobar, eds., 130–57 (Bloomfield, CT: Kumarian Press, 2005), 150.

7 Ibid., 149.

8 Silvia Federici, *Patriarchy of the Wage: Notes on Marx, Gender, and Feminism* (Oakland: PM Press, 2020).

9 Colectivo Situaciones and MTD de Solano, *La Hipótesis 891: Más allá de los piquetes* (Buenos Aires: Tinta Limón, 2002).

10 The movement of the unemployed, which reached massive levels in Argentina in the early 2000s, became known as the piquetero movement for its primary tactic of the roadblock (*piquete*), which was used to blockade major highways and bridges in support of its demands for jobs, unemployment benefits, and other forms of state support. This eventually forced the government to implement a wide range of social programs, which in many cases were managed by the movements themselves—for example, deciding which tasks would meet the work requirements for receiving benefits.

11 See Maria Mies, *Patriarchy and Accumulation on a World Scale: Women in the International Division of Labour* (London: Zed Books, 1986).

12 León Rozitchner, *Materialismo ensoñado* (Buenos Aires: Tinta Limón, 2011).

13 See Sandro Mezzadra and Verónica Gago, "In the Wake of the Plebeian Revolt: Social Movements, 'Progressive' Governments, and the Politics of Autonomy in Latin America," Liz Mason-Deese, trans., *Anthropological Theory* 17:4 (December 2017), 474–96.

14 Verónica Gago, "Financialization of Popular Life and the Extractive Operations of Capital: A Perspective from Argentina," Liz Mason-Deese, trans. *South Atlantic Quarterly* 114:1 (January 2015), 11–28.

15 Verónica Gago and Sandro Mezzadra, "A Critique of the Extractive Operations of Capital: Toward an Expanded Concept of Extractivism," Liz Mason-Deese, trans. *Rethinking Marxism* 29:4 (October 2017): 574–91; Verónica Gago, "What Are Popular Economies? Some Reflections from Argentina," Liz Mason-Deese, trans., *Radical Philosophy* 202 (2018), 31–8.

16 Randy Martin, *Financialization of Daily Life* (Philadelphia: Temple University Press, 2002).

17 Pablo Chena and Alexandre Roig, "L'exploitation financière des secteurs populaires argentins," *Revue de la régulation* 22 (2017).

18 Or, as some newspapers reported: "The government declares war against the use of 'cash.'" Pablo Wende, "Chau efectivo: Acreditarán los planes sociales en los teléfonos de los beneficiarios," *Infobae*, September 3, 2017, infobae.com

19 This was confirmed by a study by the Centro de Estudios Metropolitanos, which assures that 39 percent of those surveyed who had taken out loans used the money to "pay for everyday expenses," while another 9 percent used the loans to "pay utility bills." Randy Stagnaro, "Se endeudan para pagar gastos diarios," *Tiempo Argentino*, October 21, 2017, tiempoar.com.ar.

20 An English translation of the statement "We Want to Be Debt Free" can be found in *Critical Times* 1:1 (April 2018), 158–77.

21 Luci Cavallero and Verónica Gago, *Una lectura feminista de la deuda: ¡Vivas, libres y desendeudadas nos queremos!* (Buenos Aires: Fundación Rosa Luxemburgo, 2019).

22 Silvia Rivera Cusicanqui, *Un mundo ch'ixi es posible: Ensayos desde un presente en crisis* (Buenos Aires: Tinta Limón, 2018).

23 Raquel Gutiérrez Aguilar, *Horizontes comunitarios populares* (Madrid: Traficantes de Sueños, 2017).

24 See Graciela Toro, *La pobreza: Un gran negocio* (La Paz: Mujeres Creando, 2010), and Silvia Federici, "From Commoning to Debt: Financialization, Microcredit, and the Changing Architecture of Capital Accumulation," *South Atlantic Quarterly* 113:2 (2014), 231–44.

25 Toro, *La pobreza: Un gran negocio*.

26 Nina Madsen, "Entre a dupla jornada e a discriminação contínua: Um olhar feminista sobre o discurso da 'nova classe média,'" in *A "nova classe média" no Brasil como conceito e projeto político*, Dawid Danilo Bartelt, ed. (Río de Janeiro: Fundação Heinrich Böll, 2013).

27 See Gago and Mezzadra, "Extractive Operations of Capital"; Verónica Gago and Alexandre Roig, "Las finanzas y las cosas," in *El imperio de las finanzas: Deuda y desigualdad*, Pablo I. Chena and Pedro M. Biscary, eds. (Buenos Aires: Miño y Dávila, 2019).

28 Melinda Cooper, *Family Values: Between Neoliberalism and the New Social Conservatism* (Cambridge, MA: MIT Press, 2017).

29 Gago and Mezzadra, "Extractive Operations of Capital"; Gago and Roig, "Las finanzas y las cosas."

30 See Negri's reading of the *Grundrisse* in *Marx beyond Marx* (New York: Autonomedia, 1991).

31 Karl Marx, *Capital*, vol. 3 (London: Penguin, 1981), 599, 641.

32 Cavallero and Gago, *Una lectura feminista de la deuda.*

33 George Caffentzis, *Los límites del capital: Deuda, moneda y lucha de clases* (Buenos Aires: Tinta Limón and Fundación Rosa Luxemburgo, 2018).

34 Sandro Mezzadra and Brett Neilson, *The Politics of Operations* (Durham, NC: Duke University Press, 2019).

35 Kaushik Sunder Rajan, *Pharmocracy: Value, Politics, and Knowledge in Global Biomedicine* (Durham, NC: Duke University Press, 2017).

36 Rosa Luxemburg, *The Accumulation of Capital*, Agnes Schwarzchild, trans. (New York: Routledge, 1951 [1913]), 332.

37 Ibid.

38 Ibid., 339.

39 Ibid., 340.

40 Ibid., 342.

41 Paolo Virno, *A Grammar of the Multitude: For an Analysis of Contemporary Forms of Life* (Los Angeles: Semiotext(e), 2003).

42 Luxemburg, *Accumulation of Capital*, 343.

43 Ibid., 347.

44 Ibid., 366.

45 Ibid., 407.

46 Ibid., 408.

47 Ibid., 407.

48 Silvia Federici, *Revolution at Point Zero: Housework, Reproduction, and Feminist Struggle* (Oakland: PM Press, 2012).

49 Fraser, "Behind Marx's 'Hidden Abode.'"

50 Saskia Sassen, *Territory, Authority, Rights: From Medieval to Global Assemblages* (Princeton, NJ: Princeton University Press, 2006), 415.

5. The Assembly as a Situated Apparatus of Collective Intelligence

1 For more on the barter clubs, which numbered in the hundreds throughout Argentina at the height of its economic crisis, see Colectivo Situaciones, *19 and 20: Notes for a New Social Protagonism*, Nate Holdren and Sebastián Touza, trans. (New York: Minor Compositions, 2012).

2 Kathi Weeks, *The Problem with Work: Feminism, Marxism, Antiwork*

Politics, and Postwork Imaginaries (Durham, NC: Duke University Press, 2011).

3 "Workers United, and if you don't like it, fuck off!" The chant is usually expressed with the masculine "trabajadores," assumed to be gender neutral, but the feminist movement has reappropriated it to specifically reference women workers.

4 Keeanga-Yamahtta Taylor, *From #BlackLivesMatter to Black Liberation* (Chicago: Haymarket Books, 2016).

5 Silvia Rivera Cusicanqui, "La larga marcha por nuestra dignidad," *Cuestión Agraria* 4 (2018), 7–38.

6 There is a purely linguistic mode of resolution to that declaration of the underage status of the struggles' statements. It appears as if a maneuver of an empty signifier, which functions as an authority from above that seeks to install order and rationality (in an equivalence that claims to be egalitarian but is always subordinated to the code of lack). I am referring to the theory Ernesto Laclau elaborates in *On Populist Reason* (London and New York: Verso, 2005).

7 Gayatri Chakravorty Spivak, "Estudios de la Subalternidad: Deconstruyendo la Historiografía," in *Estudios postcoloniales* (Madrid: Traficantes de Sueños, 2008).

8 "¿Podemos oír al subalterno?," *Clarín*, November 5, 2013, clarin.com.

9 Ni Una Migrante Menos is a feminist collective made up of migrants, mostly from other Latin American countries, residing in Argentina. It emerged in 2017 and its name, a conjugation of Ni Una Menos, highlights the organizational and situated drifts of that name. The collective played a key role in the organization of the feminist strike, shedding light on the issues of migrant workers, shaping the strike's transborder character, and incorporating demands against the racist modifcations to the Immigration Law proposed by Mauricio Macri's government.

10 Verónica Gago, "Silvia Rivera Cusicanqui: Against Internal Colonialism," *Viewpoint Magazine*, October 25, 2016, viewpointmag.com.

11 Silvia Rivera Cusicanqui and Rossana Barragán, eds., *Debates Post Coloniales. Una introducción a los Estudios de la Subalternidad* (La Paz: Historia-Sephis-Aruwiyiri, 1997).

12 The others were Alison Spedding, Ana Rebeca Prada, and Rivera Cusicanqui herself.

13 Raquel Gutiérrez Aguilar, "La lectura subalterna I," in *Lectura Mundi*, September 9, 2013, video available at youtube.com.

14 Cited in Frigga Haug, *Rosa Luxemburgo y el arte de la política* (Madrid: Tierra de nadie, 2013), 79.

15 Ibid., 73.

16 Ibid., 65.

17 Santiago Maldonado was a young anarchist activist who was disappeared following a raid by the National Gendarmerie on August 1, 2017, in Pu Lof en Resistencia, a Mapuche community in the province

of Chubut, in the Argentinian Patagonia. The previous day, Maldonado had participated in a roadblock as part of the struggle for the land ancestrally occupied by the Mapuche community. His body was found in the Chubut River on October 17, 2017, after 77 days without notice of his whereabouts.

18 Sara Ahmed, *Living a Feminist Life* (Durham, NC: Duke University Press, 2017), 30.

19 Judith Butler, *Notes Toward a Performative Theory of Assembly* (London: Harvard University Press, 2015); Michael Hardt and Antonio Negri, *Assembly* (New York: Oxford University Press, 2017).

20 Hardt and Negri, *Assembly*, 293.

6. The Feminist International

1 Pastora Filigrana, "Anti-Racist Feminism or Barbarism: Moroccan Women Seasonal Strawberry Workers," *South Atlantic Quarterly* 119:3 (July 2020).

2 Raquel Gutiérrez Aguilar, "Women's Struggle against All Violence in Mexico: Gathering Fragments to Find Meaning," Liz Mason-Deese, trans. *South Atlantic Quarterly* 117:3 (July 2018), 670–81.

3 I used this image in my book *Neoliberalism from Below* (Durham, NC: Duke University Press, 2017) to account for the multinational composition of the delegates in a slum in the city of Buenos Aires. Here, with different nuance, it is displaced to the domestic "interior" that ceases to be such.

4 For more on Territorio Doméstico, see Susana Draper and Rafaela Pimental, "Making the Network That Sustains Us Visible," *Viewpoint Magazine*, February 6, 2020, viewpointmag.com.

5 The UTEP, a union that includes the Confederation of Popular Economy Workers (CTEP) as well as other organizations representing sectors of the popular economy, was launched in the end of 2019.

6 W.E.B. Du Bois, "The General Strike," in *Black Reconstruction: An Essay toward a History of the Part Which Black Folk Played in the Attempt to Reconstruct Democracy in America, 1860–1880* (New York: Harcourt Brace, 1935).

7 Cristina Vega, "Del otro lado de la huelga del 8M: Visualizando la interrupción social desde el feminismo," *Sin permiso*, February 15, 2018, sinpermiso.info.

8 David Roediger, *Class, Race, and Marxism* (London and New York: Verso, 2017), 170.

9 Kimberlé Crenshaw, "Demarginalizing the Intersection of Race and Sex: A Black Feminist Critique of Antidiscrimination Doctrine, Feminist Theory, and Antiracist Politics," *University of Chicago Legal Forum* 1989, 139–67.

10 Keeanga-Yamahtta Taylor, ed., *How We Get Free: Black Feminism and the Combahee River Collective* (Chicago: Haymarket Books, 2017).

11 Ibid., 4

12 See Geraldina Colotti, "Lo sguardo di Selma James," *Il manifesto*, March 27, 2017, ilmanifesto.it.

13 Wendy Brown, *Undoing the Demos: Neoliberalism's Stealth Revolution* (New York: Zone, 2015).

14 As I argued in *Neoliberalism from Below* (204), in politicist perspectives, questions of gender and reproduction "function as the internalized outside of the polis: its dark economy." The marginalization of these realms leads to an understanding of the political that reinforces a separation of spheres and fails to recognize the politicization of life.

15 Wendy Brown, "Apocalyptic Populism," *Eurozine*, August 30, 2017, eurozine.com.

16 Keeanga-Yamahtta Taylor, *From #BlackLivesMatter to Black Liberation* (Chicago: Haymarket Books, 2016).

17 See Paolo Virno, *A Grammar of the Multitude: For an Analysis of Contemporary Forms of Life*, Isabella Bertoletti, James Cascaito, and Andrea Casson, trans. (Los Angeles: Semiotext(e), 2004).

18 I develop this argument further in *Neoliberalism from Below*.

19 Sandro Mezzadra and Brett Neilson, *The Politics of Operations: Excavating Contemporary Capitalism* (Durham, NC: Duke University Press, 2019).

20 Nancy Fraser, "The End of Progressive Neoliberalism," *Dissent*, January 2, 2017, dissentmagazine.org.

21 Nancy Fraser, "Contradictions of Capital and Care," *New Left Review* SII, 100 (2016).

22 Melinda Cooper, *Family Values: Between Neoliberalism and the New Social Conservatism* (New York: Zone, 2017), 12.

23 Gilles Deleuze and Félix Guattari, *A Thousand Plateaus: Capitalism and Schizophrenia*, Brian Massumi, trans. (Minneapolis: University of Minnesota Press, 1987).

24 To just quote one of Laclau's opinions that demonstrates the hierarchy of articulation: "The demands of indigenous people were not responded to promptly, but neither are they central to the structuring of politics." Cited in "La real izquierda es el Kirchnerismo," *Página12*, October 2, 2011, pagina12.com.ar.

25 By the "common-multiple," I refer to the productive capacity of the social beyond the position of the demand that Laclau seems to require from the populist dynamic of democracy he theorizes.

26 Cinzia Arruzza, Tithi Bhattacharya, and Nancy Fraser, *Feminism for the 99 Percent: A Manifesto* (London and New York: Verso Books, 2019).

27 Nancy Fraser, "What Is Feminism for the 99 Percent?," March 3, 2017, La Izquierdo Diario (YouTube channel), youtube.com.

7. Counteroffensive

1   Mara Viveros Vigoya, "The Controversy surrounding Gender: A Central Question of (Sexual) Politics in Colombia," *Sexual Policy Watch*, December 9, 2016, sxpolitics.org.

2   Éric Fassin, "A Double-Edged Sword: Sexual Democracy, Gender Norms, and Racialized Rhetoric," in *The Question of Gender: Joan W. Scott's Critical Feminism*, Judith Butler and Elizabeth Weed, eds. (Indianapolis: Indiana University Press, 2011), 143–58.

3   Mary Anne Case, "Trans Formations in the Vatican's War on 'Gender Ideology,'" *Signs: Journal of Women in Culture and Society* 44:3 (Spring 2019), 639–64.

4   Sarah Bracke and David Paternotte, "Unpacking the Sin of Gender," *Religion and Gender* 6:2 (February 2016), 143–54.

5   María Alicia Gutiérrez, "Significante vacío: Ideología de género, conceptualizaciones y estrategias. Entrevista con Sonia Corrêa," *Observatorio Latinoamericano y Caribeño* 2 (2018).

6   Originally published in Italian in 2003, it was first published in English in 2006 by Human Life International in Front Royal, Virginia.

7   Mary Anne Case, "The Role of the Popes in the Invention of Complementarity and the Vatican's Anathematization of Gender," *Religion and Gender* 6:2 (February 2016), 155–72, 156.

8   Bracke and Paternotte, "Unpacking the Sin of Gender," 146.

9   Juan Varela, *Origen y desarrollo de la ideología de género, fundamentos teológicos del matrimonio y la familia*, (Barcelona: Alianza Evangélica Española), 11.

10 Roman Patternotte and David Kuhar, *Anti-gender Campaigns in Europe: Mobilizing against Equality* (London: Rowman & Littlefield, 2017).

11 Agnieszka Graff and Elżbieta Korolczuk, "Towards an Illiberal Future: Anti-genderism and Anti-globalization," *Global Dialogue* 7:1 (2017), 27–30.

12 Mario Pecheny, Daniel Jones, and Lucía Ariza, "Sexual Politics and Religious Actors in Argentina," *Religion and Gender* 6:2 (February 2016), 205–25, 221.

13 Jorge Scala, "El cardenal Bergoglio y su visión de la familia y la vida humana," *Zenit*, March 15, 2013, es.zenit.org.

14 Case, "Trans Formations," 640–1.

15 "Monseñor Héctor Aguer: 'El aumento de los femicidios tiene que ver con la desaparición del matrimonio,'" *La Nación*, January 3, 2017, lanacion.com.ar.

16 Gutiérrez, "Significante vacío," 110.

17 Helena Silvestre's analysis is especially lucid for understanding the Bolsonaro phenomonon. See "Helena Silvestre: Buscando las raíces del fenómeno Bolsonaro," Canal Abierto (YouTube channel), youtube.com.

18 "Niñas madres con mayúsculas," *La Nacion*, February 1, 2019, lanacion. com.ar.

19 The interview was later translated and published as Farès Sassine and Michel Foucault, "There Can't Be Societies without Uprisings," Alex Feldman, trans., *Foucault Studies* (October 2018), 324–50.

20 This notion is examined further in Marie Bardet and Verónica Gago, "Insurrecciones impuras y espirtualidad política," *LoboSuelto!*, 2019, lobosuelto.com.

21 Silvia Federici, *Caliban and the Witch: Women, the Body, and Primitive Accumulation* (New York: Autonomedia, 2004).

22 Barbara Ehrenreich and Deirdre English, *Witches, Midwives, and Nurses: A History of Women Healers* (New York: Feminist Press, 1973).

23 An argument that I cannot fully develop here, but that is very relevant, concerns the difference between "liberation theology" and "theology of the people," which dates back to the 1970s and opposes social liberation to a notion of the popular that is strictly linked to poverty. One of its theorists, Juan Carlos Scanonne, says that one of the characteristics of the theology of the people, which Francisco continues today, is "the critique of ideologies, both of a liberal and a Marxist nature, and in its search for hermeneutical categories based on the historical reality of Latin America, and especially the poor." Juan Carlos Scanonne, "El papa Francisco y la teología del pueblo," *Razón y Fe*, 271:1395 (2014), 31–50. Another difference that should be taken into account is that among the *villero* priests (which are nodal points in Bergoglio's structure), with respect to the doctrine that was formed in the 1980s called the "preferential option for the poor."

24 "Exposición de Karen Torres," CampAbortoLegal (YouTube channel), June 7, 2018, youtube.com.

25 Melinda Cooper, *Family Values: Between Neoliberalism and the New Social Conservatism* (New York: Zone, 2017), 22.

26 Luci Cavallero and Verónica Gago, *Una lectura feminista de la deuda: ¡Vivas, libres y desendeudadas nos queremos!* (Buenos Aires: Fundación Rosa Luxemburgo, 2019).

27 Ibid.

28 Ibid., 33.

29 "Archivo 2018: Cada 21 horas el estado asesina a una persona," CORREPI, March 15, 2019, correpi.org.

30 Judith Butler, "Anti-gender Ideology and the New Fascism," paper presented at The New School for Social Research, New York, February 21, 2019.

Index

reconceptualization of sexist violence
in, 56
as redefining labor, 48
union leaders' arguments against, 46
utopian dimension of, 242–3
feminist economics
affinity of popular economy with,
32, 241
of exploitation and extraction,
115–54
new branch of in Argentina, 240
noneconomic elements of, 16
feminist general strike, 9, 193
Feminist International, emergence of,
186
feminist internationalism, 4, 184, 188,
190, 199
Feminist Intersindical, 159–61
Feminist Interunion/feminist inter-union,
47, 160
feminist potencia, use of term, 2–3
feminist strike
alliances within, 38–42
anti-capitalism and anti-colonialism
characteristics of, 143
attempts to narrate and
conceptualize, 50
as blockade, challenge, and act of
contempt, 44
and body-territory, 17
as cartographic method, 47, 57, 157,
234
as catalyst, 4, 41
as compared to traditional labor
strike, 24–6
as critique of neoliberalism, 142
different names for, 9
disobedience as key to, 25
double dimension of, 35
evolution of, 191–2
as exercise of mass suspension
and sabotage of political and
economic order, 13
forms of time in, 27
as gesture of revulsion, 44
as lens, 5–6, 12, 37
macquilas as beginning of, 18
as not a "floating signifier," 22
as not only linked to "professions,"
24
as organizational apparatus, 47
outcomes of, 10
politicizing violence through, 13
as practical tool, 6, 13, 142, 234
as process, 6, 9, 11, 16–17, 36–7, 38,
46, 155–6, 209, 246
as producing intersections
between struggles and creating
transnational connections, 17

reinvention of, 21
as response to violence against
women and feminized bodies, 20
as shifted to terrain of reproduction,
192
temporality of, 24
as tool of refusal and contempt, 21
toward a political theory of, 9–55
as vector of transversality, 16, 21,
22, 45
finance
colonial patriarchy of, 142–6
as common code, 64
consumption and, 140–2
gender-based perspective of, 137,
247–8
as having key relation with sexist
violence, 144
popular finance, 136–40
relation to bodies, 130
financial extractivism, 89, 97, 129–33,
187
financial inclusion, 133
First International Workingmen's
Association, 196
Foucault, Michel, 54, 67, 72, 113, 201,
221
Francis (Pope), 218–19, 226
Franco, Marielle, 190, 231
Fraser, Nancy, 118, 152–3, 200, 205–8,
209
Frente de Liberación Homosexual
(Homosexual liberation front),
238–9
Freud, Sigmund, 112
*From #BlackLivesMatter to Black
Liberation* (Taylor), 256n20
future labor, 134, 140

Galeano, Eduardo, 92–3
Galindo, María, 90, 138
The Gender Agenda (O'Leary), 212
gender-based violence/gender violence,
57, 135, 220, 237
gender ideology, 212, 214, 215, 216,
217, 218, 219, 220, 225, 226, 232,
264n14
General Confederation of Labor (CGT),
44–5, 159
general strike
feminist general strike, 9, 192–3
use of term, 11
Gibson-Graham, J. K., 119, 120, 121
Graff, Agnieszka, 216
Gramsci, Antonio, 196
green tide, 101, 103, 220–1
Grundrisse (Marx), 113, 129–30, 140
Guatemala
communitarian feminism in, 91

Ideology: Theological Foundations of Marriage and the Family" (Varela), 215–16
origin stories, 50–5
"Our bodies, our territories. Where is Santiago Maldonado?" (slogan), 174

pañuelazos, 101
Paraguay, protest against poisoning with agro-toxins in, 14
Parque Nacional Isiboro Sécure (TIPNIS), protests in defense of (2011), 90, 165
Pateman, Carole, 50–1, 52, 53, 105
Paternotte, David, 215
patriarchal pact, 105
patriarchy
articulation between patriarchy, capitalism and colonialism, 29
colonial patriarchy of finance, 142–6
modern contractual patriarchy, 52
restructuring of, 145
of the wage, 33, 44, 54, 60, 61, 66, 124, 127, 143, 661
Patriarchy and Accumulation on a World Scale (Mies), 73
Patternotte, Roman, 216
Pecheny, Mario, 217
Pérez, Lucía, 22–3, 157, 194, 252n10
Peru
extractivism in, 90
feminist activities in, 190
protest in of collective "Con Mis Hijos No Te Metas" (Don't mess with my children), 219
piqueteros (unemployed workers) movement, 31, 43, 125, 126, 128–9, 136, 238, 240, 259n10
Plan Puebla-Panama, 89
plurinational, 183, 184
political spirituality, 221–3
the "poor," church of, 223–5
popular economy/economies, 7, 10, 31, 32, 42, 57, 62, 64, 94, 96, 126, 127, 128–9, 131, 133, 136–42, 144, 152, 228, 234, 239, 240, 241, 247
popular sovereignty, 162, 202, 209, 210
populism, 200, 201, 203–4, 205, 208, 209, 216
potencia, 2, 3, 251n3
power
alternative theory of, 2, 251n3
confining of women's power, 52–3
labor power, 48, 49, 91, 114, 118, 122, 123, 124, 140, 149, 204, 247
male power over female body, 106
Precarias a la Deriva (Precarious women adrift), 14

precarious tasks, 160
precarity, 5, 12, 17, 20, 22, 24, 59, 70, 79, 132, 142, 171, 179, 180, 185, 202, 242, 246
Pretti, Valentín Milton, 109
The Principle of Hope (Bloch), 221
"The Prose of Counter-Insurgency" (Guha), 169
prostitution contract, 52

radicality/radicalization, as feature of feminist movement, 4, 16, 166, 173–4, 192, 198, 226, 238, 242
Rancière, Jacques, 53
Ratzinger, Joseph, 212, 218
realism of the assembly, 23
Red de Sanadoras Ancestrales del Feminismo Comunitario Territorial (Network of ancestral healers of territorial communitarian feminism), 99
reproduction, politicization of, 125, 126, 127, 131, 139–40, 143, 240, 264n14
reproductive crisis, 227
reproductive labor, 27–8, 30, 31–2, 84, 185, 192, 206, 235
reproductive paradigm, 119
reproductive tasks, 30, 31, 32, 41, 91, 125, 127, 157, 160, 192, 206, 241, 247
"The return of the state" (slogan), 94
revolutionary realpolitik, 169–73
Rivera Cusicanqui, Silvia, 90, 135, 165–6, 168–9, 226
Roediger, David, 197
Rolnik, Suely, 22, 75–6, 77, 226
Roman Catholic Apostolic Church, as wanting to present self as anti-colonial, 226
Rozitchner, León, 130
Russia, great strike of (1905), 36, 37

Sacayán, Diana, 22
Salt of the Earth (Ratzinger), 212–13
Sassen, Saskia, 153
Scala, Jorge, 217–18
Scanonne, Juan Carlos, 266n23
The Second Sex (de Beauvoir), 80–1
Segato, Rita, 75, 77, 78
sexist violence
characterization of, 67
connection of to financialization of popular economies, 139
cruelty of, 162
as expression of impotence, 20
extractivism and, 91, 92
finance as having key relation with, 144